AF553812

Psychology
An Indian Perspective

PSYCHOLOGY AN INDIAN PERSPECTIVE

Editors

Dr. G. Aruna Mohan
Reader in Education
St. Joseph's College of Education for Women
Guntur.

Dr. D. Vijaya Bharathi
Faculty
St. Joseph's College of Education for Women
Guntur.

NEELKAMAL PUBLICATIONS PVT. LTD.
EDUCATIONAL PUBLISHERS
(EXPORTERS & IMPORTERS)
NEW DELHI HYDERABAD

PSYCHOLOGY: AN INDIAN PERSPECTIVE

Editors
Dr. G. Aruna Mohan
Dr. D. Vijaya Bharathi

First Edition : 2009
(Hardback)

ISBN : 978-81-8316-191-6

NEELKAMAL PUBLICATIONS PVT. LTD.
Sultan Bazar, Hyderabad - 500 095.
✆ 24757140, 24757197, 24757944 Fax: 040-24757951

Delhi Office:
BG5/9B, Paschim Vihar, New Delhi-110 063,
✆ 011-25285894
e-mail: sales@neelkamalpub.com; sales_neelkamal@rediffmail.com
website: www.neelkamalpub.com

Published by *Suresh Chandra Sharma* for
Neelkamal Publications Pvt. Ltd., New Delhi, Hyderabad
and printed at *Siva Sai Art Printers,* Hyderabad, India.

Preface

Psychology as of today, in academic line is almost drawn from the western perspective which starts from the external observable behaviour with experimental evidences and statistical inferences. The Indian perspective starts from the internal inner observation of 'what is'. The outer material reality is an experience that has begun internally. Science discovers relative truths which change as we experiment and discover from different dimensions. Science with its success is giving the wrong impression that truth is synonymous with science and that anything to be useful has to be scientific. Time and again the great people proved that absolute Truth cannot be arrived through reason and logic but only by inner exploration and self awareness. The realized people say that reality tends to be more and more holistic as one goes to the root.

The seers of the ancient and the recent in India, in this journey inward to find the truth, or the ultimate, God or the cause of the existence, have surpassed whatever appeared on the mental screen and journeyed through the consciousness of generations of humanity and had gone beyond in silent states of mind and experienced the Ultimate Truth. They observed the multifaceted manifestations of consciousness. Thus their perception of the inward mental phenomena was the source of data revealing the human nature in its pristine quality.

Psychology, being the mother of the discipline, education, has to bring out the facts of mind to promote attitudes and values that are fundamental and appropriate to regenerate the degenerating society. The aim of psychology from Indian perspectives is to move towards 'Holistic Psychology'. It is also a transition from

- Egoism to the spirit of oneness of humanity
- Happiness with material gains to happiness by doing dharma
- Self-interest to interest in the common good
- Narrow mindedness to broad mindedness
- Superficial living to life with deeper understanding of it.

Indian Psychology offers

- A complete understanding of the human individual by going within.
- An art of observation which is to be
    i) Self critical at some instances of life
    ii) Non-judgemental to penetrate into the layers of consciousness.
- Understanding the truth of life may give right place to knowledge, memory and thought, only where they are relevant.
- A state of being, which is not different from the Ultimate.
- A realization that one is the world, rather 'You are the world'
- The flowering of human being and human race.
- A harmonious living within oneself and with every other in existence.

– *Dr. G. Aruna Mohan*
Dr. D. Vijaya Bharathi

Psychology
An Indian Perspective

Contents

Psychology: An Indian Perspective – Introduction ... xi

Part-I

1. Psychology from Upanishads
   – *P. Datta Prasad* ... 1
2. Psychological Health: Upanishàdic Perspective
   – *Dr. L. Bhagya Lakshmi, M. Sreedevi* ... 8
3. Psycho-physical Dimensions of Human Behavior, Yoga and Meditation
   – *V. Rangacharlu* ... 25
4. Holistic Human Development in the Light of The Bhagavad Gita
   – *Lalitha Panguluri* ... 30
5. Trait and Type Theories of Bhagavadgita
   – *Dr. Ch. Lakshmi Narasamma* ... 44
6. The Inward Journey
   – *Dr. Sr. G. Theresamma* ... 50
7. The Subtle Energy Centres: Consequences of their Malfunctions & Remedies
   – *Dr. K. Jayasree* ... 60
8. Teacher's Self-critical Awareness in the Context of Jaina Theory of Liberation
   – *T. Padmavathi, B. Srilatha & P. Shanthi* ... 78

Part-II

9. **The Buddhist Psychology**
– Dr. A. Venkateswara Reddy ... 87

10. **Psychological Factors for the Selection of the Special Object of Meditation as Expounded in *Vissudhimagga***
– Prof. M.V. Ram Kumar Ratnam ... 98

11. **Buddhist Meditation: A Cure for Psychological Ill-Health**
– Valaparla Susitha Priya, Dr. J. Prasanth Kumar ... 110

12. **The Impact of Budhistic Way of Living on Mental Well-being**
– Dr. B.A. Rani ... 115

13. **Holistic Human Development: Buddhist View**
– S. Anne Sucharitha ... 129

14. **Explorations of "Sri Rama Krishna Paramahamsa's Views on Mental Health"**
– A. Srinivas ... 134

15. **Concentration: A Priceless Gift**
– Dr. D. Vijaya Bharathi ... 141

Part-III

16. **Integral Psychology in the Light of Sri Aurobindo**
– Kongara Bhaskara Rao ... 145

17. **Does Sri Aurobindo Offer an Alternative for Humankind?**
– Jackson Judan Fernandes, Sadasiva Rao ... 177

18. **Personality Development – Manifesting the Divinity Within**
– Dasapathi Rao ... 192

19. **Teacher Education: A Pleasurable Experience Principles of Integral Education**
– Prof. Y.F.W. Prasada Rao, Dr. Padma ... 198

20. **Let the Child's Mind Develop**
– P.S.A.S.K. Sudha ... 201

Part-IV

21. **Psychology from Krishnamurtis Teaching**
– G. Venkata Mohan ... 205

22. **J. Krishnamurti's Perception of Intellect, Authority and Intelligence**
– G. Yashoda ... 209

23. **A Religious Mind is Like Clear Water**
– Mubasharah Tahseen ... 213

24. **Depth and Breadth of Human Conditioning from the Teaching of Krishnamurti**
– G. Showrilu ... 220

25. **Nature: Human Nature**
– G. Sasikala ... 227

26. **Development of Integrated Individual from the Perspective of J. Krishnamurti**
– A. Srinivasa Murthy ... 237

27. **Promotive and Destructive Factors of Integrated Human Being**
– Sr. Santha ... 242

28. **Psychological Health in J. Krishnamurti's Perspective**
– J. Padmavathi ... 252

29. **Care for the Caring Nature of the Child**
– J.R. Priyadarsini ... 258

30. **Learner cannot Flower in the Field of Fear**
– Kezia. A. ... 263

31. **Need for Self-Knowledge Apart from Knowledge from the Perspective of J. Krishnamurti**
– Sr. Kochuthresia ... 268

32. **Holistic Learning: The Rhythm of Life**
– Dr. T. Swarupa Rani ... 277

33. **Explosion of Psychological Fact in the Fasting Mind, Not in the Feasting Mind**
– Dr. G. Aruna Mohan ... 290

INDEX ... 300

❖ ❖ ❖

Psychology: An Indian Perspective

Introduction

The humanity is facing the threat of violence, conflicts, war, abuse of alcohol, drug, sex, and malpractices of various sorts. The Kothari Commission 1966 stated that it should be our goal and obligation to reinterpret, and raise to a new level of understanding, the insight gained by the ancient sages as regards the fundamental problems of life -which in some ways are unique and represent the quality of deepest insight into the happenings of the world. It also said that 'man's knowledge and mastery, of outer space and his own self, are out of balance'. It is this imbalance which the mankind seeks to redress.

Psychology, being the mother of the discipline, education, has to bring out the facts of mind to promote attitudes and values that are fundamental and appropriate to regenerate the degenerating society. The Freudians found man as instinctive and impulsive, the Behaviorists found man as conditioned and mechanical, the Humanists found man with rich potential, while the Transpersonal psychologists found the divine in man. This fourth force, transpersonal psychology emerged with interest in the ultimate human capacities, concerned with the scientific study of consciousness, meta needs, B-values, transcendental states and to understand the totality of the psychological being.

Why Indian Perspectives and What is its Relevance in Psychology?

After three decades of proposed responsibility by the 1966 Education Commission, UNESCO Report of 1996 about the 21st century education titled "Learning the Treasure Within" discussed many issues.

The offered ways by Jacquis Delors, for the establishment of wider and more far reaching forms of international cooperation, to see that every thing falls into place is, "there is, ..., every reason to place renewed emphasis on the moral and cultural dimensions of education, enabling each person to grasp the individuality of other people and to understand the world's erratic progression towards a certain unity but this process must begin with self-understanding through an inner voyage, whose milestones are knowledge, meditation and the practice of self-criticism.' Self-critical awareness is essential to wipe away the illusions altogether.

Aim: The aim of psychology from Indian perspectives is to move towards 'Holistic Psychology'.

Psychology as of today, in academic line is almost drawn from the western perspective which starts from the external observable behavior with experimental evidences and statistical inferences. The Indian perspective starts from the internal inner observation of 'what is'. The outer material reality is an experience that has begun internally.

The seers of the ancient and the recent in India, in this journey inward to find the truth, or the ultimate, God or the cause of the existence, have surpassed whatever appeared on the mental screen and journeyed through the consciousness of generations of humanity and had gone beyond in silent states of mind and experienced the Ultimate, truth. They observed the multifaceted manifestations of consciousness. Thus their perception of the inward mental phenomena was the source of data revealing the human nature in its pristine quality.

What is in this Book?

This book is an anthology of the writings of thirty three authors, mostly teacher educators, whose earnest attempts to open up the human nature, development, education and wellness due to righteous way of living proposed by the ancient and the recent observers of mind like human scientists and explorers of truth are worth preserving to reach out the wider family of teacher educators and the interested readers. It even strives to fill the spiritual vacuum experienced by the humanity. It may divert the attention from attraction to the tangibles and external material progress at the cost of intangible values and inner discipline. It may draw the attention to the deeper and broader perspective of life of the humanity and other life forms. It may develop interest in unfolding one's innate potential or at least in setting right oneself through self-critical awareness.

Psychology: An Indian Perspective does not exclude anything that is currently studied in psychology but includes a great deal more. "It attempts" not only to provide an understanding of the nature of person, the causes and consequences of his conduct but also to explore the methods and means of transforming the person in pursuit of perfection in the being, certainty in knowing and happiness in feeling. Deconstruction of the ego and de-conditioning of the person are considered necessary prerequisites for one's transformation to experience truth in its pristine state'. Truth is not considered to be simple cognitive understanding".

So, it draws from a variety of sources and permits multiple interpretations. Its core area is consciousness for understanding human nature. It covers simple practical aspects of good behavior to meta-cognitive experiences. It has global relevance in the context of psychology in the West to deal with some important aspects of human nature that appear to be simply beyond its scope because of its restrictive assumptions.

This book contains the articles specifically from the Upanishads, the Bhagavad Gita, Buddhistic teaching, Aurobindo's writings and Krishnamurti's teachings. So, a humble attempt is made to introduce the essential features of these five.

Consciousness in Upanishads

India's oldest and most important scriptures, the Vedas are said to be divine revelations received by saints and seers. Upanishads are the concluding portion of the Vedic literature which embodies the first philosophical thought in India. Upanishads means knowledge that dispels, shatters and destroys the 'avidya'. The Vedas are four in number: Rik, Sama, Yajur and Atharwa. Each of these is divided into two parts -work and knowledge. The first is mainly made up of hymns, instructions regarding rites and ceremonies, and rules of conduct. The second is concerned with the highest aspect of religious truth, called 'Upanishads' - which means 'Secret Teaching' to the people who are spiritually ready to receive and profit by it. Shankara interpreted it as the knowledge of God, the knowledge of Brahman, the knowledge that destroys the bands of ignorance and leads to the supreme goal of freedom. The central theme of all the Upanishads is the divinity of man and the spiritual solidarity of the whole universe in Brahman. Freedom - physical freedom, mental freedom and spiritual freedom are the watchwords of the Upanishads.

The wisdom of the Hindu mystics with their accounts of revelations in the form of Upanishads remains as primary source of spiritual guidance for millions. Their meditations concerned overwhelming direct experiences in the midst of life and recorded insights into eternal truths. They are unified by their common search for the true nature of reality, and in the course of this search afford glimpses of supreme states of existential truths.

A characteristic of the Upanishads is their homogeneity. One Upanishad may emphasize certain ideas, or certain view, more than the rest, or may specialize as it were in a particular topic; but such differences and distinctions often seem to be accidental. The seers were concerned with reporting insights which came to them in thought or vision but not with making insights superficially coherent. They were not builders of systems but recorders of experience.

The real study is not study of themselves but study of that by which we realize the changeless. The real study is first hand experience of God. Vedas are a large body of texts handed down by generations.

Isa Upanishad embodies the spiritual unity and solidarity of all existence. The ultimate reality is declared as 'Brahman', unchangeable and everlasting reality underlying the exterior transient world. This universe is Brahman in which all the creatures merge and lose their identity as the rivers rising from the ocean and merge in the ocean and become ocean itself. It is, Brahman is truth (satyarn), consciousness (jnanam) and infinity (anantham). Upanishads declare that both the matter and spirit are subservient to Brahman.

Human development can be facilitated by the revelations in Upanishads. Mundaka Upanishad includes all knowledge about arts and science including all sacred books as apara knowledge and the imperishable and changeless reality. The one behind the many is the para knowledge, the true self of man, pure consciousness and non-dual turiya state of the being. Wealth and power are not the highest glory of man. The Upanishads don't condemn man's pursuit of worldly wealth and power. It says that there is something greater than these. Our education is largely cut off from the currents of our inheritance in self-knowing. Self-knowing alone facilitates total development of the person to have transcendental experiences beyond the sense-bound mind to realise the truths.

From the beginning two sub-currents ran through the life of people, then. Majority of people followed the social religion of the Vedas, with brahmins in charge of preserving the ancient scriptures and presiding over a complex set of rituals. Another tradition practiced the spiritual disciplines to realize directly the divine ground of life beyond the rituals of priests. The latter was considered the highest vocation of human beings. The typical Indian classical ashram tradition used to be a life of young men and women living with the teacher as part of his family in outward simplicity in order to have inner growth.

The sages of Upanishads took a different track from conventional science. They looked at human knowledge of the world outside and divided everything impermanent as the contents of consciousness and ultimately unreal. Their principle was 'neti neti atma'. "This is not the self; that is not the self". They peeled away personality like an onion, layer by layer and found nothing permanent in the mass of perceptions, thoughts, emotions, desires and memories that we call 'I'. When everything individual was stripped away, an intense awareness remains, consciousness itself. The sages called this ultimate ground of personality atman, the self.

In meditation, as the mind settles down to dwell on a single focus, attention begins to flow in a smooth unbroken stream, and is no longer connected with the organs of hearing. The body becomes like a comfortable jacket. Eventually there comes a time when one gets up from meditation and knows that he is not his body.

In the climax of meditation the barrier of individuality disappears, dissolving in a sea of pure, undifferentiated awareness. Brahman is the irreducible ground of existence, the essence of everything of the earth and sun, or all creatures, of Gods and human beings and of every power of life. The multiplicity of the perceptual world will unfold as a seed bursts into a tree in that awareness. The whole of reality is there, the inner as well as the outer: not only matter and energy but all time, space, causality and states of consciousness. Nothing can satisfy us but reunion with our real self, which the Upanishads say is sat-chit-ananda: Absolute reality, pure awareness, unconditioned joy.

The sage, the transcended person distinguishes between knowledge and wisdom, knowledge is of things, acts and relations. But wisdom is of Brahman alone; beyond all things acts and relations, he abides forever. To become one with him is the only wisdom. The sages of Upanishads did not find the world capricious. Nothing in it happens by chance not because events are predestined, but because everything is connected by cause and effect. Thoughts are included in this view, for they both cause things to happen and are aroused by things that happen. What we think has consequences for the world around us, for it conditions how we act. All these consequences are our personal responsibility. Sooner or later, because of unity of life, they will come back to us. An angry person provokes anger in others. More subtly, a man whose factory pollutes the environment will eventually have to breathe air and drink water to which he is responsible.

Upanishadic sages found that the books of karma could only be cleared within the natural world. Unpaid karmic debts and unfulfilled desires don't vanish when the physical body dies. They are forces which remain in the universe to quicken life again at the moment of conception when conditions are right for the past karma to be fulfilled. We live and act, and everything we do goes into what we think at the present moment, so that at death the mind is the sum total of everything we have done and everything we still desire to do. That sum of forces has karma to reap, and when the right context comes -the right parents, the right society, the right epoch -the bundle of energy that is the germ of personality is born again. We are not just physical creatures with a beginning in 1950 and an end after some years. We go back eons, and some of the contents of the deepest unconscious are the dark desires of an evolutionary heritage much older than the human race.

Man in his ignorance, identifies himself with the material sheaths that encompass his true self. Transcending these, he becomes one with the Brahman who is pure bliss.

Consciousness in Bhagavad Gita

Bhagavad Gita presents an elaborate analysis of the human mind. Its opening lines project the mental conflict that humans faced since ancient times, between 'what is right' and 'what is duty'. Krishna's interventions are transpersonal in nature, with the potential for transforming Arjuna, presenting him a new and lasting trans-physical and trans-social identity". Krishna's first lesson to Arjuna is about the immutable self, the nature of which is consciousness. Consciousness gives a multidimensional picture of existence. It does not come into existence like the body, having not existed before. It is the primeval being. He tried to deepen the sense of awareness to bring Arjuna out of depression. 'The only way to rescue the person from the caverns of depression is not by analysing the psychological conditions of depression but presenting him a new and integral unity'. 'The teases, consolations, questionings, traits, love and revelations that Krishna showers on Arjuna are not limited to any particular mode of counselling'.

Throughout the Gita, Krishna lauds the inevitability of self-knowledge, as the one and only means to remove self-ignorance and superimpositions. There is no purifier equal to self-knowledge. Gita talks about three kinds of yoga. They are not different techniques to yield antagonistic and varied fruits. Gitacharya says: "He who is rightly devoted to even one obtains the fruits of both". To him a yogi is: "He who, without depending on the fruits of action, performs his bounden duty, he is a sanyasin and yogin; not he who is without fire and without action". Karma yoga is the performance of work with evenness of mind in success and failure. Sanyasa is the renunciation of the false notion of ascribing agency and enjoyership to the self. All forms of actions, secular and scriptural, are done by the prakriti, using its effects, sense objects, and instruments -sense organs and organs of action. 'Actions are wrought in all cases by the energies of nature". 'It is nature that acts". It is one's nature that operates both as the direct and causative agent.

Krishna says, 'thy concern is with action alone, never with results. Let not the fruit of action be thy notice, nor let the attachment be for inaction". A pure mind is an alert mind. Peace and subtle sensitivity are the nature of an alert mind. It can be gained by 'freedom from desire for covetable experiences in the place of the seen and the unseen'. By giving up the fruits of work a yogi attains disciplined peace. He is free of craving. The individual whose mind is receptive and not selective is truly integrated. He does not react to a situation but responds spontaneously. The steady minded neither gets elated on gaining of the pleasant nor grieves on meeting with the unpleasant. Acceptance marks the transcendence of the dual.

Krishna introduced the idea that work and meditation are complementary to each other. One can meditate only if he has gained the evenness of mind through non-reactive performance of work. He says, "Better indeed is knowledge than practise; than knowledge is meditation more esteemed; than meditation the abandonment of the fruits of actions, on abandonment, peace follows spontaneously".

Gita indicates by its theory of meditation, 'a deepening and broadening of consciousness beholding all beings in consciousness and consciousness in all beings".

If self-realization is taken as the goal, then meditation is more important than scriptural knowledge. If meditation is taken as a discipline, then detached work is more important. According to Gita, a renouncing mind is a meditative mind that always abides in supreme consciousness. Krishna discusses, "He who can see in action inaction who can also see action in inaction, he is wise among men, he is integrated, he is performer of all action". This is against the popular perception that action and inaction are bipolar.

Krishna's three definitions of yoga are: yoga is the evenness of mind in terms of dualities. Yoga is skill in action, efficient performance of work. Yoga is disjunction from unhappiness, by removing. Superimpositions made on the self. A yogi according to Krishna is, 'satisfied with what comes to him by chance, rising above the pairs of opposites, free from envy, equanimous in success and failure, though acting, he is not bound'.

The Gita reiterates the importance of mental integration as the only means to win the meditative quality of mind. Thus, the Karma Yoga of Krishna helps in the context of frustration, and anxiety about work.

Consciousness in Buddha's Teachings

Gautama was Siddhartha meaning he who has achieved his object. In Buddha's time, the highest goal of the holy life for anyone was to leave the home and go into homelessness seeking after the truth. The religious mendicant was considered the ideal to which both the Kshatriyas and Brahmins aspired. It is therefore natural that Siddhartha, inclined to religious life as he was, turned his attention to this. When he was sixteen, he was married to a cousin, Yasodhara and had a son Rahula by her. At 29 years of age, leaving behind a pretty wife, a young son, and all the luxuries in which he grew up, he abandoned home for a homeless life to find a solution to life's problems. He renounced not in his old age but in the prime of manhood, not in poverty but in plenty on realising the vanity of several enjoyments while he was in place with all its worldly amusements. It was an unprecedented historic renunciation. He spent six years as the pupil of two prominent teachers and led strict ascetic life but found it unsatisfying.

On his superhuman effort for six long years his body was reduced to almost a skeleton. The more he tormented his body, the farther his goal receded from him. Benefitted by this invaluable experience, he finally decided to follow an independent course, avoiding the two extremes of self-indulgence and self-mortification. The former retards one's spiritual progress, and the latter weakens one's intellect. The new way which he himself discovered was the middle path which subsequently became one of the salient characteristics of his teaching. He attained enlightenment at the age of 35. He, endowed with deep wisdom, commensurated with his boundless compassion, devoted the remainder of his precious life to serve humanity both by example and precept, dominated by no personal motive whatsoever. He finally passed away in his 80th year after a very successful ministry of 45 long years of teaching to the humanity.

His long teaching is capsuled as the eight-fold path. But it is left for us to follow to obtain purification. The Buddha exhorts his disciples to depend on themselves for their deliverance, for both purity and defilement depend on oneself. Dependence on others means a surrender of one's effort. Parinibbana Sutta reveals how vital is self-exertion to accomplish one's object and how superficial and futile it is to seek redemption through benignant saviours and to crave for illusory happiness in an after life through the propitiation of imaginary gods or by irresponsive prayers and meaningless sacrifices. As he reached the highest possible mental state of perfection any person could aspire to, and without the close fist of a teacher he revealed the only straight path that leads thereto. Any body may aspire to that supreme state of purification if he makes the necessary exertion. He never arrogated himself to divinity. He laid stress on this important point and left no room whatsoever for anyone to fall into the error of thinking that he was an immortal divine being. Instead of disheartening his followers and reserving this exalted state only to himself he encourages and induces them to emulate him, for

Buddhahood is latent in all. In one sense all are potential Buddhas. He declared that the gates of success and prosperity are open to all in every condition of life, high or low, saints or criminals who would care to turn a new life and aspire for perfection. Irrespective of caste, colour or rank he established for both deserving men and women a democratically constituted celibate order. He did not force his followers to be slaves either to his teachings or to himself but granted complete freedom of thought. He helped the poor that were neglected. He comforted the bereaved by his consoling words. He ministered to the sick that were deserted. He ennobled the lives of the deluded, purified the corrupted lives of criminals. He encouraged the feeble, united the divided, enlightened the important, clarified the mystic, guided the benighted, elevated the base, and dignified the noble. All benefited by his words of wisdom and compassion.

Man is a mysterious being with inconceivable potentialities. Latent in him are both saintly and criminal characters. They may rise to the surface at unexpected moments in disconcerting strength. We find them dormant in varying degrees.

Within the powerful mind of the complex man are found a storehouse of virtues and a rubbish heap of evil. With the development of the respective characteristics man may become either a blessing or a curse to humanity. Those who wish to be great, noble and serviceable, who wish to sublimate themselves and serve humanity both by example and by precept, and who wish to avail themselves of this golden opportunity as human beings, endeavour their best to remove the latent vices and to cultivate the dormant virtues. But to dig up the valuable treasures latent in man, only persistent effort and enduring patience are necessary. It is strange that the vices latent in man seem to be almost natural and spontaneous. Two universal characteristics that upset the mental equipoise of man are attachment to the pleasurable and aversion to the non-pleasurable. These two opposite forces can be eliminated by developing equanimity. Buddha's teaching is basically in the form of tripitakas.

The Abhidamma investigates mind and matter, the two composite factors of the so called being, to help the understanding of the things as they truly are. He explained to us what is within and without; the Dhamma he taught is not nearly to be preferred in books, nor is it a subject to be studied from a historical or literary standpoint but to be learnt and put into practice in the course of one's daily life, for without practice, one can't appreciate the truth. Dhamma above all is to be realised, immediate realisation is its ultimate goal. Religion, means "a teaching which takes a view of life that is more than superficial, a teaching which looks into life and not merely at it, a teaching which furnishes men with a guide to conduct that is in accord with its in-look, a teaching which enables those who give it heed to face life with fortitude and death with serenity" or a system to get rid of the ills of life, then it is certainly a religion of religions.

Mind of Man

Our mind, according to Buddha is nothing but a complex compound of fleeting emotional states. One unit of consciousness consists of three phases - arising or genesis, static or development, and cessation or dissolution. Immediately after cessation stage of a thought moment, there occurs the genesis stage of the subsequent thought moment. Each momentary consciousness of this ever changing life process on passing away, transmits its whole energy, all the indelibly recorded impressions to its successor. Every fresh consciousness consists of the potentialities of the predecessors together with something more. There is, therefore, a continuous flow of consciousness like a stream without any interruption. The subsequent thought moment is neither absolutely the same nor entirely another being the same continuity of Kamma energy. There is no identical being but there is an identity in process. Every moment there is birth, every moment there is death. Conciousness - 'it persistently flows on like a river receiving from the tributary streams of sense constant accretions to its flood, and ever dispensing to the world without the thought-stuff it has gathered by the way". It has birth for its source and death for its mouth. The rapidity of flow is such that hardly is there any standard whereby it can be measured even approximately. No state once gone ever recurs nor is identical with what goes before. But we worldlings, veiled by the web of illusion, mistake this apparent continuity to be something external and go to the extent of introducing an unchanging soul, an atta, the supposed doer and receptacle of all actions to this ever-changing consciousness.

According to Abhidharma ego consists of eight kinds of consciousness. The five sense consciousnesses are out of five sense organs. The sixth consciousness in the mind is thinking. The seventh consciousness has the nature of ignorance, cloudiness and confusion. This cloudy mind is an overall structure which runs right through the six sense consciousnesses. This does not have precision. The eighth consciousness is what is called the common ground, or the unconscious ground of all this. It is the ground that makes it possible for all the other seven to operate. It has both samsara and nirvana. This eighth consciousness is not as basic as the ground. It is a kind of secondary basic level where confusion has already begun and that confusion provides an accommodation for the other seven consciousnesses to operate.

There is an evolutionary process which starts from this unconscious ground, the eighth consciousness. The cloudy consciousness arises from that and then the six sense consciousnesses. These also evolve in certain order according to the levels of experiential intensity of each of them. The most intense level is attained with sight which develops last. Abhidharma does not talk much about the all pervading basic ground. It is the source of liberation. Energies appear out of this and are the source of the development of relative situations. Relative situation contains the basic quality of ignorance.

Man has to understand the real nature of this life and the universal laws. He has to realise that the cause of suffering is due to his attachment and craving towards various things. Nibbana is the extinction of the thirst for sensual pleasures. It is generally expressed in negative terms as 'Extinction of thirst', uncompounded, unconditioned, absence of desire, cessation, blowing out, or giving up all defilements, calming of all conditioned things. One is not free from suffering so long as he is subjected to defilements.

The life of man is made perfect by his own insight due to his travel along the Noble Eight-fold path. This transcendental life can be obtained before the bodily death of man. He equates it to happiness of the highest order, accompanied too by the consciousness of the destruction of individualistic desire or selfhood. In this transcendental absolute entity man loses consciousness of his separate self and dissolves into the Nibbana state.

We want pleasures and feel that we are happy by providing more to satisfy our desires. If we observe we could find that it would be an endless job. Buddha says to calm down the senses instead of gratifying and indulging in them as slaves up to our last breath. To do so we have to understand the real nature of this life and the universal laws. Then we realise that the cause of suffering is due to attachment and craving towards various things. The eternal bliss is attained not by simply praying to a God by performing ceremonies and rituals but by being good, by abstaining from evil and by purifying our minds by ourselves.

'Calming of all conditioned things, giving up all defilements', 'liquidation of ignorance' are possible in our life itself if we travel along the Eightfold-path and break all the fetters - Right understanding, Right thought, Right speech, Right action, Right livelihood.

Then we become the very embodiment of the ten perfections due to higher life as we lose consciousness of separate selves and dissolve into the Nibbana state. The ten perfect characteristics of any transcended man are Liberality, Morality, Renunciation, Wisdom, Energy, Forgiveness, Truthfulness, Resolution, Love and Equanimity. We can obtain this transcendent life before the bodily death in the destruction of selfhood.

Consciousness in Aurobindo's Writings

He was born in Calcutta on 15 August, 1872. His father, Dr. Krishna Mohan Ghose, an England-returned doctor wanted to bring up his children in the western style only. At the age of seven, he with his two brothers was sent to England for education. At the age of 21, he left the shores of the West and returned to India.

As soon as he stepped on the Indian soil at Apollo Bandar he had a strange, experience and unexpected spiritual experience. A solid peace and an intense and a vast spiritual calm descended upon him sinking into the very cells of his physical body.

He served as the vice-principal of a college in Baroda till 1906 and studied and mastered the past glory and the powerful and undying traditions of the Indian spirit and culture. He took active part in the revolutionary movements of the day as he became surcharged with patriotism. He was arrested and put in jail as he was involved in the Alipur bomb case. In the jail his only companion was Bhagavadgita. He practised it closely and intensely. He had visions and heard voices. This one year in jail was like 'Ashramvas' to him and had intense sadhana. He was directed 'to see how the truth consciousness works in everything'. 'After the nirvana experience (with the help of yogi Bhaskar Lele) I had no thoughts of my own. Thoughts used to come from above. In fact, in Nirvana, with that peace one does not ask for anything. But the truth of the super-mind was put into me. I had no idea of it when I started sadhana and for long it was not clear to me' says Aurobindo.

At the dictates of his inner voice, he left the political scene of stress and strain and sought solitude at Pondicherry. It was at 4P.M. on 4 April, 1910 that Sri Aurobindo stepped on the soil of Pondicherry and for four decades i.e., till 5 December, 1950, till he discarded the body, he never went out of it.

The aim of his sadhana was transformation of outer nature, perfection as perfect as it can be the aim of his sadhana expanded in ever widening circles from the attainment of Brahmatejas to bringing down the divine to supramentalise the whole of the humanity itself.

His intense sadhana resulted in Siddhi in 1921 what he called the descent of overmental consciousness into physical plane. He withdrew himself into exclusive retirement. There he carried on the experimental investigation like a spiritual scientist.

Our ordinary personality is an organisation of interactions with the environment. It is intensely self-centred. It is also deeply a part of the same nature. If we dissociate from it we land in a field of wider mind, life or body, a universality. There universal focus of nature becomes a direct perception but not inferences Telepathy then becomes an exercisable function. Further inward withdrawal lands us in a luminous and blissful core consciousness which renders our wider personality, the subliminal. This is felt as self-existent and independent of circumstances. The discovery of this domain of consciousness holds the key to many problems of scientific psychology. There we feel sex is not final to life, reaction to environment is not essential and normality is not merely social conformity. It discovers a large field of consciousness of increasing luminosity and universality. It is unitary in nature, called super-consciousness or superconscient.

Man with animal inheritance through yogic discipline can live a life of spontaneous joy, unitary will and clarity of perception. Thus integrated living is a complete possibility. This has been demonstrated again and again in the lives of saints and yogis in varying forms and degrees, the change contemplated in the nature of man is really a spiritualisation of human nature.

Integral Yoga

Sri Aurobindo's integral yoga aims also at a complete transformation of human nature under the influence of the higher levels of consciousness. For this transformation a very detailed understanding of human nature is essential.

Pranayama: The real energy of our being is lying asleep and inconscient in the depths of our vital system, and is awakened by the practice of Pranayama.

Sri Aurobindo says 'To deal with this mind two things are necessary, (1) not so much to try to control or fight with or express it as to stand back from it : One looks at it and sees what it is but refuses to follow its thoughts or run about among the objects it pursues, remaining at the back of the mind quiet and separate; (2) to practise quietitude and concentration in this separateness, until the habit of quiet takes hold of the physical mind and replaces the habit of these small activities. This of course takes time and can only come by practice".

Yoga as a psychological approach aims at a radical change of consciousness which results in the immutable peace, freedom and joy and improves the spiritual faculties "Integral yoga implies, not only the realisation of god, but an entire consecration and change of the inner and outer life till it is fit to manifest a divine consciousness and become part of a divine work".

To know our inner being is the first step towards a real self-knowledge. Our concealed consciousness is our real or whole being, of which the outer is a part and a phenomenon, a selective formation for a surface use. We perceive only a part of the workings of our life and being; the inner being perceives so much that we might almost suppose that nothing escapes its view. We remember only small selection from our perception. The intelligence of inner being needs no training, but preserves the accurate form and relations of all its perceptions and memories and, though this is a proposition which may be considered doubtful or difficult to concede in its fullness can grasp immediately, when it does not possess its significance. Its perceptions are not confined to the scanty gleanings of the physical senses, but extend far beyond and use the relations between the surface will or impulsion and the subliminal urge are mistakenly described as unconscious or subconscious.

If we undertake the self-discovery and enlarge our knowledge of the subliminal self, we discover our lower subconscient and upper superconscient ends which provide the whole material of our apparent being. Man and existence are closely interconnected. Man in his constitution and make up represents the world existence. The

Pinda is a miniature Brahmanda, the microcosm and macrocosm are significant terms. The cosmos has a microform and a macroform.

Our desirable consciousness is only the little visible part of our being. It is a small field below which are depths and further depths and widths and ever wider widths which support and supply it but to which it has no visible access. Until we know all that is below or behind a little about the surface nature is understood. Below this conscient nature is the vast inconscient out of which we come. The inconscient is greater, deeper, more original, and more potent to shape and govern what we are and do. Behind our little frontal ego and nature is a whole subliminal kingdom of inner consciousness with many planes and provinces. They dictate our speech, our thoughts, feelings, and doings even more directly than the inconscient below us. Around us too is a circumconscient universal of which we are a portion. This is pouring its forces, stimuli compulsions, suggestions into us at every moment of our existence. Around us is a universal mind of which our mind is a formation modifying and transcripting its thought waves, force currents, foam of emotion and sensation, and bellows of impulse.

Consciousness or awareness is a primary, most vivid, decisive fact of human being, felt and known directly like all primary qualities of experience. Consciousness also has a dynamic and creative energy. A large part comes to us from others or from the environment, whether as raw material or as manufactured imports; but still more largely they come from universal nature or from other worlds and planes and their beings and powers and influences. Above our human mind are still greater reaches superconscient to it and from there secretly descend influences, powers, touches which are the original determinants of things here. In the superconscient part of our total existence we discover to be our higher self.

Consciousness in Krishnamurti's Teachings

Jiddu Krishnamurti was born on 11 May 1895 in a pious middle-class family in the rural town of Madanapalle in South India. He was discovered in his boyhood by the leaders of the Theosophical

Society, Mrs. Anne Besant and Bishop Leadbeater, who proclaimed that he was the world Teacher that the theosophists were waiting for. As a young man, Krishnamurti underwent certain mystical experiences that brought about a deep transformation and gave him a new vision of life. Later he dissociated himself from all organized religions and ideologies and embarked his solitary mission meeting and talking to people, not as a guru but as a friend.

From the early 1920s till his death -17th February (1986) Krishnamurti travelled around the world till the ripe age of'91, giving talks, writing, holding discussions, or sitting silently with those men and women who sought his compassionate and healing presence. His teachings were not based on book knowledge and scholarship, but on his insight into the human condition and his vision of the sacred. He did not expound any 'philosophy' but rather talked of the things that concern all of us in our everyday life. The problems of living in modern society with its corruption and violence, the individuals search for security and happiness, and the need for man to free himself from his inner burdens of greed, violence, fear and sorrow.

Declaring that his only concern was to 'set man absolutely, unconditionally free', he sought to liberate man from his deep conditioning of selfishness and sorrow. He confronted boldly the problems of contemporary society and analysed with scientific precision the workings of the human mind which is of great significance to psychology and human development.

Although he is recognised both in the East and the West as one of the greatest religious teachers of all times, he himself belonged to no religion, sect or country. Nor did he subscribe to any school of thought. On the contrary he maintained that these are the very factors that divide man from man and bring about conflict and war. He gave new meaning and content to religion by pointing to a way of life that transcends all organised religions. He is regarded by many as one who has had the most profound impact on human consciousness in modern times. He emphasized time and again that we are first and foremost human beings, that each one of us is like the rest of humanity and not different. He pointed to the importance of bringing to our daily life a deeply meditative and religious quality. Such a radical change only can bring about a new mind, and a new civilisation. Thus his teachings transcend all manmade boundaries of religious beliefs, nationalistic sentiment, and sectarian outlook. At the same time, they give a new meaning and direction to modern man's quest for truth, for the sacred.

He espouses how we are struggling to find meaning in life. But we are not using our original being, our natural capacities to observe, to listen and learn from our direct perceptions. We are simply thinking over the knowledge passed on by others and thus conditioned in many ways and also deeply to respond not to the fact but to the idea, intensely immersed in entertaining thought for each and everything and caught in it as slaves. As a result there is material affluence at the stake of healthy human relationships and thereby a loss of healthy environment, both the natural and the human environmental conditions. Due to failure in human well being there is spiritual emptiness. He finds that the social crisis and political crisis or religious crisis is due to crisis in human consciousness.

Man has not created tree or any such natural thing. But by using his mind he is creating so many forms. We are indulging in the artificial world of things created by us and losing the feeling and turning mechanical. As a result we are caring only the outward, superficial life but not the more potent faculties of human beings.

Krishnamurti's teachings mainly intend to bring in total transformation in the human consciousness. He starts with 'what is' and shows mind in its varied states and proposes the necessity for understanding of oneself to go beyond. He points out the urgent necessity for total psychological revolution in the limited, fragmented, thought-constructed self to be in the state of creative intelligence of wholeness. He points out that "what is' is not static, it is a movement. And to keep with the movement of 'what is', you need to have a very clear mind, you need to have an unprejudiced, not a distorted mind . . . .. The mind can't see 'what is', and go beyond it, if the mind is, in any way, concerned with the changing of 'what is', or trying to go beyond it, or suppress it". He emphasizes the necessity of direct seeing of the fact of what is without the self-interest.

He points out the relationship between the world situation and the individual and how human being is responsible for terrorism, environmental destruction, economic struggle, political and religious division. He projects the true relationship in consciousness. "Your brain is like the brain of every other human being. It has immense capacity, immense energy...... Our brains are not ours, they have evolved through a long period of time . . . . that brain with its consciousness is not mine because my consciousness is shared with every other human being".

He distinguishes between physical and psychological time. Lifetimes and evolutionary changes take time. When one perceives how his psyche is, how it is suffering him, he changes immediately. It does not require time 'perception is action'. But, we develop the ideal of 'not being like that or change that state later. That distance between what one is and what one wants to be is psychological time or thought which is mostly entertained by people. He shows how man is caught in the network of thought and proposes the possibility of freedom from it. "If you see the causation, or many causes, then that very perception ends the cause'.

He also indicates how the root cause of fear is thought. Thought is based on memory of past hurts, and thought projects the idea of future hurt. Thus thought, which creates this psychological time, is the cause of fear. He further helps to observe and how significant seeing is, "A scorpion is poisonous, a snake is poisonous - at the very perception of them you act . . . . observe, see, that the causation of fear is thought/time. The very perception is action. And from that you don't rely on anybody. Then you are a free person. Thus he reveals the clue to psychological freedom."

He further exposes how the self-interest originates through thoughts of the self. The self chooses to agree and disagree. When applied incorrectly it creates ideas which result in tremendous suffering. "Self-interest divides, self - interest is the greatest corruption (the word corruption means to break things apart) and where there is self-interest there is fragmentation". He further guides saying, "when you begin to be aware choicelessly of your self-interest, to stay with it, to study it, to learn about it, to observe all the intricacies of it, then you can find out for yourself where it is necessary and where it is completely unnecessary".

Here we find a hint to distinguish between physical and psychological self- interest. One has to care, look after the body well being, protect it and meet its needs. But feelings psychologically as a separate being isolates him from others and lead to self-centeredness, whereas psychologically the contents of consciousness are shared by the whole humanity.

The Mind that is both religious and Scientific

Krishnamurti explored not only the obstacles in self-knowing but also shows the urgency of change in us. Then there is the possibility of insights out of our inquiry, questioning and investigation into different states of mind. He used to be eager in awakening intelligence that is not crystalised, that is not conditioned by words. The subtlety of enquiry is such that transforms the perceptive processes.

"The scientific mind with its logic, its precision, its inquiry, investigates the outer world of nature, but this does not lead to an inward comprehension of things; but an inward comprehension brings about an understanding of the outer. We are the result of the influences of the outer. The scientific mind is precise and clear in its investigation. It is not a compassionate mind, for it has not understood itself".

—*Bombay, 8 MArch, 1961*

By penetrating in depth into the consciousness he says "The religious mind is capable of thinking precisely, not in terms of the negative and positive, therefore that mind can hold within the scientific mind. But the scientific mind does not contain the religious mind because it is based on time, knowledge, it is rooted in success and achievement. The religious mind is the real and evolutionary mind. It is not a reaction to what has been. The religious mind is the only mind that it can respond totally to the present challenge and to all challenges at all times. —*Bombay, 1 March, 1961.*

Scientific mind functions in the field of knowledge to remember, think and deal with the outer world to earn livelihood. Without the world of matter, the material world we would not be here. But when we are concerned about the totality of life knowledge, memory of it, thinking about it in many ways have no place in the life of religiosity. It is just seeing 'what is' without wanting to change it, allowing it to flower and wither away. It means that there is no naming of experience or recognising, remembering, analysing, evaluating anything seen inwardly. This seeing is not only into the superficial layers of the mind, but into the deeper layers. Religious mind thus has the explosion of the fact of the inward, both the recent and the ancient.

Sensitive, alert and attentive mind enters into the field of self-knowing

He says that the beginning of the religious life is in self-knowing but not in belief, in some scripture or doing some retreats and worshipping of idols or an image or a symbol. The mind has to be sensitive to enter into the field of self-knowing. One can't have a sensitive mind if one has not gone into oneself for deeply inquiring, searching and looking. To be sensitive and attentive the mind is to be cleansed itself of all the words, of conclusions, and images by seeing that these are the impediments to respond to anything afresh and unconditioned.

Religion as on today, is a series of beliefs, dogmas, of superstitions, of worship of idols and gurus, The ultimate truth is our projection, that is what we want that can make us happy due to this promise of certainty of moksha or a deathless state and so on. Thus the mind is stagnating as it is caught in all the promises. Greed for power is almost inexhaustible in any spiritual orgnisation though this greed is covered over by all means of sweet sounding words. Hence there is growth of conflict, intolerance, sectarianism and other ugly manifestations. Unless the mind becomes aware of that, our life becomes rather shallow, empty and meaningless. Facing the psychological fact without time interval is immediate action. This is possible in total psychological freedom.

A total human being has the heart which is full, rich, clear, capable of intense feeling, capable of seeing the beauty of a tree, a smile of a child and the agony of a woman. This extraordinary feeling, this sensitivity for everything to feel intensely, not in any particular direction, which is not an emotion, which comes and goes, but which is sensitive with nerves, with ears, eyes, body, and voice. This strong feeling makes the mind highly sensitive. To receive the truth the heart must be full and the mind must be empty. The action of seeing choicelessly is the religious way of living. This action is the action of love. All living is this action and the religious mind in this action. So religion, the mind, the life and love are one. Truth is meeting life anew from moment to moment.

In a search for reality energy creates its own discipline. The man who is seeking reality spontaneously becomes the right kind of citizen but not according to the pattern of any particular society or government. When the energy is not dissipated through conflict, violence, through the process of time, conflict, talent and when this energy has no movement at all in any direction, then something happens, it must explode. Thus the daily life of a free man is not different from religious life. He can be harmonious in his relationship and with anything and everything of the world as he is not different from the world.

Lack of self-knowledge is ignorance to Krishnamurti. We are the result of the evolution of the millennia of years. We have genetic, racial and cultural conditioning from the ancient to the present. We live by instincts and influenced by the environment around us. We are conditioned in many ways socially, politically, religiously and through education. More than any we have the mind to perceive and understand to live intelligently and be happy in our relationships.

Krishnamurti shows the common ground, consciousness of humanity. Consciousness, as we know of it, is the product of thought, with a lot of content accumulated by it. So, the human life has lost its pristine quality in its egoistic pursuits and making life meaningless with shallow purpose of achievement and success. Man's fullest potential to realise the truth, to be compassionate and unconditionally good are unlived.

If we are aware of the wholly different way of living without conflict between 'what is' and what one wants to be or to become', if we are unconditioned out of our awareness of its futility and secondhand life, if we observe ourselves inward, without creating duality by rising as the 'observer' or by dealing with the 'observed' we can pass through the whole past beyond the mind and transcend the life. The transcended life is the liberated life. Thus we are not conditioned beings but integrated beings with transpersonal nature.

❖ ❖ ❖

Psychology An Indian Perspective

Part-I

Psychology from Upanishads

– P. Datta Prasad

The earliest of the Indian Scriptures, Vedas recognized life's supreme reality. Rigveda says, 'Truth is one', the wise call it by different names. The Vedas are called sritis. The major part is called poorva meemamsa'. This was followed by the vast majority of people in those days to fulfil the worldly desires. This is a complex set of rituals. The fag end of the Vedas is Vedanthas or Upanishads. They are beyond rituals. Their purpose is to realise directly the divine ground of life through the practice of spiritual disciplines like meditation. This ideal in Vedic times was sanctioned as the highest vocation of the human beings.

There are about 1180 Upanishads, but through the centuries, many of them disappeared from human memory and only 108 have now survived. Out of them ten Upanishads were given prime importance due to their depth and content value. Sankaracharya also wrote commentaries to these ten Upanishads. They are Ishavasyopanishad, Kathopanishad Mandukopanishad, Brihadaranyakopanishad, Prasnopanishad, Kenopanishad, Chandogyopanishad, Aithareyopanishad and Taithiriyopanishad. The Sage Vyasa had written 555 Brahmasuthras, which contain the essential contents of Upanishads.

Every human being is constituted of five sense organs, five organs of action, the mind, intellect, will, and ego. Man's life clings to sensations, intellect, will, and ego only due to mind, only because of its attachment to action and result. Again the same mind unattached liberates. Some questions arise in us like –what is the purpose of the journey of life? Who has created it? Is life merely to live, eat and

✍ **P. Datta Prasad,** *Rtd. Lecturer, Hindu College, Guntur.*

finally to die? What is the cause of existence? What is the basic principle of life? Who am I? When the mind entertains such questions that mind looks from a different dimension. Looking at the state of affairs we also question –should the people of the world fragment themselves as castes, classes, religions and live quarrelling in the name of those labels? People were understood as of the three categories.

- Body conscious people: Body is everything for them. Nothing else is more important than the body.
- Ego-oriented people: They study the scriptures, feel that life is temporary and find that in this temporary life man does both good and sinful deeds. The man who is sensitively aware of this wants to do good, and be happy.
- Soul conscious people: They think that all the visible things are the manifestations of Brahman and the nature in everything is the same, which lacks these days. These people live in awareness, on studying the scriptures and with constant inquiry into themselves. They observe inward to be soul conscious. These scientists of the inward have said that one need not do any ritual, yaga and yagna to live in soul consciousness.

The opportunity for such a deep inquiry was open to anyone, to lead a life of outward simplicity in order to concentrate on inner growth. They yearned to know; to know what the human being is; what death means and whether it can be conquered. The Upanishads were individualistic in their expressions yet completely universal; these ecstatic documents belong to no particular religion but to all mankind. Each Upanishad contains the record of a darshana, literally something seen, a view not of the world of experience but of the deep still realms beneath the sense-world, accessible in deep meditation.

The eye cannot see it,
The mind cannot grasp it.
The unchanging has neither eyes nor ears neither hands nor feet.
Sages say it is infinite in the great
And in the small, everlasting and changeless,

The source of all life.
As the web issues out of the spider and is withdrawn,
As plants sprout from the earth,
As hair grows from the body,
Even so, the sages say,
This universe springs from the imperishable,
The source of all life. (Mandukopanishad. 1.1.6-7)

The early testaments of the Vedic sages were born in freedom and stamped with the joy of self-realization. They contain no trace of world denial, no shadow of fear, no sense of diffidence about our place in an alien universe. They taught that self-realization means health, vitality, long-life and a harmonious balance of inward and outward activity.

They instilled spirit into the inquiry of humans by stating that the human destiny lies ultimately in human hands for those who master the passions of the mind:

We are what our deep driving desire is. As our deep driving desire is, so is our will. As our will is, so is our deed. As our deed is, so is our destiny. (Brihadaranyaka . IV.4,5)

They insist on knowing, not the learning of facts but the direct experience of truth, the one reality underlying life's multiplicities. This is not an intellectual attainment. Knowing means realisation. To know the truth one must make it real; must live it out in thought, word and action. From that everything else of value follows.

The method these sages followed in their pursuit of truth was called Brahma vidya or Atma vidya, the supreme science. They not only taught the principles of Atmavidya but also taught the practical means of realization. Thus attention was focused intensely on the contents of conscionsness. In practice this means meditation. Brahmavidya is like a series of experiments on the mind, by the mind, which is the only instrument, with predicatble and replicable results.

The upanishadic sages looked not at the world outside but at the human knowledge of the world inside and discarded everything impermanent as ultimately unreal. Ther principle was neti, neti atma. This is not self, that is not the self. They peeled away personality like an onion, layer by layer, and found nothing permanent in the mass of perceptions, thoughts, emotions, desires and memories we call 'I'. When everything individual was stripped away, an intense awareness remained, which is conscience itself. The sages called this ultimate ground of personality atman, the self.

From the Rigveda, India's scriptures revealed, an all-pervasive order rhythm in the whole of creation that is reflected in each part. The individual according to the impressions of experience in previous lives is associated with the five karmendriyas, five jnanendriyas, the five pranas, manas and buddi. The concrete body becomes a corpse when the air leaves the body but the antharyami, the immanent spirits in the body, complex abode, the mystery that is beyond the reach, the motivating force of the impulses and intensions of that complex has no death.

There are four Mahavakyas in Upanishads. They are the following, which are preached by the guru. 'Tatvam asi'. You are that Brahman. The disciple feels, how is it possible? If so, he must be possessing supernatural powers, he does not have.

- 'Aham Brahmasmi'. I am Brahman I am, when the form and name are deleted, which atma is there that is Brahman
- 'Ayamatma Brahma', the Atman is Brahma not the forms and panchakosas.
- 'Pragnanam Brahma'. Extremely superior knowledge is Brahma.

He alone who has turned away from evil conduct, who has controlled the vagaries of his senses, who is of tranquil mind, whose mind is undisturbed even by the thought of the fruits of calmness, and who has a teacher, will attain the atman through prajnana or pure knowledge. There 'Knowing' means 'being', when the agitation of mind stops ie, the cause of desire, the sense of doership and personality are not there.

Brahma is change and changeless; the many in manifestation and the one in being. The manifest is subject to the limitations of time, space and causality. What lies above these three limitations is necessarily causeless, infinite and non-dual; it is beyond sound, touch, form, taste and smell, it knows no end. Of all disciplines and subjects of study, the Brahmavidya is the most sacred, holy and esoteric.

Panchakosas and beyond

Annamaya kosa is the body, form. The physical body is the gift of annam. Since the physical body is the transformation of food, it has an annamaya kosa. The waters in conjunction with the fire in the stomach become food. Pranamayakosa is formed of the vital airs. It is subtle and separate, different from the body. Pranamaya is the soul of the Annamaya, for it makes that function from head to foot. It cannot survive with out the prana. The one vayu is prana, apana, vyana, udana and samana. The prana moves from the heart through the nerves to the face, the nose and reaches head and motivates the various nerves flowing through the body under different names with distinct functions. To progress with the Brahmic outlook that one is Brahma and not the body, the pranamaya is the first instrument.

Manomayakosa weighs between good and bad, right and wrong out of the acquired knowledge through the senses and mind. Mind is impure when it is subject to the pressures of lust and pure when free from the lust for pleasure. The mind is formed of thought. The thoughts are spontaneous, superficial or analytical. They operate in intellect.

Vijnamayakosa functions with a purpose in view. When the self is to be realized knowledge reaches its highest consummation in perfect duality. Idam (this) is the object and aham is the subject, the two together form the intellect sheath.

Anandamayakosa is the last, innermost layer of reality. It is where the entire universe of causes and effects exists in its cosmic potentiality, where time, space and causality are entirely involutes, and where the categories of nothingness and all thingness apply with equal force. This corresponds to the anadamayakosa or bliss. In this all the stress and strain of cause and effect in suspended. We have to verify where we are, how far are we developed in terms of Kosas. 'I' in brief is beyond the five sheaths. Sat-chit-ananda is there when the residual is left over after discarding all that is not self. Sat means pure existence. Chit means pure of knowledge and ananda means ever lasting bliss.

The human condition can be better understood with all its possibility by understanding 'Avastha thrayam, the three states of life of everyday –waking, dream and deep sleep.

In the waking state the gross body perceives gross names and forms; in dream state the mental body perceives the mental creations in their manifold forms and names; in the dreamless sleep state, the identification with the body being lost, there are no perceptions. Similarly in the transcendental state identity with Brahman places the man in harmony with everything.

The dream is the combination of jagrat and sushupti. It is due to the samskaras of the jagrat state we remember dreams. We are not aware of the dream and jagrat simultaneously; still everyone recollects strange perplexities in dream. One wonders if he dreams or is awake. He argues and determines that he is only awake when he is really awake or he finds that it was only a dream.

In deep sleep the man is devoid of possessions, including his own body. Instead of being unhappy he is quite happy. Everyone desires to have sound sleep. The conclusion is that happiness is inherent in man and is not due to external causes. So one is to realise the truth of one self in order to open the store of unalloyed happiness.

The desire for happiness is a proof of ever existing happiness of the self. Man desires only that which is natural to him. If man gets rid of his misery the everpresent bliss is left. In deep sleep all thoughts disappear. There the prevailing body is anadamaya kosa.

The universe is an instrument to reveal the majesty of Brahman. He is the breath of one's breath. Since He has no specific form, He cannot be indicated by words nor can His mystery be penetrated by the senses. He is beyond the reach of ascetism, beyond the bonds of Vedic rituals. He can be known only when the intellect is cleansed of all traces of attachment and hatred of egoism and the sense of possession. Dhyana can silence the mind; Jnana alone can grant self-realization.

Every human being has the potential to realize Brahman. He can develop to the extent of being it, one with it.

References

- Chandogyopanishad Ed. no: 582. Gorakpur : Gita press.
- Eknath Eswaran, (1996) The Dhammapada, Penguin Books, India.
- Gambhiranada Swami (1996). Brahma Sutra Bhasya. Calcutta: Swami Mumukshananda Advaita Ashrama.
- Sankaracharya Sri, et.al (1980) (trans) Mahadeva Sastry Pondichery : Samata Books.
- Saraswati Swami. Tatva Vidana. (2005) Bruhadaranyokopanishad. Secundrabad: Sri Sankara Vidyapeeta Trust.
- Sri Rama Chandra. Acharya (2001) Sri Bhagavadgita Sankara Bhasyam, Hyderabad: Arsha Vignana Trust
- Vasudeva Laxmana Sharma Pansikar (Ed) (1918) The Yoga Vasistha of Valmiki. Delhi: Motilal Bansaridas
- Vidya Ranya Muni. Sri. (1999). Vivarana Prameyasan Grashai. Varanasi: Amar Publication.
- Vidyarnya Swami Varya (1927). Sri Vedanta Panchadasi. Chennai: Vavilla Rama Swami Sastrulu & Sons

Psychological Health Upanishadic Perspective

– Dr. L. Bhagya Lakshmi
M. Sreedevi

Good thoughts, Good words, Good deeds
Listening good, seeing good, being good
These confer good health on human folk,

– Bhagawan Sri Satya Sai Baba

Health is the greatest blessing. Without it man can't do even the slightest work. Health is an indispensable requisite for progress in material, moral, political, economic, artistic and spiritual fields of life. All ailments in the human body are in fact arising from the mind. Most diseases are psychological. Mental diseases are increasing in the present day world. In the modern world there are diseases, which are controlled by appropriate medicine. But some diseases do not respond to the treatment by medication. Such are the diseases pertaining to the mind. If one wants to be psychologically healthy, one must attain the qualities like taking satwic food, controlling of sense organs, inculcating positive attitude, overcoming negative emotions, practicing yoga etc, which are emphasized by Vedas and Upanishads. In the philosophy of the Upanishads one finds a constant faith in life, a jest for living. Not effort, nor rites and ceremonies, nor worship of Gods or knowledge will lead to perfection, but internal purity and goodness alone. It is the consciousness that gives life to the body-mind complex. Hence it is the essential core of the human personality.

✍ **Dr. L. Bhagya Laxmi,** *R.V.R.R. College of Education, Guntur.*
✍ **M. Sreedevi,** *A.M. College of Education, Guntur.*

The human personality consists of the body and mind, and it is necessary to have good physical health and mental health. The body is the temple of God. Health is wealth and for one's life's sojourn a healthy body is a great asset. In the same way purity of mind is essential. For only a pure mind will have the necessary discrimination to recognize the ultimate aim of life and direct the senses along the right path.

Brihadaranyakopanishad is affiliated to the Sukla Yajurveda (42) Brihadaranyakopanishad and Kathopanishad say that the sense organs have to be controlled. The entire sensory world and the senses have to be equated with the reality only. There is no use in pursuing the sense organs as ultimate and valuable.

Sai Baba says that one has to control the sense organs if one wants to be psychologically healthy. One should act as a master in controlling the senses but not the slave of the senses. Senses are packets of energy which have been bestowed to man; so, one should employ them in the right manner. Bhagavan says that the five senses have to be utilized for the laudible purpose of transcending their native downward pull. Just as the satellite has to be fixed at a speed, which will take it beyond the gravitational pull of the earth, so that it will not be pulled back to the planet, one has to flee beyond the pull of the senses through the medium of the senses alone.

Just as the mind, intellect and chitta are permitted by divinity, so also are the senses. Hence one should not treat one's senses with desire, anger etc. It is only the senses that are responsible for one's pleasure and pain, good and bad. Hence the first and the foremost job is to control the sense organs which is possible with strong determination. If one allows even one of the five senses to go out of control, one will lower himself to the level of an animal.

The senses, which are by themselves temporary, can lead only to transitory but not permanent joy. The senses are prone to be diseased and the joy they yield is fraught with illness and not true happiness. To a jaundiced eye everything looks yellow; for a malaria patient all food items taste bitter. Does the bitterness live in the man or the food? The disease causes the bitterness. So the senses, which are the gifts of God, should be used moderately. The one who violates the golden principle of moderation not only acts contrary but also courts pain and loss.

Man possesses five organs of perception -the mouth, the ears, the eyes, the nose and the skin. The eyes may be 'consuming' rajashic food (seeing ugly and undesirable things) looking here and there like crows. Thus the eyes are taking the impure food of all kinds. So one should see evil, and see what is good. The ears are for listening and an individual mostly spends his time listening to all the negative aspects. But one should be concerned mostly about his affairs and also share his good thoughts with others. So one should not hear evil but hear what is good.

The nose is meant for exhaling, inhaling and smelling. But on the other hand, one uses the nose for inhaling snuff powder, which pollutes the wind also. The misuse of the nose in this manner causes asthma and throat cancer. The diseases which are contacted by such indulgences are themselves punishments for misusing the senses.

Taittariopanishad says that tongue should be used to speak good things only i.e. *'Jihwame Madhumatthama' (P. 27) (1-4)*.

Bhagawan Baba says that the tongue is a very powerful organ. It has a double function: speech and taste. The tongue is prone to indulge in several undesirable activities like talking ill of others; talking excessively; idle gossip; and telling lies are four kinds of misbehavior by the tongue. By indulging in these four forms of abuse of the tongue, man's life is rendered unholy. Hence, the tongue has to be kept under rigorous control. The tongue, which is glorified, should not be misused for feeding on more Rajashic and Tamasic foods. Drinking and smoking are highly injurious to health and one should abstain from them. So one should use the tongue strictly for the purpose for which it has been gifted to mankind.

It should be recognized that there is divine energy in the human body. When this divine energy comes in contact with the body of a bad/good person it is likely to receive bad/good thoughts. So one should move with good company to acquire positive thoughts.

Living beings succumb to the temptations presented by the five senses of sound, smell, touch, taste and form. Lured by sounds, the deer stands still and then the hunters easily capture it. Here temptation for the sensation of sound ruins the deer. Irresistibly attracted by light, the moth rushes towards the flame and dies as a consequence. Here the sensation of sight brings doom upon the moth. Similarly, tempted by the bait of meat tied to the end of the fishing rod, the fish rushes to the bait and dies as a consequence. Here the temptation for the sensation of taste imperils the life of the fish. The bee gets choked inside the flower, fascinated by the fragrance; thereby it succumbs to the temptation of smell. The elephant succumbs to the sensation of touch and is trapped as a consequence. This is how the deer, the moth, the fish, the bee and the elephant yielding to a single sensation bring ruin upon themselves. One can imagine for oneself what havoc the combined strength of sensations can do to a man since he yields not to a single sensation but to all the five sensations. Ensnared by the senses, man has become a slave. This is how senses and materialistic pleasures hold man in bondage.

Bhagawan Baba says that these sensual pleasures vanish in a moment. Man wastes away his precious life in pursuit of these fleeting pleasures. The Upanishaths said, " Man is one who has a value". Man is the most valuable creature in the world. But unfortunately, while the value of other things has considerably increased, man's value has reached the rock bottom! This is because of misusing the sense organs, which are the precious treasures in him. So the dire need today for man is to acquire value, which helps him to promote positive thoughts or to be emotionally balanced.

Thaittriopanishad speaks that 'Satyam Vada', (P. 17) (1-11) i.e. one must always speak truth and Mandukopanishad says that 'Satyameva Jayathe Nanrutham' (P.17) (3-1-6) which means that truth is bound to succeed but not the untruth.

Bhagavan Baba says that in daily living one has to speak the truth, i.e. speak as he had seen or felt. Speaking the truth makes one's conscience clear. If one speaks untruth, one has to speak more lies to cover up. Hence lying becomes a habit. One's conscience is connected to all knowing consciousness; if ignored a time comes, when it stops guiding and does wrong things without hesitation.

Truth should be told in an acceptable way, sweetly and humbly. Sometimes it is better to keep quiet than speak a lie. Swamy Vivekananda used to say -if one practices speaking truth always for 12 years, whatever one says will come True. Such is the power of Truth. Purity of mind and intellect will lead the intellect to the highest levels.

Brihadaranyakopanishad says that speech is Brahma *'Vakyi Brahma (p.27) (4-1- 2* and also says Truth is God' *'Sathyam hyeva Brahma (p.17) (5-4-1)* and Kathopanishad says that the control of speech is very important in one's life.

Bhagawan Sri Sathya Sai Baba says that it is very important to use one's tongue to speak sweet and good words. Harsh words cause endless trouble, while sweet words give boundless joy, as words are tremendously powerful. One should mean what he says and keep one's word. One should avoid hurting others as well as speaking ill.

One should learn to talk in a well-modulated voice. Loud talk, excessive talk, excited talk, loud music all add to atmospheric pollution and destroy the peace of mind of people around, which leads to psychological ill health.

Brihadaranyakopanishad says that what we will do, that we will be paid i.e. *'Yat Karma Kuruthe thadabhi sampadyathe' (P.24) (4-4-5)*. Mandukopanishad says that if one wants to attain good results, they have to do only good things i.e. *Yesh Vah pandhaah swakruthasya Lokee' (P.23) (1-2-1)*.

Bhagawan Baba says that God is not involved in any reward or punishment. He only reflects, resounds and reacts. One decides one's own fate. So one has to do good and be good so that one gets good in return. Any instant solution would go against the fundamental quality of nature itself, as well as karmic law of cause and effect. If the individual lives in the materialistic world of desire and ego, one reaps the fruits of one's actions. This brings about revolution and devolution. As you sow, so you reap. So for every action, there is an equal and opposite reaction as said by Isac Newton in his third law of motion. The consequence of past actions clouds the light of the consciousness. Good actions cleanse the mind of its impurities.

Actions of the past bear fruit in the present. However, past is past, the future is still in the making. If one has courage to face the consequences, one will never do bad things. Every thing is like the passing cloud. It will pass off. When the result of one particular action is worked out, the fruit of the next action in the list will bring, to one's own consequences. Hence life goes on changing. Past is history, future is mystery, present is the reality. So Bhagawan says one should use the present moment best to sharpen one's skills, to broaden intelligence, expand one's, heart and to master the technique of facing the challenges of life with courage and equanimity. It is the right time to sow the seeds of good actions then and there so that it will result in good. In this way one can develop positive attitude, which helps to develop psychological health.

Mythrayani Upanishad says that mind is of two types -pure and impure i.e. *Mnno-hi Dwivitham Proktam, Suddham chaa suddha mevacha* (P.21) (6-34) and also quotes that mind is the real source for liberation or attachment i.e. *Asuddham Kamasankalpam Suddham Kama vivarjitham and Manayeva Manushyanaanam kaaranam Bandha Mokshayoh (P.21) (6-34).*

Bhagawan says that it is the mind of the individual that directs all perceptions and actions in the world. Upanishad says *'Manomoolam, idham Jagath'*. This world rests on the mind. Mind is also defined as sankalpa vikalpath makam: meaning thoughts of positive and negative type. Bhagawan Baba quotes that there is no end for the flow of these thoughts and counterthoughts. The mind is so fast that man is unable to control its speed. The mind entertains fifty million thoughts, which appear and disappear like clouds. Some pass silently, but many stay and stir the mind into activity. Positive thoughts can elicit the best from an individual and help to use all the energy in a perfect way. In order to harvest a good fruit, one should cultivate good thoughts. One can easily indulge in negative thoughts about others but it has to be remembered that one has to bear the consequences of negative thoughts. No body can escape the consequences of thoughts; good or bad. Sometimes positive thoughts and sometimes negative thoughts arise in the mind. Mind is the creation of man himself and is suffering from affects. In the modern world, most diseases are psychological. When mind is afflicted, it affects the body health causing stomachache, headache etc. Mental diseases are on the increase in the present day world. The cases of mental derangement have become very common these days and the number of persons affected is alarmingly large. The reasons for this large-scale incidence of such cases are too many.

Thoughts often lose track. Thought has no valid reason or season behind. Mind has moods of various types. It may be sorrow, love or joy. Of whatever type the thought may be, it arises out of attachment and hatred. The six evil qualities, which are enemies of man, are lust, anger, greed, delusion, pride and jealousy which arise from the mind and make it lose its original purity. Whoever is associated with a person having these evil qualities also becomes a victim of these and forgets his innate Divinity. This brings disrepute to the person. Good feelings, good behaviour, and good thoughts should be cultivated as they help man to lead a healthy and peaceful life. Mind is responsible for good and evil alike. It changes constantly. The mind attracts many objects that it sees. It promotes a variety of qualities, attitudes and attachments. Above all it encourages the inflation of the ego. Puffed up by his ego, man looses all his powers of discrimination and forgets what is permanent. One's gross body is like the outer leather cover of the football and one's subtle body is like the rubber bladder inside it. When it is inflated with the air of ego, the football of one's body receives kicks after kicks in the game of life. If the air of ego is removed, it becomes deflated and therefore receives no more kicks. It is only when the ego is defeated and eliminated that man can gradually realize the reality. Egoism is the root and the crown of all evil thought and down dragging tendencies.

Anger is a great enemy of health. As long as man is filled with anger, he can gain no peace. Anger rushes blood to the brain, the temperature rises, the composition of the blood changes, toxins enter into it in such quantities that they injure the nerves and make one old before one's time. There was a mother who was feeding her tender baby at her breast. Suddenly she plunged into a violent quarrel with her neighbours and forgot to keep her baby down. In the heat of anger, the poor child drank the toxin-mixed milk of the mother and when the flames of anger subsidized, the mother found that she had a corpse on her breast. If one bursts in anger 1000 red blood cells are destroyed. One should not listen to vile and vicious stories as they develop a diseased mind. What is heard is imprinted like a carbon copy, through the ear, on the heart. Most diseases are due to mental illness. One's body is like a camera. Heart is the film: one's mind is the lens. If one turns the lens of one's mind towards the faults of others and similar bad thoughts, the film of one's heart will be imprinted with all those negative thoughts. If one directs the lens of one's mind towards positive thoughts, one's heart will have good impressions.

The tightest bond is the ignorance of one's own reality; ignorance is caused by attachment. Attachment is identification of 'I' with the body, mind and senses. Attachment leads to desire and desire results in anger. Anger blinds reason and promotes ignorance, which breeds dualities of "mine and thine", good and bad etc.

One's heart is like the lock; and mind is the key. If one turns the key to the left, it get locked; if it is turned to the right, it becomes unlocked. Same lock and same key, just the difference is in the turning. Similarly, if one turns his mind towards outward it leads to attachment; if one turns towards inward it results in liberation. Bhagawan Baba suggests that one should be a mastermind i.e. the mind is no longer one's slave. Mastermind means a mind that is directed to doing the right path.

Brihadhrarnyakopanishad says that mind is nothing but desires, thoughts counterthoughts etc. (P.22) (1-5-3).

Bhagawan says that the mind only exists because of desires, thoughts and counterthoughts. Desire is an unfortunate thing. The desires take one to a pathetic stage. Baba often says that the mind is nothing but desires, which form its ward and woof. If one removes the thread one by one, the cloth woven will cease to exist. So also if one eliminates desires one by one then the mind will cease to exist and that results in liberation, which means just the elimination of desires. When desires disintegrate, one is liberated from bondage, which makes one to be ultimately happy.

The mind of man, because of its extreme subtlety, is capable of immense expansion. But because of the senses the mind is attracted to a variety of objects and persons. When these objects fill the mind its expansiveness is restricted. It is only when the attraction for these objectives is reduced that the mind can activate expansion. So one must progressively reduce the desires, which are the cause of all difficulties. It is true that one cannot exist without desires, but they should be within reasonable limits. There can be no happiness without the control of desires.

The vice-like grip on one's life is of the masters.

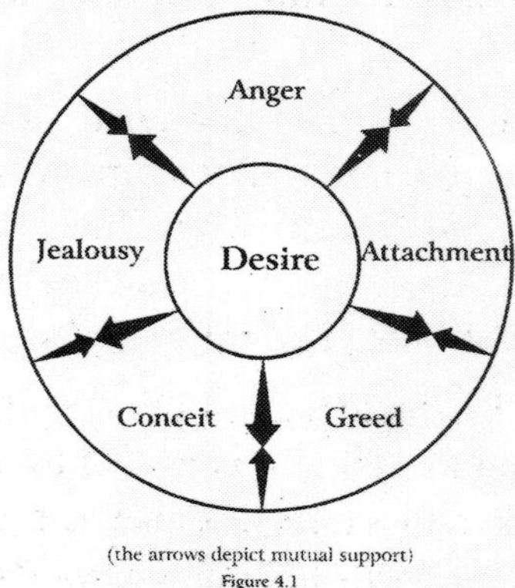

(the arrows depict mutual support)
Figure 4.1

Bhagawan Satya Sai Baba reminds of these masters virtually and tells that liberation from slavery to them is the first major step towards one's goal. In India these masters have been recognized for thousands of years. These masters are a family called selfishness made up of a mother and her five children. The mother is 'Desire'. When one intensely desires something and does not get it, two children are born: Anger and Jealousy. But if one gets what he craves for, a third child arrives: Attachment. As attachment grows stronger, another one is born: Greed for more of the same. As greed is satisfied, the fifth child takes birth: Conceit. These six masters rule one's life and become selfish individuals. Being aware that the word selfish smells bad, clever minds have coined words to camouflage it: self-centered individualism or enlightened self-interest in essence, plain selfishness.

The master who held bonded slaves has also been identified in the west. 400 years ago, the great Dutch satirist Erasmus talked of them like in the following table.

Our Masters

Title	*Named*
The Queen mother	Boundless desire
His Imperial Highness	Blinding self-love
Her Royal Highness	Flaming jealousy
Captain of Tycoons	Galloping greed
Supreme Commander of self destruction	Red-hot anger
Sultan of Sensuality	Lord lust

Bhagavan Sathya Sai Baba has pithily talked about the first step to free oneself from slavery of the family selfishness. Fish is better than selfish. Fish cleans the water but selfishness pollutes the atmosphere.

Koushithaki Upanishad quotes that one can attain every thing through mind i.e. ***Manasa sarwani Dhyananyapnothi (p.21) (3-4).***

Bhagawan Baba says man has six different kinds of minds. They are: The ordinary mind, the supermind, the higher mind, the illuminated mind, the intuitive mind, and the overmind. The starting base for the six levels of mind is the ordinary mind. At the summit level is the overmind. In the mental processes, what goes on is the ascent from the ordinary mind to the overmind, as well as a descent from the overmind to the ordinary mind. It is when the descending process and the ascending process meet that the fullness in the human being is seen.

Every human being should strive to progress towards the ultimate state of overmind consciousness, the state which has been described by seers as vijnanamayakosa. Modern science is concerned with analyzing physical objects, but the vijnanmayakosa is concerned with exploring the supreme reality, the omnipresent consciousness. This alone is true scientific inquiry. It is from the vijnanamayakosa that one proceeds to the anandamayakosa, the state of superconsciousness or total bliss. It may appear difficult to attain this state, but without making the necessary effort, it should not be treated as beyond one's capacity.

Bhagawan Baba often advises that every individual should put a question to himself: that Mahatmas and Mahapurushas who are also human beings just as he is, have attained perfection, then why not himself? Can't he succeed if he followed the methods, which have been implemented by the great people? How is he going to be benefitted by finding faults and weaknesses in others? Every individual should search for faults and weaknesses in one's own self and try to rectify them.

Chandogyopanishad says (page 100) "As the food, so the mind".

Bhagavan Baba says pure food is conducive to the purity of mind. One with a pure mind is filled with pure thoughts and bubbles with energy derived from pure love. Wisdom is the efflorescence of purity of mind. Only such persons can achieve control over the senses.

The Head of the Department of Health of Culcutta University has found that 80 out of every 100 students in Culcutta University are afflicted with poor health. In the Bombay region, the condition is even worse, affecting 90 out of every hundred. The reason is found to be in the food that the students took, and they are engaged in sensual living.

Bhagavan Baba says that all living beings exist because of food. According to the scriptures food is of three kinds, Sathwic (promoting peace and harmony), Rajashic (promoting passion and emotions, activities and adventures) and Tamasic (promoting sloth and dullness). One has to choose one's food with discrimination and control and limit the intake, if one wants to be healthy. Then the food will be health -giving medicine. If, on the other hand food is consumed indiscriminately and beyond limit, it produces illness and causes grief and pain, which leads to ill health. It assumes a fearful role. This fact is made clear in the Vedas by the probe into the word "Anna". The word anna has as its root Ad, which means 'eating' that which is taken by living beings and at the same time, it eats the person who eats; food is both beneficial and maleficent. Satwic food according to some sages consists in milk and fruit. But it is much more. It may not even be these, for the calories that one takes in through the mouth are but a small part of the intake of man. The intake by the senses is part of the food that builds the individual. The sounds heard, the sights seen, the tactile impression sought or suffered, the air breathed, the environment that attracts attention, appreciation and adoption - all these are "food". They have considerable impact on the character and care of the individual.

Bhagavan Baba says that the psychological health of the individual is maintained by regulating one's food and other living habits. Food particles should be clean and hygienic. It should be life supporting and nourishing to the mind. The vibrations of the people who handle the food are incorporated in the food and influence the minds. The food should be bought with well-earned money and prepared and eaten in a pure environment. The grain part of the food sustains the body, the subtle part of the food i.e. the vibration in it forms one's mind and subtlest part goes to form speech i.e., words. Non-vegetarian food is permeated by the feelings of the animal at the time of death; it is the worst kind of food, as it carries vibrations of anger, pain, fear, suffering, anxiety, hatred, besides the animal traits. Every action has its reaction. The suffering and pain caused to another living being will one day be reflected back. That is the law of nature. Hence animal food should be avoided completely. Intoxicants destroy the brain cells and therefore non -vegetarian food, must be avoided as it damages the psychological health. Food intake is not only through the mouth, but also through all the five sense organs. What one sees, hears, smells, tastes, the place visited, all these leave their impressions and influence on one's mind and are responsible for one's thoughts.

Food that confers Ananda to the body, mind and heart is Sathwic, that which sustains holy living: that which keeps one light, even at the end of the meal. The Sathwics are satisfied with fruits, green leafy vegetables, timely eating etc. Rajastic nature demands continuous feeding of hot stuff tasting sour, salty or pungent. Thamasics appreciate cold stale acrid taste. The grosser part of the food consumed are eliminated. The less gross parts build up muscles and bones. The subtle parts make up the nerves and the mind. Therefore one should be very careful about the quality of food one consumes. Food is the medicine for the illness of hunger, drink of thirst for the disease of bhavaragha. As the food so the mind; as is the mind so the thought; as the thought so the action.

Kathopanishad quotes that mind is greater than sense organs i.e. 'Indriyebyah Param Monaha' (Page 22) (2-3-7).

Bhagawan Baba says that the senses can do nothing by themselves. They are not independent. If the mind is brought under control, the senses can also be controlled. Some people undergo mere asceticism of the senses in order to control the mind. They are ignorant of real discipline, which is necessary. The real discipline is the distinction of desires.

Kathopanishad says that intellect is greater than mind i.e. *'Manasasthau Parabuddhihi' (Page 23) (1-3-10).*

Bhagawan Baba says that in the hierarchy of the senses, mind and intellect, it is the intellect that tells one to discriminate between what is good and what is bad, what is right and what is wrong. Similarly the intellect discriminates and decides upon the action. Therefore if one accepts the intellect as the master, there is a change and human values can be expressed out worldly.

So long as the mind is incharge as the master, one is not human by any standards. Animals too have minds and hence the mind is not an indication. Values are a sign. They are hallmarks of human beings. So one should make intellect as the master of one's life and let values guide them.

The mind creates duality or multiplicity. The intellect (like a needle is used for sticking together different pieces of cloth) seeks to grasp the unity underlying the diversity i.e. the reason why Ramana Maharshi guided people to overcome the bondage of the mind. So long as the mind is the master, one is a slave, which makes the man to be patient. Therefore one should be the intellect.

Thaittraioparishad says Mathru Devo Bhava, Pitru Devo Bhava, Aacharya Devo Bhava (1-11) (page no 34). i.e. one should give respect to his mother, father and teacher.

Bhagawan baba says that 'parent' means ' pay rent'. Children should pay the rent of respect and service to parents who gave them the room called the body. Children should always be grateful to their parents because their food, blood, money and all belong to them. Parents are the first teachers for their children. The home is the first school, where children have their initial education. Shivaji, Swami Vivekananda and Mahatma Gandhi whose lives well served as a model to others have acknowledged with reverential gratitude, the value of the wholesome training they received at the hands of their parents while young. So the children must take these great leaders as their role models. Bhagawan Baba often says that every child must be like Srawana Kumara, who dedicated his life for his old blind parents. This profound love paves way to satisfaction. Bhagawan Baba says that teachers are the second parents who educate the children in developing an allround personality. The students must respect the teachers who pave a way for them to develop good behaviour. The apex, which is the child, is equally effected by two bottom angles which are the teacher and parent. Teachers reveal the direction and goal whereas students lay the road and journey into the future. So the students must respect their teacher. Obedience to teachers helps the students to develop interest and attention in the classroom, which helps to learn in a better way.

Wisdom of Upanishads says that direct knowledge of the Brahman can be got by the eight-fold yoga of Yama, Niyama, Asana, Pranayama, Prathyahara, Dharana, Dyana and Samadhi.

According to Bhagavadgeetha, yoga is of four types –Karma yoga or the path of action, Bhakti yoga or the path of devotion, Gnana yoga or the path of knowledge, Raja yoga or Astanga yoga. This Raja yoga is the path of mind control. As the name indicates it is the king of yogas, the royal path, which blends the three yogas, mentioned above, into a harmonious whole. It integrates one's actions, emotions and intellect, into a harmonious whole.

Yama and Niyama harmonize life and integrate human personality by restraining the mental cravings and attachments to sensual pleasures. This strengthens attachment to the life divine, and gives mental purity. Asanas help in maintaining physical and mental health. Yogasanas keep the body healthy and prevent muscular degeneration. Pranayama is regulation of breath, which helps in regulating the mind. Slow and deep rhythmic breathing gives health and longivity to the body. Pratyahara is withdrawal of the senses from the sense objects and turning them inward. Dharana is concentration or holding or focusing the mind or the consciousness on some particular object. Dhyana means meditation. The first step in meditation is concentration i.e. dharana. Twelve concentrations amount to one meditation (dhyana). Twelve meditations equal to one Samadhi. Samadhi is equal mindedness, the state in which the intellect has achieved equanimity. Whether in pleasure or pain, in praise or blame, in gain or loss, in heat or cold, to be able to maintain an equal mind is Samadhi, which ultimately leads to self-realization.

Educational Implications

Modern education develops the intellect and imparts skills but does not promote positive qualities. Of what value is the acquisition of all the knowledge in the world if there is no character? Knowledge has multiplied and desires have grown, with the result one is a hero in words but zero in actions.

Sri Sathya Sai Baba (1980) says Education must enable a person to discriminate between light and darkness. It must foster and promote the precious wealth of moral strength and spiritual victory. It must purify the inner impulses of man. Mere mastery of books does not entitle a man to be known as 'educated'. Without the mastery of the inner instrument of emotion no man can be deemed to be educated. Education is meant to mould the child into an integrated personality through sustained influence, which is constantly positive in its appeal.

Bhagawan Baba advises teachers to put their heart and soul in preparing students up to the mark and for this they themselves should be value-oriented. He feels that the teacher should put into practice what they preach to the students. They should guide the students properly, as they are the most important assets of an educational institution. Bhagawan Baba says (1987), the teacher must come down to the level of the students. The baby on the floor cannot jump into the arms of the mother when she calls her. The mother has to stoop low to possess the child. In the same way the teacher should come down to the level of the pupil to teach him. This is a laudable sign of love. Sri Satya Sai Baba, like Aurobindo has been stressing repeatedly that educational institutions are the appropriate agencies for meditation. In this state the mind is still and steady.

Bhagawan Baba's WATCH method is more practicable for the students to watch themselves. He often advises students to watch their words, actions, thought, character and heart. Watching initially creates an awareness, which will progressively become a habit by repetitive behaviour. As Aristotle said we are what we repeatedly do. The values can be inculcated and internalized. The intellectual, physical, emotional, psychic and spiritual integration of the individual should be the aim of education.

Education is to purify impulses and emotions and equip one with the physical and mental disciplines needed for drawing upon the springs of calmness and joy that lie in one's own heart. So, the students should be educated because there is no penance equal to a peaceful mind, no greater happiness than contentment, no worse desire than desire and no righteousness can equal kindness. Ultimately all this brings about unity, purity and divinity to oneself, to the society and to the nation.

Lokaa Samastha Sukhino Bhavanthu
Shanthi Shanthi Shanthi

References

- Adivi Reddy, A. (1995). Uniqueness of Swami and His Teachings. Sri Satya Sai Books and Publications Trust : Prasanthi Nilayam .
- Anil Kumar Kamaraju, (2006). Sai – Chology. Sri Satya Sai Books and Publications Trust : Prasanthi Nilayam .
- Bhagavan Sri Satya Sai Baba, (2002). Sandeha Nivarini. Sri Satya Sai Books and Publications Trust : Prasanthi Nilayam .
- Bhagavan Sri Satya Sai Baba, (1997). Senses for Selfless Service. Sri Satya Sai Books and Publications Trust : Prasanthi Nilayam .
- Bhagavan Sri Satya Sai Baba, (2002). Vidya Vahini. Sri Satya Sai Books and Publication Trust : Prasanthi Nilayam

- Bhagawan Sri Sathya Sai Baba, (2003). Sutra Vahini, Sri Satya Sai Books and Publications Trust : Prasanthi Nilayam .
- Bhagawan Sri Sathya Sai Baba Prasanthi Vahini, (2002). Sri Satya Sai Books and Publications Trust : Prasanthi Nilayam .
- Bhagawan Sri Sathya Sai Baba Master the Mind and Be a Master Mind, (2007). Sri Satya Sai Books and Publications Trust: Prasanthi Nilayam .
- Bhagawan Sri Satya Sai Baba Upanishad Vahini, (2002). Sri Satya Sai Books and Publications Trust : Prasanthi Nilayam .
- Bhagavan. A Text Book of Spiritual Science Class XI. Sri Satya Sai Books and Publications Trust : Prasanthi Nilayam .
- Bhagavan. A Text Book of Spiritual Science Class XII. Sri Satya Sai Books and Publications Trust: Prasanthi Nilayam .
- Joy Thomas. (1993). Life is a Dream – Realize It. Codword Process Printers : Mangalore.
- Krishna Rao, K. (1998). Aum Sri Satya Sai Ram. Sri Lakshmi Ganapathi Binding Works : Kovvur.
- Murthy, M. V. N. The Greatest Adventure. Sri Satya Sai Books and Publications Trust: Prasanthi Nilayam .
- Madhu Kapani. Education in Human Values. Sterling Publications Pvt. Ltd: New Delhi.
- Sai Anoos, (2001). The Direct Flight to Divinity. Sri Satya Sai Books and Publications Trust: Prasanthi Nilayam .
- Sree Vishnu Bhattacharya Vedantam, (2004). Upanishaddeepikalu. Tirumala Tirupathi Devasthanam's Press: Tirupati.
- Valentina. B. Patacsil, (1999). Life, Death and Liberation. Prince Park: Bangalore.

Psycho-physical Dimensions of Human Behavior Yoga and Meditation

– V. Rangacharlu

The nature and functions of mind are very difficult to comprehend. People use the terms 'psychological', 'mental' etc. very freely. India has known the power of mind of centuries. The whole effort of Indian genius has been in search of God. In Indian philosophical writings we see the use of Mana/Manasu, it also signifies Mind because the mind is very subtle and also hidden.

The reason why so many people try to know about this mind is that many problems arise from mental conditions. Some of the physical ailments are also caused by mental conditions, which always kept Psychiatrists, Psychologists and Doctors busy. If we want to have a sound body we need to have a sound mind too.

What are the conditions essential for a sound physical body? We may list the following.

Eat wholesome food in moderate quantity and regularly. Take regular exercise, practice yoga and live in a congenial environment.

Similarly of the mind, Swami Brahmananda, many a time used to say to his Sadakas (disciples) "you have to feed the mind with nourished food, nourish it, enrich it, and strengthen it. Without nourishing the mind it is difficult to have joy, peace and wisdom".

Mind in Vedanta

The Vedanta, the science of life that helps in understanding human nature, stresses the development of the mind because human

✍ **V. Rangacharlu,** *Faculty, Mysore University, Outreach, M.Ed. - Chittore.*

development is always linked to development of mind. Our physical, intellectual, cognitive and aesthetic developments are not possible without the cultivation of mind. Mind is the source of freedom and so also bondage." Mana eva manushyanam" means man owes his existence to mind. Every individual wants nowadays to become and live what he/she is convinced of; as the thoughts so are men.

The Vedanta distinguished mind from physical body on one hand and self on the other hand. Mind is an object of study both in Philosophy and also in Psychology. The earliest method to study behavior is introspection. One's mind is observable by one directly through introspection, as the study of mind is an object and subject of knowledge, consciousness is intrinsic in mind.

According to Vedanta, mind is dark and material. Descartes, three hundred years ago in Western thought, raised the controversy of dualism between body and mind. This differentiation is due to practice to identify the mind with the self, the pure spirit, whereas in recent days the tendency is opposite. That is to identify the mind more and more with the body. Mind is just a function of the body or some sort of bodily condition. But in religious thought we have noticed that in the west this distinction is maintained. St Paul says, "the very God of peace sanctifies you wholly, and I pray God your whole Sprit and Soul and body be preserved blameless unto the coming of our Lord Jesus Christ". But if we look at Greeks, we notice three words Soul, Psyche, and Mind. These words are related to soul and mind, psyche and mind. So religion maintained the distinction between mind and pure spirit, but in Psychological and Philosophical thinking we find no difference between mind and spirit. In Vedanta the mind is called antahkarana i.e. the "Internal instrument".

What Vedanta says about Mind?

Vedanta recognized different functions of mind, such as cognition, conation and volition. The functions of the mind are memory, imagination, love and hatred, hope, despair and fear. All these belong to the mind. Vedanta considers cognitive functions of mind as primary to feeling and willing and these depend on the cognitive aspects of the mind. Mind even though like a material external object, is also composed of finer subtle powers. That's why eyes to perceive, the hands to touch. During sleep eyes do not see and hands cannot grasp (because) consciousness almost completely recedes from the physical arena. Vedanta also studies mind particularly, as the seat of impressions. Vedanta analyzed cognitive functions of mind and took into account its four states of deliberations (manas), determination (bhudhi), egoism (ahankara), and recollection (citta). In every external perception all these four are involved. The four functions represent four different states of the mind. Vedanta studies the mind as seat of impressions and these impressions are left on the mind not only by the perceptions of objects but also through their activities. Just like the functions of organs of cognition leave some impressions on the mind so also the organs of action. The structure and composition of mind and intellect are founded upon one's own vasanas (vasanas are impressions left on the mind by actions of senses). Vasanas or tendencies are prime movers of all desires and actions. Human inclinations are called vasanas (vasanas in Sanskrit means fragrance). These vasanas are the cause of egocentric thoughts and sensuous actions. Lord Krishna says in the Githa that men act and behave in accordance with one's own nature many a time conditioned by vasanas. The sensuous vasanas increase one's personality composition. The more these sub-conscious urges and motivating factors in the individual are, more are his/her desires which ultimately lead to an agitating mind or a disturbed mind.

The Vedanta advocates Vasanaksharya as a remedy to redeem the mind from bondage

According to Vedanta the mind stores all these impressions. Vedanta also does not divide the mind into 'conscious & unconscious. ' What may be conscious today may become unconscious tomorrow. These impressions that are unmanifested are actually in subconscious level too. In Vedanta there is also the Superconscious state. Many of our impressions lie overpowered under the stress of circumstances. There are many impressions and tendencies that lye dormant in the mind. As long as they are asleep they do not do any harm. No mind is perfect, and free from weaknesses.

Vedanta stresses the cultivation and development of the conscious mind with self-determination. The suggested practice for development of the mind is the critical analysis of mental conditions. Vedanta prescribes self-discipline for purification of mind. Another course suggested by Vedanta is 'meditation'.

Meditation: An Ancient Technique for More Brain Power

Everywhere in India and also the world over there is growing desire for meditation and Yoga especially among the educated.

One of the purposes of meditation is removing impurities both gross and subtle within the mind. In a secular society like ours scientific observance of religious life is essential. If we desire to lead physically agile and mentally alert productive life, people need to understand and adopt the art of living. Unfolding secrets hidden in our scriptures and practices need the realistic application of Philosophy with Psychology. This paper considers Bhagavath Githa as the first philosophical treatise. Applied psychological aspect of the Githa attempted to counsel grief-stricken Arjuna in the battlefield to Kurukshethra and motivate Arjuna to fight the righteous war. The long treatise on the battlefield is a universal gospel to all manvas (men who are in confusion) and struck with attachments, forgetting the very divine nature of human being. Religion is always a transcendental experience, deals with eternal relationship between God and the Soul. Religion enables one to become spiritual. Without the spiritual ideal, enlightened self-interest and economic scurrility only serve as instruments of exploitation. Work and worship should be equally emphasized. Meditation without work ends in laziness, selfishness and self-deception. Religion needs to adopt and accept scientific laws like evolution, gravitation, cosmology etc. Scientific method itself may be taken as a boon bestowed upon human beings by benevolent God. The moral foundation of every religion is moral discipline. Occult non-religious experiences are viewed as projections of the mind. Every religion has been kept alive by saints and sages, but not by theologians or philosophers.

Sleep Vs. Meditation

During sleep, people rest and relax; as a result the need for oxygen is reduced. We consume less oxygen. Lower oxygen consumption means a more relaxed state. It means we relax more in meditation than in sleep.

Yoga and meditation practice for psychophysical well-being

Yoga and Meditation greatly help in developing concentration of mind. Meditation means our conscious growth into Infinite. When we try to meditate, we try to expand ourselves like a bird spreading its wings. Githa in Chapter II elaborated on the qualities of Sthithapragna (a personality who has established equanimity of mind and human tendencies). Yoga is the control of thought waves in the mind. Waves of mind subside and become calm; only then is the bottom, the superconscious revelation experienced. Meditation is not an escape to Himalayan caves; it is the acceptance of life in its totality with a view to transforming mind to the highest manifestation. Upanishads mention of three kinds of meditation; gross meditation, subtle meditation, and transcendental meditation. Maharishi Mahesh Yogi popularized and scientifically expounded TM to the Western World. In the advanced countries interest in TM popularized by Mahershiji evoked scientific research to find out the effects of meditation on body, mind and performance. Scientific researches on TM showed that the TM practice produces a state of rest and relaxation deeper than sleep, reduces anxiety, lowers BP and stress, and strengthens immune system. Meditation is, depending on the quality of meditation, a more or less scientific means of contacting the soul, and of eventually becoming one with the soul. That is the basic purpose of meditation of any kind. The long-term benefit seems to be slowing down of the aging process.

References

- Swami Prabhavananda, (2004). *Patanjali Yoga Ssutras*. Chennai: Sri Ramakishna Math.
- Praveen Kapadia, (2002). *"Yoga Simplified"*. Hyderabad: Gandhi Gyan Mandir Yoga Kendra.
- Martha Davis, (1996). "*The Relaxation and Stress Reduction Work Book*". Jaico publishing House.
- Nagendra. H.R and Nagaratna.R, (1986). "*New Perceptives in Stress Management*". Bangalore. Swami Vivekananda Yoga Prakasana.
- Jnaneswara Swamy. 2000.*Traditional Yoga and Meditation of the Himalayan Masters-The Yoga Sutras*. Vedanta, Samaya Sri Vidya.

❖ ❖ ❖

Holistic Human Development in the Light of The Bhagavad Gita

– Lalitha Panguluri

It is quite amazing that the age-old wisdom of the Indian seers is becoming more relevant and meaningful to address the present day problems of management and development in the modern world of highly scientific and technological progress.

The timeless wisdom of the Bhagavad-Gita is the Light of Life, lit by the Supreme to save humanity from the darkness of ignorance and suffering. It is the scripture of scriptures, which outlives time, and can be acknowledged as indispensable to the life of any man in any age. It is the encyclopaedia of life.

The Blessed Lord Sri Krishna said:

- Fearlessness, purity of heart, perseverance in acquiring wisdom and in practicing yoga, charity, subjection of the senses, performance of holy rites, study of the scriptures, self-discipline, straightforwardness (chap 16-1);
- Non-injury, truthfulness, freedom from wrath, renunciation, peacefulness, non-slanderousness, compassion for all creatures, gentleness, modesty, lack of restlessness, absence of greed (chap 16-2);
- Radiance of character, forgiveness, patience, cleanliness, freedom from hate, absence of conceit-(chap 16-3);

are the soul qualities that make man Supreme-like. A person with all these divine qualities is a dear one to all, wherever he is.

The Bhagavad Gita is the science of body, mind and soul. The approach of the Bhagavadgita for individual development is holistic and integrated one i.e. physical, intellectual and spiritual. One to the

✍ **Lalitha Panguluri**, *Research Scholar, Mother Teresa University.*

exclusion of the other may, for a time, help but eventually it is the composite approach which helps to develop a rounded personality, not easily disturbed by the strains or stresses while going through the life's journey.

This holistic personal development differs from traditional approaches to personal development by having one primary prerequisite: an inner connection to the source of being. That is the awakening of conscious awareness. When that is made, personal development becomes a process of effortless mastery.

"The holistic development of an individual means touching all parameters such as his work, family, personal and spiritual zones." A focus on these factors will improve their attitudes, which is directly related to the progress of their lives.

The Bhagavad Gita explains every aspect of our life viz, what to eat, what to do, how to do, how to think etc in a systematic way. Bhagavad Gita is the advice and prescription for holistic development.

Value of the Food

Food is very necessary to anyone, not only for survival, but also to discharge the responsibilities and duties of the materialistic world in a proper way. It influences the spiritual progress also.

What the modern health and nutrition explains was already explained in the ancient wisdom of Sri Krishna

Foods that increase the longevity purify one's existence and give strength, health, happiness and satisfaction. Such foods that are juicy, fatty, wholesome, and pleasing to the heart are liked by those in the mode of goodness (Satvic) (BG 17.8)

Foods that are too bitter, too sour, salty, hot, pungent, dry and burning are dear to those in the mode of passion (rajasic). Such foods cause distress, misery and disease. (BG 17.9)

Food prepared more than three hours before being eaten, food that is tasteless, decomposed and putrid, and food consisting of remnants and untouchable things is dear to those in the mode of darkness (tamasic.) (BG 17.10)

Satvic foods, in general are sweet fresh fruits and vegetables (raw or properly prepared), whole grains and legumes, fresh dairy products, nuts, natural sweets such as honey and dates (minimizing refined sugars) and nominal amounts of fat from dairy or vegetable sources only. Prepared foods should be combined and cooked in a manner that retains and enhances their nutrients. They should be aesthetically pleasing to the eye and tasteful to the palate (mildly seasoned) and agreeable to the body's constitution. Since food has a major effect on the body and the mind, a Sattvic diet should be adhered to in order to enhance both the health of the body as well as purity and strength of the mind. This type of food is being prescribed by the present day dieticians also to promote good health and to avoid long run health problems

Sri Krishna specifically emphasizes moderation in eating and sleeping.

"There is no possibility of one' becoming a yogi, ..., if one eats too much, or eats too little, sleeps too much or does not sleep enough." (B.G 6-16)

The modern doctors also agree that overconsumption of food leads to many health problems and suggest the foods that promote health only, and warn us not to use the foods that are too oily, too salty, too hot, too spicy, which affect the health. The present scientific knowledge is already well explained by the age-old Divine doctor Sri Krishna. But it is our ignorance for not caring the age-old wisdom, and inviting many health problems, viz gastric problems, diabetes, hypertension, urinary problems, obesity, heart problems, respiratory problems etc.

The Way of Work

The Divine Teacher Sri Krishna, as a Management Guru explained all the secrets of performing the duties in the Holy Script, The Bhagavad Gita

"You have a right to perform your prescribed duty, but you are not entitled to the fruits of action. Never consider yourself the cause of the results of your activities, and never be attached to not doing your duty" (BG 2.47).

"Perform your duty equipoised,….., abandoning all attachment to success or failure. Such equanimity is called yoga" (BG 2.48).

Everyone must engage in some sort of activity in this material world. But actions can either bind one to this world or liberate one from it. By acting for the pleasure of the Supreme, without selfish motives, one can be liberated from the law of karma (action and reaction) and attain transcendental knowledge of the self and the Supreme.

Whatever action a great man performs, common men follow. And whatever standards he sets by exemplary acts, all the world pursues.(BG 3.21)

As the ignorant perform their duties with attachment to results, the learned may similarly act, but without attachment, for the sake of leading people on the right path. (BG 3.25)

One who sees inaction in action, and action in inaction, is intelligent among men, and he is in the transcendental position, although engaged in all sorts of activities. (BG 4.18)

Having accepted strict vows, some become enlightened by sacrificing their possessions, and others by performing severe austerities, by practicing the yoga of eight-fold mysticism, or by studying the Vedas to advance in transcendental knowledge. (BG 4.28)

Outwardly performing all actions but inwardly renouncing their fruits, the wise man, purified by the fire of transcendental knowledge, attains peace, detachment, forbearance, spiritual vision and bliss (Chapter 5).

A man engaged in devotional service rids himself of both good and bad actions even in this life. Therefore strive for yoga, which is the art of all work. (BG 2.50)

The Way of Yoga

The Lord Sri Krishna explained Dhyana Yoga to Arjuna to become one with the Supreme. (chap 6.) Yoga is for spiritual cleansing.

A person is said to be elevated in yoga when, having renounced all material desires, he neither acts for sense gratification nor engages in fruitive activities (BG 6.4).

For one who has conquered the mind, the Supersoul is already reached, for he has attained tranquillity. To such a man happiness and distress, heat and cold, honor and dishonor are all the same; but for one who has failed to do so, his mind will remain the greatest enemy. (BG 6.6-7)

A person is said to be established in self-realization and is called a yogî [or mystic] when he is fully satisfied by virtue of acquired knowledge and realization. Such a person is situated in transcendence and is self-controlled. He sees everything - whether it be pebbles, stones or gold, as the same. (BG 6.8)

A person is considered still further advanced when he regards honest well-wishers, affectionate benefactors, the neutral, mediators, the envious, friends and enemies, the pious and the sinners all with an equal mind. (BG 6.9)

One should hold one's body, neck and head erect in a straight line and stare steadily at the tip of the nose. Thus, with an unagitated, subdued mind, devoid of fear, completely free from sex life, one should meditate upon Me within the heart and make Me the ultimate goal of life. (BG 6.13-14)

Thus practicing constant control of the body, mind and activities, the mystic transcendentalist, his mind regulated, attains to the kingdom of The Supreme or the abode of Kròsònòa by cessation of material existence. (BG 6.15)

He who is regulated in his habits of eating, sleeping, recreation and work can mitigate all material pains by practicing the yoga system. (BG 6.17)

In the stage of perfection called trance, or samâdhi, one's mind is completely restrained from material mental activities by practice of yoga. This perfection is characterized by one's ability to see the self by the pure mind and to relish and rejoice in the self. In that joyous state, one is situated in boundless transcendental happiness, realized through transcendental senses. Established thus, one never departs from the truth, and upon gaining this he thinks there is no greater gain. Being situated in such a position, one is never shaken, even in the midst of greatest difficulty. This indeed is actual freedom from all miseries arising from material contact. (BG 6. 20-23)

One should engage oneself in the practice of yoga with determination and faith and not be deviated from the path. One should abandon, without exception, all material desires born of mental speculation and thus control all the senses on all sides by the mind. (BG 6.24)

Lord Úrî Kròsònòa said: .., it is undoubtedly very difficult to curb the restless mind, but it is possible by suitable practice and by detachment. (BG 6.35)

A yogî is greater than the ascetic, greater than the empiricist and greater than the fruitive worker. Therefore, ... in all circumstances, be a yogi. (BG 6.46)

Behavioral Principles or Mental Attitude

Each individual tries to give donation as it is said to be a good quality. But the divine teacher Sri Krishna advised observing some measures even while doing Dana to get more spiritual benefits.

The good or sattvic gift is one made for the sake of righteousness, without expectation of anything in return, and is bestowed in proper time and place on a deserving person. (17 - 20)

There are three kinds of sattvic gifts: material, mental, and spiritual. On the physical plane to give food and money to a poor man is good; to give him a job is better. To help him become well qualified to obtain work is better still. Continued material aid to a man makes him enslaved and dependent, so it is wise to encourage him to remedy his ills by self-help.

On the mental plane, to aid in enlightening an ignorant person is good; and to offer further education to an intelligent man is better, for he can in turn be more helpful to many others.

On the spiritual plane, to give elevating instruction to willing man, whose life has been sunk in materialism, is good. To impart divine wisdom to an ardent seeker is better.

That gift is deemed rajasic, which is offered with reluctance or in the thought of receiving a return or of gaining merit. (17-21)

A tamasic gift is one bestowed at a wrong time and place on an unworthy person, contemptuously or without goodwill. (17-22)

Three-fold Austerity

Austerity of the body consists in worship of the Supreme Lord, the brâhmanòas, the spiritual master, and superiors like the father and mother, and in cleanliness, simplicity, celibacy and nonviolence. (BG 17-14)

Austerity of speech consists in speaking words that are truthful, pleasing, beneficial, and not agitating to others, and also in regularly reciting Vedic literature. (BG 17.15)

And satisfaction, simplicity, gravity, self-control and purification of one's existence are the austerities of the mind. (BG 17.16)

This threefold austerity, performed with transcendental faith by men not expecting material benefits but engaged only for the sake of the Supreme, is called austerity in goodness. (BG 17.17)

Undivided Spiritual Nature

One who performs his duty without association with the modes of material nature, without false ego, with great determination and enthusiasm, and without wavering in success or failure is said to be a worker in the mode of goodness. (BG 18.26)

That knowledge by which one undivided spiritual nature is seen in all living entities, though they are divided into innumerable forms, you should understand to be in the mode of goodness. (BG 18.20)

That knowledge by which one sees that in every different body there is a different type of living entity you should understand to be in the mode of passion. (BG 18.21)

And that knowledge by which one is attached to one kind of work as the all in all, without knowledge of the truth, and which is very meager, is said to be in the mode of darkness. (BG 18.22)

Determination which is unbreakable, which is sustained with steadfastness by yoga practice, and which thus controls the activities of the mind, life and senses is determination in the mode of goodness. (BG 18.33)

That which in the beginning may be just like poison but at the end is just like nectar and which awakens one to self-realization is said to be happiness in the mode of goodness. (BG 18.37)

Spiritual Way

The blessed Lord Sri Krishna explained so many methods and principles, to get the divine grace and to become one with him ...the person who is not disturbed by happiness and distress and is steady in both is certainly eligible for liberation. (BG2.15)

As a person puts on new garments, giving up old ones, the soul similarly accepts new material bodies, giving up the old and useless ones. (BG 2.22)

A person who is not disturbed by the incessant flow of desires that enter like rivers into the ocean, which is ever being filled but is always still can alone achieve peace, and not the man who strives to satisfy such desires. (BG 2.70)

A person who has given up all desires for sense gratification, who lives free from desires, who has given up all sense of proprietorship and is devoid of false ego he alone can attain real peace. (BG 2.71)

Being freed from attachment, fear and anger, being fully absorbed in Me and taking refuge in me, many, many persons in the past became purified by knowledge of Me and thus they all attained transcendental love for Me. (BG 4.10)

As a blazing fire turns firewood to ashes, ..., so does the fire of knowledge burn to ashes all reactions to material activities. (BG 4.37)

In this world, there is nothing so sublime and pure as transcendental knowledge. Such knowledge is the mature fruit of all mysticism. And one who has become accomplished in the practice of devotional service enjoys this knowledge within himself in due course of time. (BG 4.38)

A faithful man who is dedicated to transcendental knowledge and who subdues his senses is eligible to achieve such knowledge, and having achieved it he quickly attains the supreme spiritual peace. (BG 4.39)

A person who neither rejoices upon achieving something pleasant nor laments upon obtaining something unpleasant, who is self-intelligent, who is unbewildered, and who knows the science of God, is already situated in transcendence. (BG 5.20)

Such a liberated person is not attracted to material sense pleasure but is always in trance, enjoying the pleasure within. In this way the self-realized person enjoys unlimited happiness, for he concentrates on the Supreme. (BG 5.21)

An intelligent person does not take part in the sources of misery, which are due to contact with the material senses....., such pleasures have a beginning and an end, and so the wise man does not delight in them. (BG 5.22)

Before giving up this present body, if one is able to tolerate the urges of the material senses and check the force of desire and anger, he is well situated and is happy in this world. (BG 5.23)

Those who are beyond the dualities that arise from doubts, whose minds are engaged within, who are always busy working for the welfare of all living beings, and who are free from all sins achieve liberation in the Supreme. (BG 5.25)

Those who are free from anger and all material desires, who are self-realized, self-disciplined and constantly endeavoring for perfection, are assured of liberation in the Supreme in the very near future. (BG 5.26)

Shutting out all external sense objects, keeping the eyes and vision concentrated between the two eyebrows, suspending the inward and outward breaths within the nostrils, and thus controlling the mind, senses and intelligence, the transcendentalist aiming at liberation becomes free from desire, fear and anger. One who is always in this state is certainly liberated. (BG 5.27-28)

A person in full of consciousness of Me, knowing Me to be the ultimate beneficiary of all sacrifices and austerities, the Supreme Lord of all planets and demigods, and the benefactor and well-wisher of all living entities, attains peace from the pangs of material miseries. (BG 5.29)

And whoever, at the end of his life, quits his body, remembering Me alone, at once attains My nature. Of this there is no doubt. (BG 8.5)

Whatever state of being one remembers when he quits his body, ..., that state he will attain without fail. (BG 8.6)

A person who accepts the path of devotional service is not bereft of the results derived from studying the Vedas, performing austere sacrifices, giving charity or pursuing philosophical and fruitive activities. Simply by performing devotional service, he attains all these, and at the end he reaches the supreme eternal abode. (BG 8.28)

If you cannot practice the regulations of bhakti-yoga, then just try to work for Me, because by working for Me you will come to the perfect stage. (BG 12.10)

If, however, you are unable to work in this consciousness of Me, then try to act giving up all results of your work and try to be self-situated. (BG 12.11)

If you cannot take to this practice, then engage yourself in the cultivation of knowledge. Better than knowledge, however, is meditation, and better than meditation is renunciation of the fruits of action, for by such renunciation one can attain peace of mind. (BG 12.12)

He for whom no one is put into difficulty and who is not disturbed by anyone, who is equipoised in happiness and distress, fear and anxiety, is very dear to me. (BG 12.15)

Meaning of Knowledge

Humility; pridelessness; nonviolence; tolerance; simplicity; approaching a bona fide spiritual master; cleanliness; steadiness; self-control; renunciation of the objects of sense gratification; absence of ego; the perception of the evil of birth, death, old age and disease;

detachment; freedom from entanglement with children, wife, home and the rest; even-mindedness amid pleasant and unpleasant events; constant and unalloyed devotion to Me; aspiring to live in a solitary place; detachment from the general mass of people; accepting the importance of self-realization; and philosophical search for the Absolute Truth - all these I declare to be knowledge, and besides this whatever there may be is ignorance. (BG 13.8-12)

The Qualities of the Dear ones of the Supreme

One who is not envious but is a kind friend to all living entities, who does not think himself a proprietor and is free from false ego, who is equal in both happiness and distress, who is tolerant, always satisfied, self-controlled, and engaged in devotional service with determination, his mind and intelligence fixed on Supreme

One who is equal to friends and enemies, who is equipoised in honor and dishonor, heat and cold, happiness and distress, fame and infame, who is always free from contaminating association, always silent and satisfied with anything, who doesn't care for any residence, who is fixed in knowledge and who is engaged in devotional service.

One who is not dependent on the ordinary course of activities, who is pure, expert, without cares, free from all pains, and not striving for some result...One who neither rejoices nor grieves, who neither laments nor desires, and who renounces both auspicious and inauspicious things.. Those who follow this imperishable path of devotional service and who completely engage themselves with faith, making the supreme, the divine goal, are very, very dear. (BG 12chap;13-20)

Elimination of Demonic or negative Qualities

The development of a person not only means inculcating good or positive qualities but to eliminate the bad or negative qualities.

In every civilized human society there is some set of scriptural rules and regulations, which is followed from the beginning. Those who adopt the civilization rules are known as the most advanced civilized peoples, those who do not follow the scriptural injunctions are supposed to be demons.

Lord Sri Krishna clearly explained the ungodly traits of those who create in themselves a demonic nature.

Pride, arrogance, conceit, anger, harshness and ignorance -these qualities belong to those of demonic nature. (BG 16.4)

The transcendental qualities are conducive to liberation, whereas the demonic qualities make for bondage. (BG 16.5)

Those who are demonic do not know what is to be done and what is not to be done. Neither cleanliness nor proper behavior nor truth is found in them. (BG 16.7)

Self-complacent and always impudent, deluded by wealth and false prestige, they sometimes proudly perform sacrifices in name only, without following any rules or regulations. Bewildered by false ego, strength, pride, lust and anger, the demons become envious of the Supreme Personality of Godhead. (BG 16.17-19)

There are three gates leading to this hell - lust, anger and greed. Every sane man should give these up, for they lead to the degradation of the soul: The man who has escaped these three gates of hell,.., performs acts conducive to self-realization and thus gradually attains the supreme destination. (BG 16.21-.22)

He who discards scriptural injunctions and acts according to his own whims attains neither perfection, nor happiness, nor the supreme destination.: One should therefore understand what is duty and what is not duty by the regulations of the scriptures. Knowing such rules and regulations, one should act so that he may gradually be elevated.(BG 16.23-24)

The Bhagavad- Gita is considered by eastern and western scholars alike to be among the greatest spiritual books the world has ever known. The main objective of the Gita is to help people struggling in the darkness of ignorance. It can be experienced as a powerful catalyst for transformation.

Each of the eighteen chapters presents a yoga or graduated means of linking the separate individuality with the selfless Self. If each individual who experiences an inner calling could work in accordance with his or her capacity to forge this connection, there would be peace and contentment within the individual, the family, the society and the world.

The Bhagavad Gita is a message addressed to each and every human individual to help him or her to solve the vexing problem of overcoming the present and progressing towards a bright future.

"Every age will interpret Gita according to its own times and will find new meanings, inspirations and strength to cope with newer situations. Different people may find different meanings in Gita, because the philosophy of Gita is holistic and eternally dynamic."

In order to gain a spiritual frame of mind, personal discipline, austerity, penance, good conduct, selfless service, yogic practices, meditation, worship, prayer, rituals, and study of scriptures, as well as the company of holy persons, pilgrimage, chanting of the holy names of God, and Self-inquiry are needed to purify the body, mind, and intellect. One must learn to give up lust, anger, greed, and establish mastery over the six senses (hearing, touch, sight, taste, smell, and mind) by the purified intellect. One should always remember that all works are done by the energy of nature and that he or she is not the doer but only an instrument. One must strive for excellence in all undertakings but maintain equanimity in success and failure, gain and loss, and pain and pleasure. Everyone is a student in this world to seek the knowledge from the right persons to meet the demands of life at different phases of life. They may be materialistic or spiritual.

By surrendering thyself (to the guru), by questioning (the guru and thine perceptions) and by service . . . . .(to the guru), the sages who have realized truth will impart that wisdom to thee.(4.34).

With the righteous knowledge, guidance and blessings of the guru, a realized teacher, one can be developed holistically and will be enlighted in the divine path. The Bhagavad Gita is a prescription for life here and hereafter.

Sri Krishna's message in the Holy book Bhagavad Gita is the perfect answer for the modern age, and any age which explains the Yoga of dutiful action, leaving the fruits to God, yoga of non-attachment (chap.2-47, 48) and of meditation for God-realization (chap.6). The path advocated by Sri Krishna in the Bhagavad Gita is moderate, medium, balanced golden path, both for the busy man of the world and for the highest spiritual aspirant. Indian spirituality is waiting to serve the humanity in all the areas of life. The need is for, an awareness of it.

References

– Sri Sri Paramahansa Yogananda. (2002). God Speaks with Arjuna. The Bhagavad Gita. Kolkata: Yoga Satsang Soceity of India.

– Sri Vidya Prakasananda Swamy. (1994). Sri Bhagavad Gita. Kalahasthi: Suka Brahmasramam.

– Swami Vivekananda. (1999). Personality Development. Kolkata: Advaita Ashrama.

– Sri Jayadayalji Goenka. (2007). Srimad Bhagavad Gita. Gorakhpur: Gita Press.

– Sri Aurobindo. (1922). Essays On the Gita. Pondichery : Sir Aurobindo Ashramam.

❖ ❖ ❖

Trait and Type Theories of Bhagavadgita

– Dr. Ch. Lakshmi Narasamma

The present psychology is developed in the United States. The Western viewpoint is materialistic. The main aim of every human being is to be well adjusted to his environment. He has to become a productive citizen so that his contribution helps others also to be prosperous.

In spite of the development the underlying human nature is not well studied by the Western psychology whereas in India the human nature has been well studied by Rishis. The greatest script Sreemad Bhagavadgeeta explains all human characteristics. One important personality theory, which classified human beings on the traits drafted, is relevant to identify the nature of people.

The Geetacharya explained the divine traits as well as the destructive traits in Daiwasura Sapadwibhaga Yoga, which means the division of the wealth of Divine and Demon.

The sixteenth chapter of Bhagawad Geeta aims at what we need, what we should not aspire. The traits, which are aspirable, are as follow: They are twenty-six in number.

- **Fearlessness:** This is an essential quality to achieve. One should not be doubtful about his abilities. The fear arises out of thought of defeat or calamities. Those who never care for means but simply aim at goals undergo this emotion frequently. So the students should choose proper means along with suitable goals.

✍ ***Dr. Ch. Lakshmi Narasamma,*** *Lecturer, D.N.R. College, Bhimavaram.*

- **Purity of mind:** When a person looses attention so many things enter into the mind and make the mental state imbalanced. When a person pays attention to what he is doing by keeping all other thoughts in the margin then his mind becomes pure and he becomes aware of what to do to get what he wants.
- **Dedication:** Dedication is an essential ingredient in all activities. It can be achieved by knowing the worth of a thing, how it helps the individual and society. So one should evaluate every activity before undertaking it.
- **Charity:** Usually people think that charity means donating some money to the needy. But it is not of that narrow nature. It is supplying what others are in dire need of, like showing a correct route to a stranger in a city, or helping a student of a lower class in solving his educational problem.
- **Controlling the Senses:** The sense organs serve as the gateways of knowledge (information from external world). If information enters the mind, it is impossible to erase it. So there should be a filtering mechanism for every individual so as to choose and select what to see, eat, hear, touch, smell etc. This is called Indria Nigraha, that is bringing the sense organs under the control of our mind. The present day youth scatter their energies in different activities other than education, thus bringing their achievement to lower levels.
- **Yagna:** Yagna means an exchange, what we know and what has to be known come under Yagna. So there should always be a revival of our knowledge. Some new knowledge has to come and enrich our treasure of knowledge.
- **Reading:** The student should not confine his reading to his class textbook. He has to supplement his knowledge by inculcating a good habit of reading which will help him in developing the power of imagination, reasoning, problem-solving and judgement.
- **Tapas:** It is for making our body and mind healthy. The yoga practices and physical work help to get strength. Good food habits, a timetable for doing every activity etc come under Tapas.

- **Flexibility:** The students should not be rigid. Now the world has become a global village. So a student should know the greatness of all the cultures, religions and countries, and he should respect others by becoming open minded.
- **Ahimsa:** It is not simply stopping the killing of animals but stopping hurting others in any form, either by thought, word or deed. So, verify the worth of words and actions before practicing them.
- **Truthfulness:** It is saying as it is, not by enlarging or reducing the true nature of anything. So we should not see anything through glasses (Concave or tinted convex) i.e. developing objectivity is one of the aims of education.
- **Not Having Anger:** Anger arises when we are hindered by some obstacle while reaching some thing we want. By giving overemphasis to things we usually become angry. To get rid of the consequences of anger, we have to wait for sometime before taking any decision. By getting angry one loses the capacity of reasoning. So it is better to stop taking a decision during the moments of anger.
- **Sacrifice:** The true happiness lies in sacrificing something. It is difficult, because we also need the same thing. But by thinking that the others are in more need than us, we give, and feel an enlightened bliss in our mind. It leads to perfect health.
- **Peace:** The peace generates in our mind. Usually people try but fail to push out unpleasant thoughts from mind. But it is very difficult to push out thoughts from our mind. It can be done only by filling our mind with good and optimistic thoughts, which leaves no room for unnecessary thoughts.
- **Uncomplaining Nature:** The complaining nature is exhibited by those who want to get the favour of others by making others inferior. Every human has to build on his merits than on the limitations of others.
- **Mercy:** It is treating things of nature with dignity. The animals, trees, rivers and hills all have their right to exist in the

nature but man, imagining himself as a superior being, wants to control the elements of nature. He is not estimating the calamities waiting in the future where he will become helpless and will be punished. So he should develop mercy and sympathy towards the salient elements of nature.

- **Simplicity:** The youth should not be pompous and exhibitive in their nature. They should be simple, humble, in dressing and in their aspirations; they should be helpful, respect elders and become role models for the younger generations. Soft natured people become achievers by winning hearts of all.
- **Integrity:** The purity of the three organs, the mind, mouth and hand. The word should coincide with the activity we take, and that should be our inner idea. If, there is a conflict between these three it leads to maladjustment in the individual. If it is severe it leads to mental disorders.
- **Glow:** This is not the external beauty as thought by all. It is the divinity that makes man attractive and approachable. By practicing good deeds one becomes truly beautiful.
- **Patience:** Everyone at one time or the other suffers from difficulties. If he becomes impatient by thinking that these difficulties will exist forever he will lose all his potentialities to face the problem. Everyone should develop patience so that there is a time for thinking over the real causes of the difficulties. By knowing the nature of a problem there is a chance to take correct decision,
- **Bravery:** It evolves out of the abilities of a person. A person will become brave only when he knows that his path is correct i.e. not harming self and society. The one who evaluates himself well is the bravest person in the world.
- **Cleanliness:** We need healthy body to discharge all our duties well. We have to keep our body and surroundings clean. Man with ignorance is spoiling nature with a number of pollutants. Cleanliness can be achieved by good habits.
- **Being Fair:** The guilt arises when someone cheats the other, and the other suffers because he is cheated and the fellow who has cheated becomes guilty. This influences his mental health.

- **Unbiased:** The feeling that someone belongs to us whereas others do not makes one biased. On the basis of caste, religion, nationality or race, one distances oneself from others. It damages the group mindedness, which reduces the productivity. It leads to growth of enemies.

The student should learn the positive things. But the teacher who is a guide and counselor should know well about the bad traits also, so, that he can treat the child with consideration and patience. Those having the above traits lack evil mind.

Asuara traits are explained as the following:

- **Lack of Discriminating Capacity:** Such people do not discriminate good from bad. So they always prefer the easiest ways, which are usually faulty. They prefer individual goals rather than social goals.
- **Bad Practice:** The objects the wrong people choose are harmful to others.
- **Materialistic View:** They believe in immediate **results,** they never think of effects.
- **Greed:** They never get satisfied with what they have but always want excess which is relative and impossible.
- **Pride:** They always compare themselves with the inferior people and feel that they are highly placed.
- **Ignorance:** They never try to know the real knowledge. They feel what they know is enough and is every thing.
- **Earning in Improper Ways:** They want to get more money to enjoy the earthly pleasures and select harmful ways as their vocation and profession to get money. They become proud of this money they have collected in a wrong way.
- **Disobedience:** Always want to violate the rules and regulations, which are formed for smooth running of society.

If we see traces of these wrong things in the child then they have to be deconditioned.

The teacher selects observation and interview as his chief methods to study so that they give him a lot of information about the inner nature of the child.

Bhagawad Gita also classified the personality of the people on the basis of the food they eat. Soft people like the food, which is tasty and well cooked. They take food, which helps them to be tireless in work. This type of food makes the people live long, be intellectual, strong, hygienic, comfortable and enlightened.

Whereas the people who are Rajas are short tempered, they like very sour, salty, spicy, hottest, and dry food.

The evil-minded people like spoiled and unhygienic food, which is stale.

According to Indian Philosophy the food we eat decides and controls our temperament, behavior and the mind. The air we breathe enters the mind and does all the thinking. So with pranayama we can control our thought process.

❖ ❖ ❖

The Inward Journey

– Dr. Sr. G. Theresamma

The journey inwards though the longest is the most valuable

Our age has achieved marvels in outer space by landing men on the moon, sending probes to Venus and Mars, and exploring the unknown. But we have not been as successful in exploring our inner space, or even in sensing its value and importance. Self-realization is the ocean that exists in each one of us to seek our divine core. That core, though never absent in anyone, remains latent within everyone. It is not an outward quest for a Holy Grail that lives beyond, but an inward journey to allow the inner core to reveal itself.

By Hindu world vision every person must have a four-fold goal in life. These are of two kinds, one is the ultimate, and the other is the proximate. Ultimate cannot be more than one, proximate by nature can be many, three plus one - four. Now these three goals are not neglected but transcended and integrated. We cannot go to the ultimate without passing through and dealing with all the implications and exigencies, of the first three goals.

Four Aims of Life

Purusarthas are man's four aims in life –dharma (sense of duty), artha (purpose and means of life), kama (enjoyments of life), and moksha (freedom from worldly pleasures).

According to Patanjali the four aims of life that must be accomplished are dharma, artha, kama, and moksha. He spoke of the culmination of purusarthas and gunas as the highest goal of yoga sadhana.

✍ ***Dr. Sr. G. Theresamma,*** *Principal, St. Joseph's College of Education for Women, Guntur.*

Dharma is doing one's duty by living in the right way. Dharma is that which upholds, sustains, and supports one who has fallen or is falling, or is about to fall in the sphere of ethics, physical or mental practices, or spiritual discipline. Dharma is the careful observation of one's ethical, social, intellectual and religious duties in daily life. Strictly speaking this is taught at the level of studentship, to be followed throughout life. Without dharma, spiritual attainment is not possible. Patanjali's whole concept of yoga is based on dharma, the law handed down in perpetuity through Vedic tradition. The goal of law of dharma is emancipation.

Artha is the self-reliance on earning one's own living. Artha is acquisition of wealth in order to progress towards higher pursuits of life including understanding the main purpose of life. If one does not earn one's own way, dependence on another will result in leading a parasitic life. One is not meant to be greedy while accumulating wealth, but only to meet one's needs, so that one's body is kept nourished and one may be free from worries and anxieties. If one comes to understand human love through friendship and compassion, one may later develop a universal fellowship leading to the realization of divine love. The householder is expected to fulfill his responsibilities of bringing up his children and helping his fellow men. Married life has never been considered a hindrance to happiness, to divine love or to the union with the supreme soul.

Kama – the pleasures of love and human enjoyment. Kama means enjoyment of the pleasures of life provided one does not lose physical health, or harmony and balance of mind. The self cannot be experienced by a weakling. The body, the temple of the soul, has to be treated with care and respect. Asana, pranayama and dhyana therefore, are essential to purify the body, stabilize the mind and clarify the intelligence. One must learn to use the body as a bow, and asana, pranayama, and dhyana as arrows to be aimed at the target, the soul.

Moksha - is freedom from a thousand little things that we accomplish each day. It is our training for the greatest detachment that leads to the ultimate freedom, Kaivalya. Anything, however small, that restricts our freedom to act, that is to act from source, from our core, is a cause of tension and stress. Freedom is to be gained incrementally and over a time.

The inward journey is like a river flowing between the two banks that control its course. One bank is dharma, the science of religion, or the righteous duty that upholds, sustains, and supports our humanity and observance of universal or ethical principles, not limited by culture, time, or place. The other bank of river is moksha, freedom, that is, acting with detachment in all the little things of here and now. The river of love, pleasure, prosperity and wealth flows between these guiding banks.

One way to sum up the four aims of life would be to say that provided we behave ethically on the one hand, surrender to God on the other, between these two, we will love, labour, and laugh.

Dharma is universal. It is about the search for enduring ethical principles, about the cultivation of right behaviour in physical, moral, mental, psychological, and spiritual dimensions. This behaviour must always relate to the growth of the individual with the goal of realizing the soul. If it does not, if it is culturally limited or warped, then it falls short of the definition of dharma. Sadhana, the practitioner's inward journey, admits no barriers between individuals, cultures, races, or creeds, so, neither can dharma. The discovery of the universal soul through the realization of individual soul is an experience that, by definition, can leave no frontiers intact. Kaivalya, liberation, comes when the yogi has fulfilled the purusharthas, the fourfold aim of life, and has transcended the gunas. Aims and gunas return to their source, and consciousness is established, in its own natural purity.

Four padas –Samadhi, Sadana, Vibhuti and Kaivalya are consciously or unconsciously, founded on these four aims and stages of activity. The four aims of life are closely related to four stages of life (Ashramas) – Brahmacharyasrama, gruhasthasrama, vanaprastha-srama, and sannyasasrama.

Patanjali made it clear in his penultimate verse (sutra) that enlightenment and freedom come to one who has lived life fully and completely. The yogis and sages of India formulated ways and means for creating a harmonious and peaceful life by classifying men's minds according to their vocations (varnas), their stages of life (asramas) and their aims in life (Purusarthas).

Lord Krishna says in theBhagavad-Gita (IV.13) that men are born according to their acquired moral, mental, intellectual and spiritual growth. These are known as duties of communities (varna dharma). Varna is the psychological characteristic of man according to his words, thoughts and deeds.

According to the Bhagavad-Gita (VIII. 40-44) 'Serenity, faith, self-restraint, austerity, purity, forbearance, uprightness and knowledge, to lead a pure and divine life are said to be the characteristics of a brahmana. A Brahmana is one who knows about the self (Purusha), and has understood and realized the divinity in himself.

As per the theory of cycles all life's activities –as science has been discovering the truth in more and more fields, are cyclic. The application of this law can be found in the "theory of four yugas". The idea of the four Yugas was once, part of the universal religion, which was the original "Vedic Hinduism" of the Masters and Maha Rishis.

So in the land of Bharata, time, according to the scriptures, is divided into four long ages or chaturyugas. The first was the age of dharma, the Kritayuga –satyayuga –Morning of civilization. Here, virtue walked on four feet, majestic and proud. Satya or truth reigned supreme. All of man's deeds were clothed in purity; all of man's thoughts were divine. Soon, however, came the Tretayuga –Noon day of kingship, when evil marked its entry, and man's soul was slowly sucked into sin. And dharma lost a leg. By the time, the third age, the Dwaparayuga came - onset of commerce and wealth, made their presence felt, adharma occupied centre-stage and the very fabric of life began to decay.

Now, the age we are living in, Kaliyuga, the 'Mid Night' of man, is the absolute nadir of civilization. Deceit and deception dominate, wickedness whispers in the veins, mere materialism motivates man and virtue has been crippled, hobbling on just a single foot. A crisis reigns on earth -a spiritual crisis as well as material crisis. A crisis which, sadly enough, is the result of the sorry state man has made of his own affairs -on this Earth. Today man is chained by shackles of his own science mended by weapons given by his own chemistry and bombed by his nuclear physics to ashes. Man is imprisoned by the laws, which he himself has invented for others.

Modern age is marked by lack of faith in divine nature of man (Materialism), and interest in his body not in his soul. Kaliyuga is therefore called -the age of wars and war of wars. There will be intrigue, treachery, sabotage, espionage, murder, lust, rapacious greed for wealth, revolutions, massacres, wars and bloodshed –mankind has to pass on from a dark cycle of troubles, tribulation and wars, a veritable moral nightmare –into a golden morning of soul.

In this era of darkness, man is blinded by corruption, served by power and over-whelmed by vanity, when greed and gluttony consume the world, corruption and cunning tear it apart, selfishness and insanity stalk on it.

So man's consciousness has to flower to perfection, which is possible only by means of self-realization. Here the individual self realizes its fullest expression as a universal world personality while still residing in the body. In order to attain it man has to embrace an inward journey.

Yoga: The Inward Journey

The Indian perspective starts from the internal inner observation of 'what is'. Time and again the great people proved that absolute truth couldn't be arrived through reason and logic but only by inner exploration and self-methods, paths and approaches like meditation, yoga, etc.

All yoga as practiced today is based on the yoga sutras -a collection of aphorisims offered, more than 2000 years ago, by the Indian sage, Patanjali. The sutras were the earliest and are still the most profound and enlightening study of the human psyche. Yoga is an art, a science and a philosophy. It touches the life of man at every level, physical, mental and spiritual. It is a practical method for making one's life purposeful, useful and noble. It ensures revitalization of the body metabolism by total relaxation of the system. It frees one from the stress and strain, which have become part and parcel of modern life.

Yogasanas are time-tested exercises for the harmonious development of a sound body and mind. This is a science of body culture, which has come down to us from the ancient sages as a part of our great cultural heritage. Yoga as it was understood by its sages is designed to satisfy all the human needs in a comprehensive, seamless whole. Its goal is nothing less than to attain the integrity of oneness with ourselves and as a consequence oneness with all that lives beyond ourselves. We become the harmonious microcosm in the universal macrocosm. Oneness, what is often called as integration, is the foundation for wholeness, inner peace, and ultimate freedom.

The therapeutic value of the yogasanas is well known. Yoga transforms and even sublimates the mind giving the power of self-control, confidence and overcome obstacles to one's spiritual evolution. In this way one can attain the goal of yoga, Kaivalya, liberation from the bondage of worldly desires and actions, and union with the divine. It is also a discipline, which seeks to evoke the INDIVIDUAL to the UNIVERSAL. It is both a means to acquire that union as well as the state of that union. Health is the supreme foundation of virtue, wealth, enjoyment and salvation. Diseases are destroyers of health, of good life, and even of life itself. Charaka, one of the oldest physicians of India, made this statement about 2500 year ago; a statement that rings true for all times.

B.K.S. Iyengar says, yoga is like music, the rhythm of the body, the melody of the mind, and the harmony of the soul, which creates the symphony of life.

The inward journey will allow us to explore and to integrate each of these aspects of our being. From our physical body, we will journey inward to discover our subtle bodies -our very body, where breath and emotions reside, our mental body, where thoughts and obsessions can be mastered; our intellectual body where intelligence and wisdom can be found; and our divine body where the universal soul can be glimpsed.

We do not need to seek freedom in some distant land, for it exists within our own body, heart, mind, and soul. Illuminated emancipation, freedom, unalloyed and untainted bliss await us, but we must choose to embark on the inward journey to discover it.

In order to find out how to reveal our inner most being, the sages explored the various sheaths of existence, starting from body and progressing through mind and intelligence, and ultimately to soul. The yogic journey guides us from our periphery, the body, to the center of our being, the soul, to integrate the various layers so that the inner divinity shines out as through a clear glass.

The Five Kosas: The Sheaths of Being

Before one embarks on a long journey into unfamiliar territory, it's helpful to have a map. Over 3,000 years ago yogic sages developed the map of the Koshas (bodies) to navigate an inner journey –starting from the periphery (physical body) and moving towards the core of the self (the embodied soul). We are composed of five layers, shealths, or bodies. Like Russian dolls, or the layers of an onion, each metaphorical 'body' is contained within the next. These include physical body (annamaya kosa), energetic body or the breath body (pranamaya kosa), psycho – emotional body or the mental body (manomaya kosa), intellectual or wisdom body (vijnanamaya kosa), and ultimately our blissful body or soul body (anandamaya kosa).

The koshas are interwoven together like a tapestry. Without a doubt we have all experienced this interconnection in our own body. Whenever we feel tension or stress, we find our breath becoming shallow and our mind in a state of agitation while wisdom and joy seem far away. But when we feel joy and are in communion with life, positive energy permeates our entire being.

From the kosha perspective, yoga or any other meditative practice allows us to bring alignment of the layers to allow connection with the bliss body. The individual ceases to exist and becomes one with all that is beautiful. This is the center of our being where unconditional love arises and communion with spirit happens. Learning about the different bodies and how they work together is the journey that leads to enlightenment. Nature (Prakruti) includes the physical body, and soul (Purusha). As we explore the soul, it is important to remember that their exploration will take place within nature (the body), for that is where we are and what we are. Our specific field of exploration is ourselves, from skin to unknown center. Yoga is concerned with the fusion of nature and soul because this is the essence of human life with all of its challenges, contradictions, and joys.

There is something in the world, which is not superseded, an imperishable absolute, Brahman. This experience of infinity is given to us all on some occasions. The Upanishads declare, "If there were no spirit of joy in the universe, who could live and breathe in this world of life?" Brahman, revealing itself in all, is the permanent background of the world process. The Rig-Veda tells us of one supreme reality, Ekam Sat, of which the learned speak variously. Another verse says; 'The man of action finds his God in fire, the man of feeling in the heart, the feeble-minded in the idol, but the strong in spirit finds God every where.'

The aim of life is the gradual revelation, in our human existence, of the eternal in us. 'Whoever comes to me through whatsoever form, I reach him' says the Lord in the Gita. However, distinctions are made on the basis of the threefold activity of human consciousness, into the Jnanamarga or the path of knowledge and illumination, Bhakti marga or the path of faith and devotion, and karma marga or the path of work and service. Thought, feeling and will are not isolated faculties, but only distinguishable aspects of experience. Each of them makes its own contribution to the whole and is penetrated by the others. These three -right knowledge, right desire and right action –go together. The first reveals to us the truth; the second instills a love for it and the third moulds life. All the three enter into the integral experience of a perfect life.

The Gita says; 'There is no purifier like unto Jnana or wisdom'. This jnana is not dialectical learning. Man in his essential nature has freedom of spirit and wisdom. Our limitation shuts us away from the reality of ourselves and subjects us to error. This jnana is independent of symbols and senses, as life living itself in the very heart of reality.

The cognitive pursuit of God is rather slow and painful. The father and mother of this whole world are hard to find, and when one has found Him, to declare Him to all is impossible. Our life is so short and the search is so slow. The practical minded man tries to realize his divine destiny by the performance of duty, karma, social service, and yajna. Freedom is the nature of man; bondage is due to the barriers that shut us from ourselves. Our slavery is complete when we begin to hug it. If we break our selfishness, which walls us off from the world, and identify ourselves with the larger ends we can gradually develop the love that casts out fear, disarms all hatred, and breaks all springs of bitterness. Mere mechanical morality is not likely to lead us to the end. It has to be led by a vital union with God. Then shall we realize that in every man there is a ray of the eternal light emanating from the central sun. When we love man, we are conscious of our unity with him in the central spirit and we give effect to this consciousness in our lives. The great statement by which the Upanishads are known to the world is 'tat tvam asi' – 'you are that'. The potential divinity of the human soul is asserted thereby.

Of all sciences, the science of the self is the greatest adhyatmavidya. The Upanishad tells us: atmanam viddhi, 'know thyself'. Sankara lays down an essential condition of spiritual life, atma-anatama-vastu-viveka; the knowledge of the distinction between the soul and the non-soul. There is nothing higher in this world than the possession of one's soul.

Kabir says, 'The way to the knowledge of God is through self-surrender which it is not ceremonial piety'. The Kathopanishads says that man turned outward by his services and so lost contact with himself. The Upanishads require us to acquire Brahmavidya (knowledge of God) or atmavidya (self-knowledge). This will make us to attain Bliss. Truth, peace, equanimity, forgiveness, renunciation, detachment, and kindness light up the true seeker's consciousness keeping one in perpetual awareness.

The heart of the spiritual journey is to know and to live the truth of who you really are. – *Rick*

References

- SeethaRam A.R.Dr. Yoga Therapy for Holistic Health with Chittarama Yoga Sutra. Mysore: Paramalawsa Yoga Therapy Centre Bogadi.
- Sri Sri Ravi Shankar. (2007) Wisdom for the New Millennium Mumbai: Jaico Publishing House.
- Sri Mad Ray Chowdary: Chandrika (Trans) [2006] Atma – Siddhi, Insearch of the Soul, Mumbai: Vakds, feffer and simons Pvt. Ltd. Marathe Marg.
- Heinrieh Zimmer [1974] Philosophies of India (ld) Joseph Campbell. Princeton, New Jersey: Princeton University Press [2006]
- Radha Krishnan. S. Indian Religious Thought. New Delhi. Orient paper backs.(A Division Vision Books Pvt. Ltd.)
- Gambhirananda Swami (TV) [2003]. Eight Upanisads with the commentary of Sankaracarya (Vol.2) Kolkata. Advvai Ashrama, Swami Mushananda. President.
- Gambhirananda Swami (TV) [2003]. Eight Upanisads with the commentary of Sankaracarya (Vol.1)
- Sri Sri Ravi Shankar [2007]. Celebrating Silence. Hyderabad. Jaico Publishing House.
- Iyengar. B.K.S. Light on life [2005] London Rodale International Ltd. [2000]
- Amalorananda Swami Atmapurna Anubhava. Mysore. Anjali Ashcam.

The Subtle Energy Centres Consequences of their Malfunctions & Remedies

– *Dr. K. Jayasree*

Om – Sahanavavathu – Sahanow Bhunaktu – Sahaveeryamkaravavahai
Thejaswinavavadeetha mastu – Mavidwishavahai
Ohm Shanti Shanti Shantih

– Kataupanishad Shanti patam

Let the mortal clay (self) be the immortal God. (Rigveda VIII-1)

Human body is the most highly evolved of all the existing bodies that express themselves through behaviour. It is capable of self-expression and the realization of truth beyond the realm of sensory perception. With the help of memory, imagination and intuition, the human organism can understand and grasp laws inherent in nature and can put those mysterious forces to work for its benefit, growth and development. So human body is the most perfect instrument for the expression of consciousness, which is the ultimate irreducible reality out of which and by whose power mind and matter proceed. The chief centres of consciousness in human beings are found in the cerebrospinal system and in the upper brain.

In order to attain a full understanding of human kind, the psychie dimensions - not simply the physical ones -must be examined thoroughly. In essence, cosmic consciousness and individual consciousness are one, because both are consciousness and are indivisible. Realization of one's divine nature brings release from the trap of one's animal nature, which causes subjectivity and limited vision. In the language of yoga this is called the 'mind trap'. For modern psychologists mind denotes the functional aspect of the brain

---

✍ ***Dr. K. Jayasree,*** *Lecturer, St. Joseph's College of Education for Women, Guntur.*

that is responsible for thought, volition and feelings. Yogis approach the psyche by searching for its cause in the mind and consciousness. Psychologists on the other hand seek to define it by studying behaviour. According to 'Tantra Yoga', a combination of Raja, Jnana, Karma, Bakthi and Hatha yoga, body and mind are considered to be one and the body is believed to be a vehicle of the mind.

The functioning of the entire human body is controlled by the cerebrospinal system, and the psychic centres are located in this system. For many centuries this knowledge has been handed down through the Hindu tantra tradition, which terms these psychic centres as 'chakras'. There are seven stations or chakras along the spinal column through which the Kundalini passes on awakening. Kundalini a vital force, is an aspect of the externally, supreme consciousness, which is both with and without attributes. (Yoga Kundalini-1st verse, Yoga Chudamanyo-panishad - 7th verse, Trisaki Brahmopanishad - 25th verse) In the nirguna aspect it is the will of the cosmic consciousness and is pure consciousness. In the Saguna attributes, their energy is often personified as Kundalini. When awakened, this dormant energy works through nadis, means 'stream' as per Rigveda.

Nadis are linked with the chakras. The central canal, Sushumna plays a vital role in yogic and tantric practices. Mention of these nadis is given in Sandilyopanishad (1:11) and Varahopanishad (5:2) Some of the gross nadis such as physical nerves, veins and arteries are only known in modern medical science.

According to the tantric treatise 'shiva samhita' there are fourteen principal nadies. Of these Ida, other Pingala and Sushumna are considered the most important; all nadies are subordinate to sushumna. Mention of these is also given in Kshurikopanishad-3: 5, 8, 9 and 16; Dhyana Bindupanishad - 1:52-54; Trisaki Brahmanopashad - 31; Yoga Chudamanyopanishad-4 and 5; Varahopanishad chapter 5; Darsanopanishad chapter 4:2 & 3; Prasnopanishad 3rd chapter - 6 & 7.

Like all other forces, Kundalini is itself invisible; but in the human body it clothes itself in a curious nest of hollow concentric spheres of astral and etheric matter, one within another. There appear to be seven such concentric spheres resting within the root chakra, in and around the last real cell or hollow of the spine close to the coccyx, but only in the outer most of these spheres is the force active in the ordinary man. In the others, it is sleeping, it is only when the man attempts to arouse the energy latent in those inner layers that the dangerous phenomena of the fire begin to show themselves. The harmless fire of the outer skin of the ball flows up the spinal column using the three lines of sushumna, ida and pingala simultaneously.

Prana travels through sushumna from the pelvic plexus to Brahma Randra ('The cave of the Brahman'; the hallow space between the two hemispheres of the brain), which is situated in the interior of the cerebro spinal axis. Muladhara chakra is the meeting place of the three main nadis, and is known as Yukta Triveni. Sushumna is centrally situated and passes through the merudanda (spinal column). Shadilya upanishad names Muladhara as the seat of Sushumna. So it originates in Muladhara chakra, runs up the body and pierces the talu (palate at the base of the Skull) and joins Sahasrara (the plexus of one thousand nadis at the top of the skull known as the thousand petalled lotus). This nadi divides into two branches: anterior and posterior. The anterior branch goes to Ajna chakra, which is situated in the alignment with the eyebrows and joins the Brahma Randra. Yogasikhopanishad chapter 5 verse 3 had given about this and place of Ida and Pingala. The posterior branch passes from behind the skull and joins the Brahma Randra. It's a soft spot open when child is born but begins to harden after six months and will be opened only through the special practices.

In the space outside the merudanda to the left and right are the nadis Ida and Pingala. Ida is the self-channel, carrier of lunar currents, is feminine in nature and the storehouse of life producing maternal energy. Mention of these nadies is given in Varahopanishad chapter 5: 2 & 3 verses. In Svara yoga it represents the 'left' breath, which is described as magnetic, female, visual and emotional in nature. Ida is neither a nerve nor a sympathetic cord; it's a manovahinadi. In India, the moon (chandra) is related to the psyche. In the Purushasukta it is said "chandramamanaso jatah. Even though it is not possible to locate Ida with modern technical devices, its pranavahi aspect can clearly be felt through the effects of Svara Sadhana.

Pingala is the right channel, carrier of solar currents, is masculine in nature and a storehouse of destructive energy. In its own way, it is also purifying but its cleaning is like fire. In svarayoga it represents right breath. Right is electrical, male, verbal and rational in nature. The Sun is related to the eyes of virata Purusha. As per Purusha Sukta "chakshore surya ajayatah". Arousal of Kundalini through the Ida / Pingala manifests their negative aspects but arousal through sushmna leads one to the kingdom of God (Sat-Chit - Ananda). The two nadis Ida and Pingala create ripples through their respective powers and the points where these ripples meet are called chakras, which are vortices of energy moving in clockwise direction.

Chakras are psychic centres on the surface of the etheric double with their corresponding centres in the spine in the body that are active at all times, whether we are conscious of them or not. Energy moves through the chakras to produce different psychic states. Mention was being made in varahopanishad chapter 5 : 5. Modern biological science explains this as the chemical changes produced by the endocrine glands, ductless glands whose secretions mix into the body's blood stream directly and instantaneously. Ancient philosophers of East related those changes with the five basic tattvas or elements -earth, water, fire, air and akasha (either) knowledge about chakras can be a valuable key to introspection.

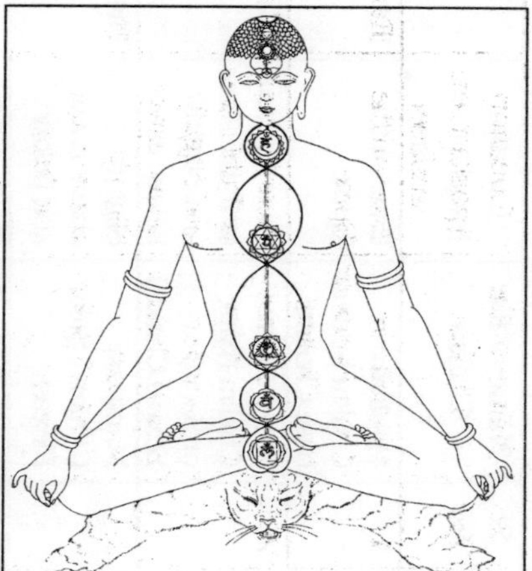

Muladhara, Swadhisthana, Manipura, Anahata, Visuddha and Agna, which in the physical body are said to have their correspondences in the principal nerveplexuses and organs, commencing from what is possibly the sacro-coccygeal plexus to the space between the eyebrows which some identify with pineal gland, the centre of the third or spiritual

S. No	Name of the Chakra	Location (position on surface)	Element	Colour	Corresponding Nerve plexus	Corresponding Endocrine gland	System
1	Mooladhara Chakra (root or base Chakra)	Base on the Spine	Earth	Red	Root Plexus or Pelvic Plexus or Coccygeal Plexus (4th Sacral)	Adrenal	Excretory Muscle Skeleton
2	Swadhisthana Chakra (hara or Sacral or Sexual Chakra)	Near Sacrum or Pubic Area and Slightly below navel	Water	Red – orange	Sacral Plexus or Hypogastric plexus or Aortic Plexus (1st Lunar)	Gonads	Reproductive
3	Manipura Chakra (Solor Plexus)	Slightly above navel and below ribs	Fire	Yellow	Solar Plexus or Coelioc Plexus (8th Thoroic)	Pancreas	Digestive
4	Anahata Chakra or Hart Chakra	Centre of Chest at the height of heart	Air	Green	Cordioc Plexus (8th cervical)	Thymus	Circulatory
5	Vishuddhi Chakra (Throat)	Hollow of Throat	Ether (Space or Akasa)	Blue	Pharyngeal Plexus or cervical Plexus or Brochial Plexus (3rd cervical)	Thyroid	Lymphatic
6	Ajna Chakra (Brow or Third Eye)	Between the Eyebrows	Ether (Space or Akasa)	Indigo	Cavernous Plexus or Nasociliary Plexus (1st cervical)	Pituitary	Autonomic Nervous
7	Sahasra Chakra (crown)	Top of Head	Ether (Space or Akasa)	Violet White	*	Pineal	Cerebrospinal Nervous

eye and others with the cerebellus. Description of seven major chakras is given in tabular form. Mention of the place/ position of the chakra is given in Yogashikopanishad 5:1 & 2; Kshurikopanishad-7 & 11 versus and DhyanaBindopanishad 1:43; Yogachudamani upanishad 2 & 3: Yogakundalini 3:7; Amrutanadaupanishad 4:35 - 39.

The first or Muladhara - chakra, (foundation which is so called from its being the root of sushumna where kundalini rests is at the place of meeting of Kanda (root of all the nadis) and the sushumna - nadi and in the region between anus and genitals (pelvic, plexus). The base of the spine; the first three vertebrate as shown in the table.

It is not meant that the chakra proper is in the region of the gross body described but is the subtle centre of the gross region; such centre exists in the spinal column, which forms its axis. Chakras are symbolised by lotus correspondence to three different levels of spirituality. It is rooted in the mud -ignorance, endevours through water to reach the top -action; and finally reaches out in the air to receive the light from the sun –enlightenment; this represents the quest of man from dusk to dawn.

This crimson Muladhara lotus is described as one of four petals, the virtues of which are the four forms of bliss known as Paramananda, Sahajananda, Yogananda and Virananda. The petals are configurations made by the position of the Nadis at any particular centre, and are in themselves, Prana sakti, manifested by Prana vayu in the living body. This lotus is the centre of the yellow prithivi or earth tattva with its quadrangular (square) mandala inorder to facilitate the flow of energy. Of the seven types of desires, security is associated with muladhara. (Its vibration helps to create a passage inside the Brahmanadi). The chakra's predominant 'sense' is smell, sense organ -nose, work organ -Anus, Vayu (air) is Apanavayu, the air that expels the semen from the male organ; Urine for both sexes and that which pushes child from womb during birth. Loka is Bhu, and Rulling Planet is mars.

The four lotus petals represent ganglions that are formed at four important nerve endings, the colour of the petals is vermillion mixed with a small amount of 'Crimson Red'.

The seat of the vital life force, kundalini shakti in the form of a coiled serpent, with her mouth open, face upward, is connected with the path of sushumna. The unawakened kundalini shakti remains cooled, wrapped around the lingam with her tail in her mouth because her mouth faces downward, the flow of energy is downward. As soon as one begins working with the first chakra, this dormant energy rises to head and flows freely into the channel of sushumna. In Humsopanishad 6th versus, passage of kundalini from 1st to 7th chakra is given.

Muladhara chakra represents the manifestation of the individual consciousness into human form that is physical birth. Meditation on the tip of the nose induces the beginning of awareness, freedom from disease, lightness, inspiration, vitality, vigor, stamina, security, an understanding of inner purity, and softness in the voice and in the inner melody.

Behavioural Characteristics of Muladhara Chakra

A person who acts wisely and with moderation (who acts in harmony with natural laws) explores his body and mind as vehicles of liberation from the lower realm.

Normally a child from the ages of one to seven years acts out of first chakra motivations. The earth is being grasped as a new experience. The infant must ground himself and establish the laws of his world, learning to regulate his patterns of eating, drinking and sleeping as the proper behaviour necessary for securing his worldly identity. The young child will be self-centered and highly concerned with his own physical survival.

The main problem of child/adult acting from first chakra motivation is violent behaviour based on insecurity. The person dominated by this chakra generally sleeps on his stomach (for 10-12 hours). This chakra encompasses the places of generic, illusion, anger, greed, delusion avarice and sensuality, which are fundamental to human existence. The desire for more experience and information acts as a motivating force, a basic impetus for individual development.

The Swadhisthana chakra is the second lotus proceeding upwards and is a vermilion lotus of six petals placed in the spinal centre of the region at the root of the genitals. Water is the tatva of this chakra, the colour of the tatva being light blue whose shape is circle and chakras sense organ is tongue, work organ genitals and its vayu (air) is Apanavayu. This chakra belongs to the astral plane whose ruling planet is Mercury. Three fourths of the earth is covered with water. The ocean tides are governed by the moon. Three fourths of a person's body weight is water. The moon affects people in the form of "emotional tides". Women have a monthly cycle, which is synchronized with the moon cycle. The Swadhistnana chakra is the centre of procreation, which is directly related with the moon. The vital relationship between water and the moon is shown by the crescent yantra within the white circle of the water chakra. The moon plays a great role in the life of a 'second-chakra' person who goes through many emotional fluctuations during the changing phases of the moon.

The six details of the lotus represent six important nerve endings in the second chakra; these petals show energy flowing from six dimensions. The linear awareness of first chakra becomes circular with more movement and flow.

The crocodiles (Vehicle of Bija) habits of hunting, trickery, floating and fantasing are qualities of a second chakraperson, centering on this chakra enable the mind to reflect the world. One acquires the ability to use creative and sustaining energy to elevate himself to refined arts, and pure relationship with others, having become free of lust, anger, greed, unsettledness, and jealousy.

Behavioural Characteristics of Swadhistana Chakra

Normally a person between the ages of eight and fourteen acts from swadhistana chakra's motivation; he sleeps between eight to ten hours in fetal position. The child begins to reach out to his family and friends for physical contact. The imagination increases. Once the need for food and shelter is met the person is free to visualize any environment or circumstances that he desires. Sensitivity enters into relationship as a new awareness of physical body evolves. The second chakra can have a downward, whirlpool effect on the psyche, causing a person to be restless and confused. He changes roles, maintains self-esteem and is chivalrous. When the world is seen with a negative mind nothing excites, nothing pleases; all is lost. Envy and jealousy arise from a desire to possess the time or qualities of another. This results in a destructive state of restless anxiety. The plane of joy brings a feeling of a deep satisfaction, which penetrates the entire consciousness of the person who has evolved beyond the aspects of the second chakra.

The third chakra, the Manipura chakra (the city of gems) located at solar plexus; epigastic plexus; navel, whose tatva is fire, shape of the tatva being triangle. The predominant sense is sight, the sense organ being eyes and work organs being feet and legs. Saman vayu, the vayu that dwells in the upper abdomen in the area of the navel, helps the digestive system. It causes the blood and chemicals produced in the solar plexus through assimilation with the help of saman vayu; the rasa or essence of food is produced, assimilated and carried to the entire body. Svaloka (celestial plane) is the plane of this chakra, ruling planet being Sun. Yantra is in the form of inverted triangle.

Behavioural Characteristics of Manipura Chakra

Between the ages of fourteen to twenty-one a person is ruled by Manipura chakra. The motivation energy of this chakra impels the person to develop his ego, his identity in the world. A person dominated by the third chakra will strive for personal power and recognition, even to the detriment of family and friends. Such a person will sleep from 6 to 8 hours during nights on his back. The plane of Manipura chakra encompasses karma, charity, and atonement for one's errors, good and bad company, selfless service, sorrow, the plane of dharma and the celestial plane. Dharma is the timeless law of nature that interconnects all that exists. Every person must be aware of his actions in order to achieve a balance in the life. Once this balance is attained, a person may enter the celestial plane of illumination.

The fourth chakra -Anahata chakra (unstricken) is located in the cardiac plexus (the heart). Its aspects are attaining balance between the three chakras above the heart and the three chakras below it. Colourless air (formless with out smell or taste) is its tatva, whose shape is hexagram, predominant sense is touch, sense organ is skin and work organ is hand. Prana vayu dwelling in the chest region is the vayu of chakra, whose plane is maha loka, ruling planet being Venus. Twelve million petals surround the gray green hexagon of Anahata chakra. Within Ananta chakra is an eight petalled lotus, in the centre of which rests the spiritual, etheric heart known as Anahata Kanda towards the right side. These eight petals are connected with different emotions and when energy flows through them the desire related to that petal is experienced.

Behavioural Characteristics of Anahata Chakra

From 21 to 28 years of age one vibrates in this chakra. This chakra encompasses sudharma; one becomes aware of his karma, his life's actions.

The fifth chakra Vishuddha chakra (pure) is located in the carotia plexus; throat. Its aspects are knowledge, the human plane, with smoky purple colour akasha; sound is its tatva, whose shape is crescent with hearing as predominant sense, its sense organ being ears and work organ being mouth (vocal cords). Udana vayu, which dwells in the throat region of the head, is its vayu, whose tendency is to carry air up through the head, aiding in the production of sound. Janaloka (human plane) is its plane and Jupiter is the ruling planet. The yantra is a silver crescent within a white circle shining as a full moon surrounded by sixteen petals.

Behavioural Characteristics of Vishuddha Chakra

One who enters this chakra becomes master of one's entire self. Here all elements dissolve into pure, Akasha. Only the Tanmatras remain - subtle frequencies of those elements. This chakra governs between the ages of 28 to 35. This chakra encompasses the five planes of Jnana. Thus bestowing bliss the vishuddhi chakra embodies chit or cosmic consciousness.

The sixth chakra-Agna chakra (authority, command, unlimited power) is located in medula plexus; pineal plexus; point between the eyebrows. Mahatattva, which consists of three gunas and includes manas, Buddhi, Ahamkara, and Chitha is its tattva.

Transparent, luminescent, bluish or camphor which is the colour of tattva, belongs to Tapas Loka, whose ruling planet is Saturn. Yantra is in the form of a white circle with two luminescent petals. (These petals are the tabernulae of the pineal gland). In Agna chakra one becomes sat and this embodies Sat-Chit-Ananda or being conscious of bliss.

Behavioural Characteristics of Agna Chakra

When a person enters Agna Chakra, light will form around his head-aura. He maintains continual state of samadhi during all actions; the sixth chakra encompasses the plane of conscience (Vivaka) plane of neutrality, Solar plane, Lunarplane, Plane of austerity, Plane of violence, Earthly plane, Liquid plane, and the plane of Spiritual devotion. The Yogi himself becomes a divine manifestation.

Sahasrara Chakra "Thousand Petaled" also called Shunya chakra and Niralambapuri Chakra is the 7th Chakra, which is located on the top of the cranium, cerebral plexus. Belonging to satyam loka, the ruling planet is ketu yantra whose form is circle as a full moon. Above the sphere is an umbrella of one thousand lotus petals arranged in the variegated colours of the rainbow. Planes encompassed in sahasrara chakra are Tejas loka, Om kara, Vayu Loka, Subudhi Loka, durbuddhi, Sukha Loka, Tamas Loka. According to shastras, Sahasrara is the seat of the self-luminescent soul or chitta, the essence of being. In the presence of cosmic self it is possible for any one to feel the divine and indeed to realise the divinity with in himself.

The function of each chakra, its physical organs controlled, mental aspects governed and diseases due to its malfunctioning is given in table 2.

Name of Chakra	Function	Physical organs controlled	Mental aspects governed	Diseases due to mal functioning of Chakras	Remarks
Mooladhra	Kundalini Security Survival Grounding Fear Physical energy	1. Muscular and Skeletal system, 2. Spine, 3. Adrenal Glands, 4. The production and quality of blood, 5. body heat, 6. General vitality, 7. Growth of children, 8. Kidneys	Self-protection, Survival Instinct fear, insecurity	1. Arthritis, 2. Spinal ailments, 3. Blood ailments, 4. Cancer (Bone cancer, Leukemia), 5. Allergy, 6. Growth problem, 7. Low vitality, 8. Slow healing of wounds and broken bones	Persons with healthy root Chakra tend to be robust and healthy, full of vitality, persons with weak Root Chakra lend to be weak and drained of vitality. Old people usually have deplete Root Chakra.
Swadhisthana	Anger/Action Sexuality, Peace	2. Sex glands (ovaries, testicles), 2. Sexual organs, 3. Kidney, 4. Adrenal glands, 5. Controls B.P., 6. Lower parts of liver, pancreas, spleen and intestines 7. Bladder, excretion, 8. Uterus	Desire and craving for sexual and other sensual pleasures, seat of negative feeling of guilt, hurt and frustration	1. Sex related problem, 2. High B.P., 3. Back problems, 4. Kidney problems, 5. Bladder ailments, 6. Constipation	It transmits vital energy throughout body via spleen chakra and back Hara chakra.
Manipura	Emotion Power Wisdom Action	1. Stomach, 2. Intestines, 3. Spleen, 4. Gall bladder, 5. Diaphragm, 6. To some degree adrenal glands, heart, lungs, 7. Liver, 8. Pancreas	Ego, craving for name, fame, status, power, control, high ambitions and aggressiveness, negative emotions like anger, jealousy, envy, hatred, greed, violence, cruelty	1. Digestive disorders, 2. Ulcer, 3.Constipation, 4. Diabetes, 5. Hepatitis, 6. Jaundice, 7. Colitis and Diarrhea, 8. Skin problem and allergies, 9. Heart problems and high B.P., 10. Asthma	

Anahata	Group Consciousness Love Compassion Life Force	1. Heart, 2. Lungs, 3. Thymus gland, 4. Circulatory system	Love and compassion, center of higher and refined emotions	1. Heart and circulatory ailments, 2. Lung ailments (Bronchitis, asthma, tuberculosis etc.)	This chakra is the end receiving point of panic energy from where it is distributed to arms and hands.
Vishuddhi	Communication Self-expression Creative energy And sound	1. Throat, 2. Voice Box (Larynx), 3. Air tube (Trachea), 4. Thyroid and Parathyroid glands, 5. Lymphatic system, 6. Arms, hands, 7. Mouth, tongue, 8. Neck.	Communication, speech, self-expression, creativity (musical and artistic talents etc.), Aesthetics	Throat related diseases like 1. Goiter, 2. Sore throat, 3. Speech or voice problems 4. Tonsillitis, 5. Cervical pain	Strength of a person in his speech comes from vishuddhi chakra. Shouting, anger and use of foul language full of ego blocks this Chakra.
Ajna	Third Eye Intuition Clairvoyance Intelligence, Light, Telepathy	1. Hypothalamus, 2. Pituitary and other endocrine glands, 3. Autonomic Nervous System and Lower brain, 4. Left eye, 5. Ears, 6. Nose.	Intuition, intellect, Occult powers/ESP (e.g. Clairvoyance, telepathy etc.)	1. Diseases related to endocrine glands, 2. Diseases related to Autonomic Nervous system (A.N.S) and lower brain, 3. Diseases related to sight, hearing and smell, 4. Sinusitis, swollen adenoids	It is called the master chakra and controls all other major charkas.
Sahasrara	Spiritual Vision Enlightenment	1. Pineal gland 2. Upper or higher Brain, 3. Right eye	Cosmic consciousness, self-realization	Diseases related to pineal gland and the cerebral cortex.	It is also the entry point for Prani energy, Sahasrara Chakra is seen in mediation as a one thousand petalled lotus Upon enlightenment, it looks like a burning bundle of flames.

Some Useful Notes about Chakras

- Colour Mentioned against each chakra are astral colours and closer counterparts of physical colours are seen while chakras are perceived with trancevision.
- Every chakra (except root and crown chakra) has two portions: a) Front, b) Back.
- When chakras become blocked or insensitive due to catches (adverse physical and mental factors), central channel (Sushumma nadi) remains closed and Kundalini can't ascend through it.
- Chakras, in fact the whole bioplasmic body, are greatly influenced by the mental activity especially the negative emotions in the mind.
- The front heart chakra is closely connected to the front solar plexus chakra by several big bioplasmic channels and is also energized by the front solar plexus chakra to a certain degree.
- Throat Chakra and Hara Chakra - Ajna Chakra and Root Chakra are interrelated and form pairs.
- If a person's vital body is strong then his probability of contracting a disease due to external factors like bacteria / virus, pollutants etc. is greatly reduced because body's aura and defence mechanism will easily counter the effects of external irritants.
- Activation of certain chakras may result in the development of these psychic faculties or siddhis. Activation of Ajna chakra results in powers of clairvoyance, clairaudience, etc. Activation of Palm chakra (minor chakra) results in sensing subtle pranic energy.
- Inhalation of smoke particularly cigarette smoke and use of foul language and shouting damages Vishuddhi Chakra or Throat centre.
- Ajna chakra gets cleared by developing the quality of forgiveness. When Ajna chakra opens, Kundalini can pass through it to Sahasrara Chakra.

- Yogis who perceived these chakras in deep meditation saw that they resembled lotus flowers of different shades with different number of petals. Each chakra has a certain number of petals, which correspond to subplexus just as main chakra corresponds to major plexus.
- Lower three chakras (Root, Hara and Solar plexus) indicate lower level of consciousness in the scale of evolution while higher chakras (Heart, Thraoat, Ajna, Sahasrar) correspond to higher levels of consciousness.
- When a person's energy is primarily focussed on the lower level chakras, his mental attitudes or traits are governed by the psychological aspects of these chakras as mentioned in the table of chakras. Similarly when a person operates from the level of higher chakras, his mental traits correspond to the psychological aspects of these chakras as mentioned in the table. This happens only when the energy is allowed to leave the domain of the lower level chakras and enter in the domain of higher-level chakras.
- Each chakra is associated with a yantra (geometrical figure). If we focus on these yantras, we can awaken that chakra easily.

Energy Imbalance: Root Cause of All Problems

- When body and mind are misused, functioning unhealthily, abnormally or are overexerted, energy flow becomes imbalanced, i.e. energy becomes blocked and congested at one place, and depleted at another place leading to some kind of disease (dis-ease) in body.
- If any Rajasik or Tamasik activity disturbs the energy flow of the body then it generates negative energy. Satwik lifestyle and activities promote the balanced and free flow of prana and generate positive energy. Whatever organs or systems get damaged due to the negative physical factors, pranic flow in the corresponding nadis and chakras get disturbed.

Mental Factors Causing Imbalance

- Negative thinking like not accepting and understanding the things as they really are, disturb the flow of prana and health of chakras.
- Unnecessary fear, overestimation, feelings like "I know they will happen like this", wrong notions about people, things , places, pride, ego, prejudice, and disappointment don't allow us to be integrated, whole and complete in our personality.
- We should start accepting and integrating and everything finally leads us to a state of unity, wholeness and completeness. Suppression brings about separation, which creates loneliness, discomfort and a feeling of dis-ease.

Balance at the Centre (Sushumna)

We transcend time and space by opening of Sushumna and Kundalini awakening. As we develop, a process of integration takes place among all alienated or conflicting aspects of ourselves leading to increased happiness and satisfaction. When our consciousness is fully developed, we finally reach that state of enlightenment and equilibrium from which all can be understood, appreciated and accepted. As consciousness gradually becomes expanded and integrated, we become less self-centered with more concerned for others. This, in spiritual parlance, is also stated as moving from a state of separation (selfishness) to the state of unity (selflessness).

When personality is not integrated it is reflected in our behaviour as various forms like negative emotion, desires and expectations, craving and passion for name, fame, power, status etc., various vikaras like greed, attachment, selfishness, ego etc. unsteadiness, and distractions in mind and inability to focus. These negative mental factors create corresponding vibrations in our astral body. Since astral body is connected to etheric or pranic body at the point of chakra or energy centres, corresponding chakras get affected and start malfunctioning. Now the organs to which these chakras feed energy also start malfunctioning as a result. Mention of the different Kosas or bodies is given in Taitraya and Varahopanishad. So doing regular meditation in thoughtless awareness (pure perception) and leading virtuous life is vital inorder to cure the diseases connected with the imbalance of chakras. We should also ensure that our lifestyle is such that which keeps our energy body clean, positive and strong.

Some of the Measures, which will help in keeping our energy body Pure and Strong

- Apart from exercise and meditation, good food, good hygiene, the right amount of rest, right clothes, home, pleasure, personal challenge, intimacy and friends mixed with a good amount of love, will reap great rewards.
- Do occasional fasting with water and fresh fruit juices, to keep our system clean.
- Stop or minimise caffeine drink as it creates imbalance in the nervous and endocrine system and hence in the energy body.
- Alcohol/drugs/smoking also leads to several psychological ailments. So not only physical hygiene, etheric, emotional and mental hygiene are also important. So positive emotions like happiness, kindness, joy, enthusiasm and others have beneficial effects.
- Cruelty to fellow human beings and animals is one of the major causes of severe painful ailments. So proper human relationships are to be maintained.
- The act of forgiving is therapeutic and is necessary for good health. Forgiveness and loving kindness help to normalise the solar plexus chakra and the other affected chakras.
- Prolonged stress is a psychological ailment. Meditation would definitely help a lot in coping with stress conditions.
- Excessive involvement in watching T.V, reading stray magazines distracts the mind and thereby effect the balance of energy body.
- Drink water stored in copper vessels at least (if not gold or silver) Water charged with these metals becomes filled with positive energy. Magnetized water is equally good.

- Walk bare foot on earth especially near river and on grass wet with morning dew.
- Laugh a lot, also develop the habit of cutting and hearing jokes frequently within limits of decency.
- Be aware of negative emotions.
- Foodgrains especially rice (uncooked) have the capacity to absorb and transmute negative energies.
- Tulasi leaves are very effective in destroying the negative energy and purifying the atmosphere

The positive energy atmosphere thus generated by the above measures will tend to neutralize negative energy in our energy body and increase positive energy and help in keeping our energy body pure and strong.

Hence

Let the light of love, compassion, truth, justice, peace, pleasure, joy, serenity, tranquility and smiling face work out from moment to moment throughout life for our perfect health and liberation of soul.

Sarve Jano Sukhino Bhavantu
OM Shanti Shanti Shanti

Teacher's Self-critical Awareness in the Context of Jaina Theory of Liberation

– *T. Padmavathi, B. Srilatha & P. Shanthi*

Abstract

The central theme of Jainism considers religion as a science of ethical practice. The ultimate end and purpose of all life and activity in Jainism is to realize the free and blissful state of our true being. Jains seek, in the first place, to control harming actions engendered by negative emotions and harmony is given the secondary place. Jainism thought the idea of supremacy of human life and stressed the importance of positive attitudes towards life. Jainism lays down a definite course of practical moral discipline, contemplation of the highest truth and reorientation of life in light of these for attaining ultimate reality of truth. Jainism advocates that one should first try to know, comprehend and understand the nature of reality, one's own self-religious goal and path.

"*Education is something which makes a man self-reliant and selfless*"
- ***Rigveda***

"*Education is that whose end product is salvation (Liberation)*"
- ***Upanishads***

Awareness means bringing their mind closer and closer to the body, penetrating the body with awareness and when it happens, a great thrill passes through the whole body mechanism, and then it is no more a mechanism at all. It becomes an organic

---

✍ **T. Padmavathi,** *Lecturer, St. Joseph's College of Education For Women, Guntur.*
✍ **B. Srilatha,** *Lecturer with the same institution.*
✍ **P. Shanthi,** *Lecturer with the same institution.*

unity with the soul. Then the body vibrates in unison. Jainism considers self-awareness and knowledge of ways and means of escaping; this may go a long way in the adjustment of the human beings to life's situations. It has a therapeutic value inherent in it. This should, therefore constitute an aim, a function of education to impart this knowledge to the students. Knowledge of all these ways or means of Jaina may contribute to students' moral and spiritual development. Realiasing the fact that one's own desires and aspirations are a cause of tensions, emotions, pains and miseries, he may try to control his desires at least asocial and conflicting desires which may lessen his miseries. This kind of awareness must form a part of education.

The greatest message of Jainism is observing self-awareness and righteousness, which should constitute essential values to be taught and developed in students through education. It is a non-theistic religion of moral purity and excellence. It aims at liberating man out of the degradation and sufferings but not worshipping gods and going through rituals. The path of pure ethical conduct was considered good enough for this purpose. Man is the true reality for Jainism. He himself is capable of attaining infinite power, infinite knowledge, infinite faith and infinite bliss. This is the tragedy that we are carrying an unconscious of which we are not even aware. What kind of animality, criminality will come up from the unconscious when the opportunity is there? The unconscious should be changed into consciousness so that nothing remains inside us that we don't know. This is the only possibility that we may not fall into darkness and do things, which are inhuman, and not go in the ways of evil. The only possibility is that our only mind is made of simply consciousness leaving no unconscious part at all. And this is one of the greatest contributions of Jainism.

According to Jainism knowledge is the supreme means of liberation. With regards to knowledge the Jain philosophy firmly states that the whole knowledge cannot be observed from a single viewpoint. To understand the reality it is essential to acknowledge the multiple perspectives of knowledge. According to Jains the knowledge is of two kinds -Pramana and Naya. Naya knowledge has three theories namely

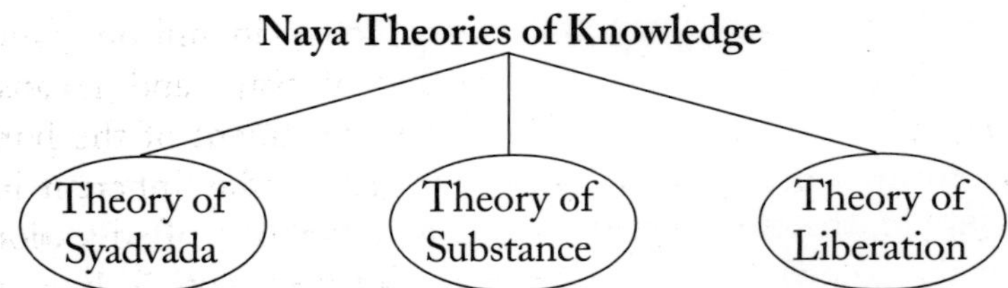

Theory of Syadvada

Syadvada is the theory of the relativity of knowledge. In its practical implication, it means a healthy spirit of sympathetic understanding of other people's views, reconciliation, tolerance, cooperation, and coexistence. It is a national creed opposed to blind faith and fantacism.

Theory of Substance

According to Jains the natural and supernatural things of the universe can be traced back to seven fundamental elements i.e jiva, ajiva, asrava, bandha, samvara, nirjara. Much importance has been given to these seven elements in Jaina theory of substance, as everyone would aspire for (liberation).

Theory of Liberation

Liberation is the freedom for all karmic matter, owing to the non-existence of the cause of bondage and the shedding of all the karmas. Thus, complete freedom of the soul from karmic matter is called liberation. From the basic principles of Jainism a person will obtain the real and everlasting happiness only when the karmas are completely removed from the soul. Jainism firmly believes that even though man is imperfect at present, it is quite possible for him to rid himself of the karmas by his own personal efforts. The highest happiness is to escape from the cycle of births and deaths and be a liberated soul. This world is full of sorrow and troubles and it is quite necessary to attain liberation by different ways or means. The different ways to attain liberation are as follows:

1. Carefulness (Samitian)

To attain liberation carefulness should be followed in five external means. They are

1. Proper care in walking (Erya)
2. Proper care in speaking (Bhasa)
3. Proper care in begging (Aisna)
4. Proper care in lifting or laying down the things (Adanikshapana)
5. Refusing alms (Pratisthapana)

The teacher should walk carefully looking forward, so as not to cause the pain or death of any living being. The teacher should avoid faults of speech during conversation like anger, pride, deceit, laughter, fear, and gossip etc. Always use sinless and concise speech. Teacher should lay down or take up an article of use very carefully so as not to endanger the things.

"Anything that can feel pain should not be put to pain"

-R.M .Dolgin

2. Preservation (Guptian)

To attain liberation preservation or control of different activities of the body are necessary. They are as follows:

1. Proper control over body (Kaya)
2. Proper control over speech (Vag)
3. Proper control over mind (Mano)

The teacher should guard movement of his body so as not to hurt others. The teacher should guard his speech so that it might not utter harmful, harsh, careless, foul, senseless, embarrassing or bad language. The teacher should guard his mind from impure thoughts such as anger, hate, curse, and greed, jealousy, ego etc. Always be forgiving and devote the mind to pious meditation.

The teacher should not daydream while doing any activity. He should develop decent behavior and manners. Guptis are prohibitions against sinful activities of mind, speech and body.

"Silence and self-control is non-violence" ***- Mahavira***

3. Five vows (Panchamahavrata)

Right knowledge, right faith and right conduct are the three most essential principles for attaining liberation. In order to acquire these one must follow these five vows.

1. Non-violence (Ahimsa)
2. Truthfulness (Satya)
3. Non-stealing (Asteya)
4. Chastity (Brahmacharya)
5. Non-attachment (Aparigraha)

The teacher should be non-violent and honest in his action, speech, and thought. The teacher should conquer greed, fear, anger, jealousy and ego to speak the truth. The teacher should withdraw from all attachments, which will develop greed, jealousy, selfishness, ego, hatred, violence etc.

"Non-violence and kindness to living being is kindness to oneself."
- Mahavira

4. Religious virtues (Dharma)

Liberation from suffering and attaining enlightenment could be possible simply by following the path of dharma i.e.

1. Forgiveness (Kshama)
2. Sweetness (Mruduta)
3. Simplicity (Saralatha)
4. Cleanliness (Souch)
5. Truth (Satya)
6. Self-control (Samyam)
7. Hard work (Tap)
8. Sacrifice (Tyag)
9. Indifference (Audacenya)
10. Celibacy (Brahmacharya)

The teacher has to understand the need for personal and environmental cleanliness for promoting personal health and pupil's health. The teacher should speak with good intention. It should not be harmful to others, criticizing others to lookdown upon others, rebuking, abusing and teasing others. The teacher by hard work, self-control and continuous effort can achieve success of high order and excellence in the teaching-learning process.

"Be true in your inner being and all religion are fulfilled"

-Jainism

5. Reflection (Anupreksayen)

By following these 12 reflections liberation can be attained to make life beautiful.

1. Impermanence of the world (Anitya)
2. No one provides protection (Asharana)
3. No permanent relationships in the universe (Sansara)
4. Solitude of the soul (Ekathva)
5. Separateness (Anyathva)
6. Impurity of the body (Ashuchi)
7. Influx of karma (Ashrava)
8. Stoppage of influx of karma (Sanvar)
9. Shedding of karma (Nirjara)
10. Transitoriness of the universe (Loka)
11. Feeling of proper understanding, knowledge, and character as difficult to obtain (Bodhidurlabhathva)
12. Feeling of introducing stability (Dharmanupreksha)

These reflections give a significant emphasis on the thought process of a teacher. They cover a wide field of teaching processes. They are reflections upon the fundamental facts of life, intended to develop purity of thought. They give scope for pure thoughts for teachers.

"Know thyself, recognize thyself, be immersed by thyself.
You will attain God-hood" **-Mahavira**

6. Subduing of things (Purisaha)

Man's sufferings are 22. If he overcomes all these sufferings he attains liberation easily. They are as follows:

1. Hunger
2. Thirst
3. Cold
4. Heat
5. Mosquito bite
6. Nakedness
7. Detachment to sex
8. Living in solitude
9. To be undeviating from posture
10. Shayya
11. Anger
12. Murder
13. Pleading
14. Sickness
15. Tnasparnsha
16. Being obvious to any dirt
17. Hospitality
18. Reward
19. Knowledge
20. Ignorance
21. Non-perception
22. Non-attainment

The teacher should be non-attached to material possessions like desire for money, things of comfort, clothes, food and other avoidable things considered undesirable. It requires that attraction for worldly pleasures and possessions should be avoided.

"Non violence is the highest religion" *- Mahavira*

7. Conduct (Charita)

It is necessary to generate the following five characters to attain salvation.

1. Calmness of mind or temper (Samyak charita)
2. Confession of one's mistakes (Dosasthapana)
3. Ideal and passionless conduct (Pariharavishuddi)
4. Non-creation of negative emotions (Suksma samparaya)
5. Negation of all negative emotions (Yathakhyata)

The teacher should emphasise on the observance of conduct, observance of equanimity, viewing all the living beings as one's own self, conception of equality, harmonious state of one's behaviour, integration personality as well as righteousness of the mind, body and speech. Charita means a tensionless state of consciousness or a state of self-absorption. The teacher has to practice attaining equanimity while as an end it is the state in which self is completely free from the flickering of alternative desires and wishes as well as excitements and emotional disorders.

> *"When your consciousness becomes a still mirror, a still lake,*
> *a silent reservoir of energy, god is reflected in it."* **-Jainism**

Conclusion

Teacher acts as an inspiring role model by his kind, sympathetic and encouraging behaviour and leads and guides the child through the maze and intricacies of self-awareness. The teacher should acquire mental and moral qualities and live by them in order to inspire his students. He should be a scholar himself if it is desired that the student develop a passion for knowledge. He should have good moral character and manifest virtues and human excellence, if the students are desired to be so. He should be an enlightened person; excellent human being and self-disciplined and lead his students in the same way. The teacher can be self-critically aware of himself to establish right speech, right movement, ahimsa, satya, self-realization, forgiveness, indifference, self-control, sacrifice, truth, simplicity, cleanliness, real knowledge, and right character. Such a teacher with self-critical awareness transfers similar virtues to the learners.

When the teacher practices all these means of liberation she can manage ego problems, emotions, and develop an integrated personality, which is the very aim of education.

References

- Dr.H.M.Shailaji, Rajeev, P. Gundale, PG Dept. of Education, Karnatak University, Darwad.
- Jainism and its relevance to education, Quest in Education, October 2006. Gandhi Shikshan Bhavan, Juhu (North) Mumbai.
- Mohammad Nagis Modern Value Education, Anmol Publications Pvt. Ltd.

- O.P DHIMAN, Foundation of Education, Atma Ram & Sons – Delhi (Pg 18-19)
- Dr. Vatsyayan, Indian Philosophy, Kedarnath Ramnath, Meerut.
- Pravin Shah., Path of Liberation: http://www.jcnc.org/jainism/intro_jainism.htm
- Indra Chandra, Jain Theory of Knowledge, IPC 3.2, 1958, Page 83-89, http://faculty.washington.edu/kpotter/xabr.htm
- Glossary of Jaina Words: www.cs.colostate.edu/~malaiya/jaingloss.html
- www.fas.harvard.edu/~pluralsm/affiliates/jainism/workshop Pathashal%20Workshop98.PDF

Part-II

The Buddhist Psychology

– Dr. A. Venkateswara Reddy

This paper seeks to investigate the distinctive features of Buddhist Psychology and its relation to depth Psychology.

Ever since humanization took place, men have been looking within and without to understand themselves both mentally and physically. In the East we see man's experiences are preserved in the form of religious faiths. Asian Psychologies are interwoven in religions. Yogis, monks, priests, seers, and shamans knew them fully well, but for the faith they are as good as non-existent. These are always applied psychologies, as it were.

They always tried to transform the individual into an ideal one, whatever this ideal may mean. But these procedures were never systematized.

In the West, the systematic study of mental phenomena began in the late 19th century and made great strides. It became a separate discipline from its matrix philosophy in 1912. This nascent science began initially defining itself as the study of mental life, but later, during 1920-1950 came to be defined as the study of behavior. Today most psychologists would like to make room for both the definitions and redefine it as the scientific study of behavior and mental process and how organisms affect them, physical and mental states and external environment. To make this definition more complete we may have to add the methodology. It depends upon and the way it interprets the data. As human behavior is more complex, it cannot be studied in full to our satisfaction.

As the Buddha is a rationalist, humanist, empiricist, the philosophy and psychology that flows from him cannot be different.

✍ ***Dr. A. Venkateswara Reddy,*** *Editor, 'MISIMI', Hyderabad.*

That is why he does not subscribe anything to any postulated, speculative concepts like soul, god or Brahman or supra-rational reality. While most of the Indian psychologies are otherworldly, the Buddhist psychology is earth-bound and this worldly. Hence Buddhism as taught by the Buddha never undertakes any discussions of eschatology, which discusses what happens after death.

Buddhist Psychology

The Humane Buddha 'through self-culture' cleansed his mind from all 'Asavas' and gave the world his Dhamma, which till the beginning of the last century was the largest religion in the world. The Buddha made excursions and incursions into the inner provinces of human nature and the nature of the world and gave the world, the insights. And we can make an ontological premise basing on those insights: "The first and foremost ontological premise of Buddhism is pure flux. There are no enduring entities, the so-called substances either within man or without man. Therefore all talk about substances of souls, whether of Aristotle, Spinoza, Kant, Sankara and the like of Upanishads is talk about fiction and figments of imagination. They say that soul or substances would not undergo change under any circumanstances. But here the Buddhist asks -does anybody ever experience substance or soul? According to him whatever are experienced are only – Stream of dharmas nothing more nothing less. Thus the Buddha stands off from the rest." (Puligandala 1991 P136). Basing on the Buddha such as contained in the above quote, the Abhidhamma evolved a comprehensive theory of Individuality.

According to this theory man or individual is a psychophysical continuum or organization, which is described as "Nama –Rupa (Mind and body). The mind part of this continuum contains four components, which are feeling (vedana) perception (sanna) i.e., sense impressions, images or ideas and concepts; mental formations (sankhara) or conative ideas and their concomitants and the fourth one consciousness (Vijnana). All these four non-physical factors are collectively regarded as "mind." Here it is the name part of the individual. The other part of the continuum of the individual is rupa –the material part. The four components of the mind with the physical factor body-clubbed –all the five factors are collectively called Pancha Skandhas (five aggregates.)

In Buddhism a very high place is given to the mind, when Buddha says:

"Well monk, the world is led by mind (thought)

By mind the world is drawn along.

All have gone under the sway of mind, the one Dhamma"

"Mind is the forerunner of all (evil) states"; mind is chief, mind made are they; if one speaks or acts with wicked mind, because of that, suffering follows one, even as the wheel follows the hoof of drought ox"...........

Now a little elucidation of the four components of the mind is in order. The first of them is vedana or feeling which accompanies our impressions and ideas. Only on the basis of contact of sense with the object accompanied by mind, feeling arises. This may be pleasant, unpleasant or neutral. In Buddhist psychology "manindria" or mind is considered to be the sixth sense, in addition to the five usual senses (indrias). Hence the feeling is of six fold as there are six senses.

The function of aggregate of perception (Sanna skhandha) is recognition of objects. It is also six-fold like feeling. There is a close affinity between perception and vijnana (awareness); while consciousness becomes aware of an object, simultaneously perception makes the object distinct from others. This distinctive function of perception enables one to recognise an object when we see it for a second or third time. It leads to the faculty of memory. Sometimes perceptions may lead one to illusions (Vipallas) when our minds are clouded with views. When a sanna vipallasa (perverted perceptions) is entrenched in the mind, occurring frequently, it is hard to free the mind and the result would be disastrous. Sutta Nipata says:

Who is free from sense perceptions

In him no more bonds exist

Who by insight freedom gains

All delusions cease in him

But he who clings to sense perceptions and to bring points wrong and false he lives wrangling in the world.7

Next is sankhara, which is popularly described as samskara in Sanskrit, mental or volitional formations in English. Abhidhamma speaks of 52 mental formations or factors (cetasika). Though feeling and perception are included in these 52 mental formations, strictly speaking, these two are not mental formations. The remaining fifty are collectively regarded as Sankharas.

To understand the function of consciousness it is very vital to gain awareness of the external world. We cannot be aware of an object by simple "sense-object contact with it or indriyardha sannikarsa": This sense-object contact becomes meaningful only with the accompaniment of consciousness. As per the ontological premise of Buddhism, which is extensively quoted in this paper already, everything is in a state of flux and everything arises out of causes and conditions and consciousness is an exception. It is also conditioned, subject to change and hence it is not a spirit or soul as opposed to matter. Vijnana occupies a very high place in Buddhism as it plays an important role as Patisandhi vijnana, relinking or rebirth consciousness, the discussion of which does not fall under the purview of this paper.

It has been already stated that consciousness is evanescent and fleeting as a stream and is conditioned. By what is it conditioned?

Abhidhamma speaks of two kinds of minds, one vidhi citta which functions in waking state and two Bhavanga citta, which functions in both conscious and unconscious states. This Bhavanga citta which roughly can be translated as "life continuum" by reason of which the stream of consciousness is kept going. Bhavanga (Bhava = existence, life becoming) may be defined as the foundation or condition of existence, as the sine qua non of life. It is the nature of process, literally a flux or stream (sota). It has been tried till now by way of discussion and description of nama-rupa its components and their functions, to give an idea of individuality or personality. To be more specific what exactly is "self in Abhidhamma? We have to face this question squarely. On the basis of the basic original insights of the Buddha's, which were sprinkled all over the Pali canonical literature, the Abhidhamma thinkers evolved a beautiful psychology, a psychology yet to be surpassed. No psychology including the modern ones, did reach the heights the Abhidhamma psychology reached, till now.

The Abhidhamma evolved a psychology of ideal type of personality around which its analysis of the workings of the mind is oriented. As a modern Buddhist monk scholar puts it: "In the Buddhist doctrine mind is the starting point, the focal point and also as liberated and purified mind of the saint, the culminating point". (Jnanaponika 1962 P12)

What the western psychology denotes by the word 'personality' roughly equates to the Atta, of the Abhidhamma. But the ontological premise of Buddhism, as has been already referred to, is Anatma or no-soul. According to this premise, there is no abiding soul. Self is impersonal aggregates of processes that come and go. The semblance of a personality springs from the intermingling and quick succession of these impersonal processes. What appears to be personality is the sum total of the body parts, thoughts, sensations, desires, emotions, memories and so on.

The only continuity is Bhavanga, the continuity of consciousness over time. We may identify the "self" with the psychological activities like our own thoughts, memories or perceptions etc. Yet all these phenomena are a part of continuous flow. According to Abhidhamma, the human personality is like a river that appears to be in a constant form, in a single identity, though not a single drop of it is the same as a moment ago; one cannot step into the same river twice means the same. According to this view there is no actor apart from action, no percipient apart from perception, no thinker apart from thought, no subject apart from consciousness. Samyutta succinctly puts the above:

"Just as when parts are set together

There arises the word chariot

So does a notion of being

When aggregates are present" Wood Ward 1972 P1.35

A being though not abiding in the sense of a soul as in other religions, comprises five aggregates and is only a manifestation of ever changing psychophysical organisation, which the Abhidhamma calls Nama-rupa.

The nama which is composed of non-material components plays a vital role. Vijnana or consciousness connotes a deeper meaning than what the westerns are inclined to endow it with. It is striking that the definition of mind given by James Derver, in his Dictionary of Psychology is closely parallel to the Abhidhamma conception of 'Nama'. Derver defines mind as "The organised totality of psychophysical structures and processes, conscious and unconscious, and endopsychic, philosphically rather than psychologically, the entity or substratum underlying these structures and processes". James Drever 1952 P

This definition of mind apart from structures and substratum, "which suggest" the taste of "static," contains the word "processes" suggesting the dynamic aspect.

Buddhist Psychology and Depth Psychology

Buddhist psychology differs from Freudian depth psychology in almost every aspect -in subject matter, methodology, orientation and goal.

The Buddhist psychology has one goal to achieve. It is the transformation of the individual into an ideal perfect being. To achieve this, it sought to describe the nature of person's immediate experiences. To carry out this operation, Buddhism adapted the method of meditation. The meditation, it adapted is vipassana i.e., insightful meditation, which served as a window to observe the stream of consciousness.

Sigmund Freud who did not have any inkling either of the Buddha or of his psychology, which delved deep into the inner provinces of human nature, may have lumped it under theologies.

The attitude of psychologists towards Buddhist psychology can be seen for the first time in the paper "Buddhist Training as Artificial Catatonia" by Franz Alexander. Jung who made an extensive study of Eastern myths and religions saw much of value in Buddhism, but he believed that it would be of no value to the west. We can include, in our list of modern psychologists who worked for an understanding of Buddhist psychology by bringing parallels and correspondences with western psychology, the names of Abraham Maslow of "self-actualisation," Allport of "Functional Autonomy," and Adler of "Creative Selfhood."

Though not a psychologist himself we can include Alan Watts in the list. After making a good study of the East and the West, he wrote in his book "Psycho Therapy -East and West" (1961) that Eastern ways of liberation resemble very much the Western psychotherapy. Both of these the East and West are concerned with changing people's feelings about themselves and their relations to others and to the world of nature.

After these eminent psychologists came on to the scene, introducing Buddhist psychology to the West, a deeper understanding came to the fore.

There came to be identified certain characteristics common to both and the one that is more important of them is determinism, which applies to the individual personality. The Buddha says in the Dhammapada: "All that we are is the result of what we thought; it is founded in our thoughts."

Freud also expressed the same, when he spoke to Putnam, "we are what we are because we have been what we have been"

Buddhist psychology denies "self", but psychoanalysis affirms 'it'. Whereas the psychoanalyists help their psychotic and character disorder patients develop a sense of 'self' i.e. a sense of ongoingness in existence, a sense of stability, predictability and personal continuity across time and place and states of our consciousness. But contrastingly Buddhist psychology holds that these very characteristics are the very roots of suffering. The seeming opposition can be resolved says Jack Engler by recognising that there are stages in the development of self or more accurately in the images or representations of self." It seems that the western traditions have mapped out the early stages of that development and the Buddhist tradition has mapped out later or more advanced stages in which "decentering" from the "ego-centrism" of early development culminates in selfless altruism. And neither tradition knows much about the other. They are about the same continuum of development but about different segments of it!!" Jack Engler 1999 P112.

Both the Buddha and Freud speak of mind as many layered. The deepest layer of the mind, the Buddha calls, is Bhavanga, which comprises the contents or samskaras of several previous births. Bhavanga, if expressed in modern psychological terms, would be subconscious or unconscious. Some pandits saw a close parallel with ID too, as Bhavanga shares some of the characteristics of the same. The deepest zone of the mind, to the Buddha, is a continuum from previous existences and contains many things such as "Anusays" (Proclivites) and Sanskaras (Samkharas) which are carried over from existence to existence from immemorial times, which often surge out to reach out to the upper layers of mind, taking hold of it.

Bhavanga may be rendered as subconscious, which is similar to but not identical with the Freudian usage of the term. Bhavanga is explained in the commentaries as the foundation or condition of existence (bhava), the sine qua non of life, having the nature of a process, literally a flux or stream (Sota). Herein, since times immemorial, all impressions and experiences are, as it were, stored up or better said functioning, but concealed as such to full consciousness from where, however, they occasionally emerge as subconscious phenomena and approach the threshold of full conscious, or crossing it become fully conscious. This so called "subconscious life stream or undercurrent of life is that by which might be explained the faculty of memory, paranormal psychic phenomena, mental and physical growth, karma and rebirth etc – an alternative rendering of life continuum."

The Bhavanga partakes the functions of the ID and unconscious layers of the personality as conceived by Freud. There is agreement in many respects: In Bhavanga, impressions, experiences and memories etc., are stored up concealed from the conscious, but waiting for an opportunity to cross the threshold. Same is the case with the unconscious of Freud. Both Bhavanga, and unconscious act as storehouses of experience, memories etc. Experiences, impressions etc., do not remain quiet or dormant. They are dynamic forces, which strive to seek the audience of the conscious. The unconscious, which in Freudian theory of psychoanalysis plays a major role, and contains mental causes for a nervous breakdown, has been amply discussed by Freud, with number of case studies, in his Psycho-Pathology of Every day Life. When the dark forces from the inner chamber of unconscious surge up, the preconscious censors in the case of Freudian psychoanalysis, but the same is absent in Bhavanga. Even while they are in dormant stage, they influence the conscious behavior in both the cases.

In Buddhism, by means of Bhavanga or the under current of life, the faculty of memory, paranormal psychic phenomena, mental and physical growth are explained. Karma and rebirth too.

Again Bhavanga is comparable to ID. Freud describes ID in his "An Outline of Psychoanalysis" as follows: "To the oldest of the mental provinces we give the name ID. It contains everything inherited, that is present at birth, that is fixed in the constitution and above all therefore the instincts, which arise in the somatic organisation in ID, in forms unknown to us."

From the description of the ID, given by Freud, it follows that as Bhavanga is a reservoir of experiences and impressions of previous births from times immemorial, so is the ID a reservoir of the past inheritance.

There are three important concepts of Freud, which are comparable to the three types of Tanha or craving. The Freudian concept Eros that means sexual love, the principle of life perpetuating. Eros is the name of a Greek god who perpetuates life, taken over by Freud. This Eros of Freud is comparable to one of the three-fold Tanha "Kama Tanha," which is craving for pleasures, which means sustaining life.

Another kind of Tanha, which is associated with eternal belief in eternal existence is called craving for becoming or existence -Bhava Tanha. This is comparable to Freudian Libido, which is sexual energy or psychic energy or mental energy, which is contained in the reservoir ID.

Again the third type Tanha, which is craving for non-existence, destruction, is Vibhava Tanha. This can be compared Thanatos –the death instinct. Thanatos the name of a Greek god used to describe destructive, aggressive instinct.

Therapy: Psychoanalysis brings out and ventilates the hidden conflicts, unwanted memories and experiences, charged with emotions, from the unconscious by means of psychoanalytic techniques such as hypnosis, talking out, dream analysis, free association to the conscious rationality. When the unconscious material is exposed to reason i.e., conscious, it is dissipated and the patient becomes normal.

We find a very similar technique in the Buddha's teaching of self-culture. He taught us in Satipatthana Sutta the four foundations of mindfulness; literally awareness of mindfulness is a practical way to the self-culture. It contains four types or foundations of contemplation. The first one is Kayanupassana –contemplation of the body; the second one is vedananupassana -contemplation of feeling, the third one is cittanupassana -contemplation of consciousness, and the fourth one is Dhammanupassana -the contemplation of mind objects.

In particular our attention is drawn to Kayanupassana. This contemplation leads to a thorough psycho-physiological relaxation resulting in perfectly wakeful awareness, a conscious that is capable of ventilating the unconscious material.

And cittanupassana –contemplation of mind, which leads to self-analysis, renders the cure of psychoanalysis superficial. Through this self-analysis one gains access into the innermost provinces of the mind ie., unconscious and gets a clear inspection of what is there.

At present, appreciative attempts at cross-pollination and integration of Buddhism and psychoanalysis are being made. Jeffrey B. Rubin Ph.D. private practice, New York for example authored a book, Psychotherapy and Buddhism: Toward an Integration and A psychoanalysis for our Time: Exploring the Blindness of seeing 'I'.

There is a tendency now in the Western psychiatrists to make use of the Buddhist meditation in their treatment of the mentally disturbed patients. Both the doctor and the patient undergo practicing vipassana – an exclusive method of meditation of Buddhism – the cure attained as a result of this practice in vipassana is long lasting and deep, than it is through psychoanalysis alone. The difference is that through vipassana – satipatthana – the practitioner is enabled to have direct, conscious inspection of dark-spots in the unconscious.

Now the West is fast embracing Buddhism as it contains the solution, not only to mental problems, but also to problems arising out of the discontents of civilization, to use a phrase of Sigmund Freud.

References

- Radha Krishna, S. (1946) Indian Philosophy Vol. 1, OUP Indian Edition, 1946.
- Brhadaranyakopanisad, IV. 3.17
- Katapanisad VI.17
- Puligandala. R. (1991) The Buddhist Analysis of Identity and its psychological implications, in from Sambhasa, ed., Adhikari, Mahabodhi centinary commemorative volume, Ministry of Education, Srilanka, 1991,
- Anguttara Nikaya, ii.177
- Dhammapada, 1.1
- Sutta Nipata, V.847
- Jnanaponika, M. 1962 The Heart of Buddhist Meditation, Rider,
- Wood Ward, F.L (trans) 1972 Samyutta Nikaya London, P.T.S.

Psychological Factors for the Selection of the Special Object of Meditation as Expounded in *Vissudhimagga*

– ***Prof. M.V. Ram Kumar Ratnam***

The *Vissudhimagga* states that mans' freedom from suffering (dukhka) can be attained by cultivation and developing the path of virtue (sila), concentration (samadhi) and knowledge (panna). The process of purifying the consciousness (vinnana) from the triple germs of attachment (raga, hatred (dvesa) and delusion (moha) plays a pivotal role by providing an insight into the existential reality governing all things in nature namely; impermanence(anicca), esssencelessness (anatta) and suffering (dukhka) leading the aspirant (yogavarain) to attain liberation- nirvana.

Early Buddhists prescribe meditation as the means to achieve the cultivation of purified states of consciousness and thereby the de-ontologisation of the consciousness is achieved. The aspirant to practice meditation has to select both the general object and special object of meditation from the forty objects of meditation. The kalyanamitta1 guides the aspirant to select the special object (pariharuya) based on the dominant psychological parameter of temperament expressed by the aspirant.

The Visuddhimagga2 speaks of six types of temperament namely:

1. Greedy temperament; 2. Hating temperament; 3. Delusion temperament; 4. Faithful temperament; 5. Intelligent temperament; 6. Speculative temperament.

✍ **Prof. M.V. Ram Kumar Ratnam,** *Centre for Mahayana Buddhist Studies, Acharya Nagarjuna University.*

i) The role of Kalyana-Mitta

The Bhikkhu after having overcome the ten impediments approaches a Kalyana-Mitta, a spiritual guide. A Kalyana-Mitta is a person, who acts as a good friend, guide and philosopher to the Bhikkhu in selecting the object of meditation, depending upon his temperament. He should be a man of wisdom *(panna),* one possessing an insight into the teachings of the Buddha.[3] The *kalyanamitta* prescribes the two-fold meditational objects: (i) Generally useful meditational objects and (ii) Special object for meditation. The first category of general meditational object involves cultivation of loving kindness towards other fellow Bhikkhus and all beings of the world. Later, he has to develop mindfulness of death and foulness.[4] It helps him to realise the transitory nature of all things and he cultivates the practice of detachment.

The *kalyanamitta* also prescribes the special object of meditation from amongst the forty objects of meditation,[5] depending upon the temperament of the Bhikkhu. Everyman exhibits a certain trait or character more prominently than the others. These dominant traits constitute the temperament of that person.[6] The mental dispositions of 1) Greed, 2) Hatred, 3) Delusion, 4) Faithfulness, 5) Intelligence and 6) Reasoning are displayed depending upon their temperament. The object of special meditation should be chosen bearing in mind that it should not only counteract these traits, but should also render them conducive to meditation. This is decided by the *kalyanamitta* after careful observation and study of the temperament displayed by the Bhikkhu.[7] For instance, a Bhikkhu who has a greedy temperament, the ten kinds of foulness *(asubhas)*[8] are recommended as useful. Selecting the object of meditation therefore, is a technique, which is not possible for all. For instance, Elder Sariputta, as a *kalyanamitta* of a young Bhikkhu, chose a special meditation object to help him to meditate and thereby attain freedom from lust. But the Bhikkhu failed to attain freedom from lust as the object of meditation did not correspond to the temperament displayed by the Bhikkhu. They approached the Buddha to suggest a special meditation object. Buddha with his deep insight into the past history of the Bhikkhu who happened to be a goldsmith in his past life, decided to prescribe a lotus made of gold, as the special object of meditation. The object being suitable to the Bhikkhu's temperament helped him to concentrate and realise the three marks of conditioned existence of impermanence (annica), esssencelessness (anatta) and suffering (dukkha) leading to the attainment of Arhantship.[9]

ii) Relation between the Temperaments

In the Visuddhimagga[10] relation between the various temperaments has been presented. Herein, the faithful temperament is treated as parallel to greedy temperament because faith is strong when profitable (kusula kamma) occurs in one of greedy temperaments, due to the special qualities being near to those of greed. In an unprofitable way greed is affectionate and not austere and in a profitable way is faith. The greedy seeks attachment with sense desires whereas the faithful seeks the special qualities of virtues. The greedy does not give up anything harmful while faithful does not give up anything beneficial. (Vis.M.III,75)

Similarly, the intelligent temperament is parallel to hating temperament because understanding is strong when profitable (kusula kamma) occurs in one of hating temperament, due to the special qualities being near to those of hate. In an unprofitable way hate is affectionate and not austere and in a profitable way is understanding. The hater seeks only unreal facts whereas the understanding seeks only the real faults. Hate involves condemning living while understanding involves condemning formations[11]. (Vis.M.III,76)

Speculative temperament is parallel to deluding temperament because obstructive applied thoughts arise often in a deluded man who is striving to arise the unarisen profitable states due to their special qualities and its proximity to delusion. Delusion makes one restless due to perplexity and the applied thoughts are due to thinking on various aspects. The deluded vacillates due to superficiality while applied thoughts are vacillating due to facile conjecturing[12]. (Vis.M.III,77)

The Vissudhimagga[13] speaks of six types of persons based on the prominence of temperaments stated above which are determined by the rebirth producing kamma.

Tempera-ment	*Previous Habit*	*Element in Prominence*
Greedy	Plenty of desirale tasks and gratifying works to do. Heaven	Air, Water, Earth and Water are equal.
Hating	Plenty of stabbing, torturing and brutal work to do. Hell	Air and Water
Deluded	Addicted to Intoxicants-neglected learning and questioning-Animal	Earth and Fire

Based on the observations of the processes of posture, action, eating, seeing and other related activities the kalyanamitta is able to recognise the dominant temperament and then decides the special object of meditation conducive for attaining purified consciousness.

iii) Temperament can be gauged by the kalyana-mitta based on observation of the following activities of the yogavarain

1. POSTURE
2. ACTION
3. EATING
4. SEEING
5. KINDS OF STATES OF CONSCIOUSNESS[14]

1. POSTURE - a) Walking[15]

Tempera-ment	*Putting the foot*	*Lifting the foot*	*Step*	*Gait*
Greedy	Slowly & Evenly	Slowly & Evenly	Springly	Careful
Hating	Digging	Quickly	Dragging	Stiff
Deluded	Confused	Pressed down suddenly	Hesitant	Perplexed

b) Stance, Sitting[16] etc.

Temperament	*Stance*	*Sitting*
Greedy	Confident & Graceful	Confident & Graceful
Hating	Rigid	Rigid
Deluded	Muddled	Muddled

c) Activities connected with Sleeping[17]

Tempera-ment	*Bed Making*	*Daying Down*	*State of Sleep*	*Reaction when Woken*
Greedy	Unhurried	Composed limbs	Confident	Slow & doubtful
Hating	Hastily	Flung down	Scowl	Quickly but annoyed
Deluded	All Awry	Face downward	Sprawling	Slowly saying *Hum*

II. ACTIONS - SWEEPING[18]

Tempera-ment	*Grasp*	*Resultant*
Greedy	Strong	Clean, evenly without hurrying or scattering
Hating	Tightly	Unclean, unevenly with a noise hurrying & scattering
Deluded	Loosely	Neither clean nor evenly mixing the cleaned & uncleaned

a) WASHING OR DYEING[19]

Temperament	*Resultant*
Greedy	Skillful, gentle, even and careful
Hating	Tense, stiff & uneven
Deluded	Unskillful, muddled, uneven & indecisive

b) ROBING[20]

Temperament	*Resultant*
Greedy	Neither tight nor loosely, confident, level all round
Hating	Too tight & not leveled
Deluded	Loosely and muddled

III EATING[21]

Tempera-ment	*Food liked*	*Size of Lump*	*Process*	*Tasting*
Greedy	Rich, Sweet	Rounded not to big	Unhurried & Enjoys	Savoring
Hating	Rough, Sour	Filling the mouth	Hurried & Aggrieved	Without Savoring
Deluded	No settled choice	Small & unrounded	Drops bits & Smears face	Mind is astray

IV. SEEING / HEARING[22] ETC.

Tempera-ment	*Perception of ob*	*Gaze*	*Liking*	*Departing*
Greedy	Even Slightly pleasant	Long, surprised	Seizes trivial virtues	Unwilling to leave
Hating	Even Slightly unpleasant	Long, tired	Picks trivial faults	Anxious to leave
Deluded	Any sort of object	Copies others	Critizes when others	Equamity of unknown

V. KINDS OF STATES OF CONSCIOUSNESS OCCURRING[23]

1. GREEDY - Deceit, Fraud, Pride, Evilness of wishes, Discontent, Foppery and Personal vanity.
2. HATING - Anger, Enmity, Disparing, Domineering, Envy and Avarice.
3. DELUDED - Stiffness, Torpor, Agitation, Worry, Uncertainty, Holding on tenaciously with refusal to relinquish.
4. FAITHFUL - Free generosity, Desire to see Noble Ones, Hear the Dhamma, Great Gladness, Ingeniousness, Honesty, Trust in things that inspire trust.
5. INTELLIGENT- Readiness to be spoken to, Possession of good friends, Knowledge of right amount of eating, Mindfulness and Full

Awareness, Sense of Urgency, Wise directed endeavors.

6. SPECULATIVE - Talkativeness, Sociability, Boredom with devotion to profitable, Failure to furnish undertaking, Planning during night putting them into action in day.

iv. Relation between Accumulated Kamma and Resultant Behaviour[24]

S. No.	*Strong Characters*	*Weak Character*	*Rebirth Dominant Character*	*Knowledge & Understanding*	*Behaviour*
1.	G, NH, ND,	NG, H, D	Greedy	Strong	Good natured Not angry
2.	G, H, ND	NG, NH, D	Greedy & Hate	Strong	Dull, Good natured Not angry
3.	G, NH, D	NG, H, ND	Greedy	Slow	Dull, Good natured Not angry
4.	G, H, D	NG, NH, ND	Greed & Hate	Slow	Deluded
5.	NG, H, D	G, NH, ND	Hate	Slow	Unshakeful Good tempered
6.	NG, NH, D	G, H, ND	No Greed & No Hate	Understanding	Good tempered
7.	NG, H, ND	G, NH, D	No Greed but Has Hate	Understanding	Irascible
8.	NG, NH, ND	G, H, D	No Greed & No Hate	Understanding	Good tempered

G-Greed; NG-Non-Greed; H-Hate; NH-Non-Hate; D-delusion; ND-Non-delusion.

- No Greed & No Hate - Faithful temperament
- Possess Understanding - Understanding temperament
- Non-Delusion - Intelligent temperament
- Thought of sense desires - Speculative temperament

The kalyanamitta typecasts the yogavacarin based on the above classification and then decides the object of meditation suitable from the forty objects of meditation.

v. The Forty Objects of Meditation[25]

I.	Ten Kasinas	- Earth, water, fire, air: Blue, yellow, red, white, light and limited space.
II.	Ten kinds of foulness	- The bloated, livid, festering, cut-up, gnawed, scattered, hacked and scattered, bleeding, worm infested, and skeleton.
III.	Ten recollections	- Buddha, Dhamma, Sangha, Virtue, Generosity, Deities, Mindfulness of Death, Mindfulness occupied with the body, Mindfulness of breathing, Recollection of Peace.
IV.	Four divine abidings	- Loving kindness, compassion, gladness, equanimity
V.	Four immaterial states	- Boundless space, boundless consciousness, nothingness, neither perception nor non-perception.
VI.	One perception	- Repulsiveness of nutriment.
VII.	One defining	- Defining of the four elements

vi. Temperament and the Object of Meditation[26]

❖	Greedy temperament	- Ten foulness and mindfulness occupied with the body and eleven meditation subjects.
❖	Hating temperament	- Four divine abidings, four colors kasinas and suitable objects
❖	Deluded temperament	- Mindfulness of Breathing is one meditation subject.
❖	Speculative temperament	- Mindfulness of Breathing is one meditation subject.

- Faithful temperament - First six recollections.
- Intelligent temperament - Mindfulness of death, Recollection of Peace, Defining four elements, Perception of repulsiveness of nutriment.

The remaining Kasinas and immaterial states are suitable for all kinds of temperaments.

Educational Implications

- The psychological temperament and the resultant behaviour assessment methodology mentioned in the Visuddhimagga can be used by educators to identify the temperament of the student.
- Based on the temperament and resultant behaviour the area of interest and the subject to be pursued for higher studies can be arrived upon. This identification will satisfy the creative needs and generate intrinsic motivation in the student, whereby the student is able to realize the meaning and purpose of living.
- The philosophy of defining tasks for a particular individual student will also eliminate the tendency of students selecting their specialization based on empirical factors and parential influences.

References

Visuddhimagga-*Path of Purification*-a post canonical work, is referred to as a compendium by western Buddhist scholars for it systematically summarises and interprets the teaching of Buddha as expounded in the Pali Tripitakas. This master piece is one of the thirty works, was authored by Bhandantacariya Buddhagosa (4th C.A.D.), a native of Andhradesa who migrated to Ceylon, present day Sri Lanka during the reign of king Mahanama (412-434 A.D.) in the monastery at Anuradhapura. For further details refer to *Path of Purification*, translated by Nanamoli Bhikkhu, Buddhist publication Society, Kandy, Sri Lanka.

1. Visuddhimagga III.57,61-66
2. Visuddhimagga III.

3. Qualities of a kalyanamitta are described in Ang. Nikaya iv. 32; Sam. Nikaya, i. 88; Visuddhimagga p.66(BVB);
4. Visuddhimagga III, p.104;
5. Visuddhimagga III. 74, p.102;
6. Visuddhimagga p.77(BVB);
7. Visuddhimagga III. 77.
8. Visuddhimagga III. 89
9. Visuddhimagga III. 75
10. Visuddhimagga III. 77
11. Visuddhimagga 80-82
12. Visuddhimagga III. 88
13. Visuddhimagga III. 87
14. The thirty two parts of the body are prescribed for meditation.
15. Visuddhimagga III. 89
16. Visuddhimagga III. 91
17. Visuddhimagga III. 92
18. Visuddhimagga III. 92
19. Visuddhimagga III. 93
20. Visuddhimagga III. 94
21. Visuddhimagga III. 95
22. Visuddhimagga III. 83 to 86
23. Visuddhimagga III. 104
24. Visuddhimagga III. 121
25. Ibid
26. Ibid

The fourteen modes of consciousness

1. **Rebirth linking:** This refers to that mode of consciousness wherein the sign of kamma that appeared at the time of dying.

2. **Life continuum:** In this mode of consciousness wherein the same kamma of rebirth linking- Gives arise to the living faculties thereby the apprehending processes get working. Visible datum comes into eye's focus- eye sensitivity arises.
3. **Adverting:** In this mode due to disturbance in life continuum ceases and functioning of the mind element processes begins making the sense datum its object.
4. **Eye consciousness:** This mode of consciousness arises accompanying the function of seeing.
5. **Ear consciousness:** This mode of consciousness arises accompanying the function of hearing.
6. **Nose consciousness:** This mode of consciousness arises accompanying the function of smelling.
7. **Tongue consciousness:** This mode of consciousness arises accompanying the function of tasting.
8. **Body consciousness:** This mode of consciousness arises accompanying the function of touching –tactile.
9. **Receiving consciousness:** This mode of consciousness arises with the cessation of eye- herein the mind, mentation; the appropriate mind element has received the same objective fields.
10. **Investigating Consciousness:** In this mode of consciousness the appropriate mind consciousness element resultants received by the mind element are investigated.
11. **Determining consciousness:** In this mode of consciousness the process of determining the same objective field is done.
12. **Impulsion consciousness:** In this mode of consciousness the impulsions with respect to the same objective field are determined.
13. **Registration consciousness:** In this mode of consciousness the registration with respect to the same objective field is done.
14. **Death consciousness:** In this the life continuum resumes its occurrence and its following modes of consciousness occur until

the life continuum consciousness of one becoming is exhausted.

Eight-Fold Path - *Ariyo Attangiko Maggo*

SILA	Ethical Perfection	Right Speech (Samma Vaco) Right Conduct (Samma Kamanto) Right Livelihood (Samma Ajivo)
Samadhi	Critical Reflection	Right Effort (Samma Vayamo) Right Contemplation (Samma Sati) Right Concentration (Samma Samadhi)
Panna	Epistemic Perfectrion	Right View (Samma Ditthi) Right Resolution (Samma Sankappo)

Buddhist Meditation
A Cure for Psychological Ill-Health

– Valaparla Susitha Priya,
Dr. J. Prasanth Kumar

The world today is not what it was half a century ago. Ideas of good and bad are changing fast, moral attitudes are in flux and the general outlook of people is very different.

Today's Life

We live in an age of rush and speed. Tension is everywhere. If we stand at the corner of a busy street and scan the faces of the people hurrying feverishly by, we notice that most of them are restless. They carry with them an atmosphere of stress. They are mostly pictures of rush and worry. Rarely you will find a picture of calm, content and repose in any of these faces. Such is the modern world.

Need of Meditation

Those who live in big cities have no time to think of noise; they are conditioned by it and are accustomed to it. This noise, stress and strain have done much damage by way of ailments –heart diseases, cancer, ulcers, nervous tension and insomnia. Many of our illnesses are caused by anxiety, nervous tension, economic distress and emotional unrest –all products of modern life.

Let us bear in mind that certain aloofness, a withdrawing of the mind from the business of life is a requisite to mental hygiene. Whenever we get an opportunity, we wish to be away from the town,

✍ ***Valaparla Susitha Priya,*** *Lecturer in Education, A.L. College of Education, Guntur.*

✍ ***Dr. J. Prasanth Kumar,*** *Principal with the same institution.*

its busy life and engage ourselves in quiet contemplation, call it concentration or meditation.

Buddhist Meditation

The meditation taught in Buddhism is neither for gaining union with any supreme being, nor for bringing about mystical experiences, nor for any self-hypnosis, it is for gaining tranquility of mind.

According to Buddha, Meditation (Bhavana) begins with concentration (Samadhi). Concentration is a state of no distraction. The three factors of the samadhi, namely, right effort, right mindfulness and right concentration, function together in support of each other. They comprise real concentration.

Samadhi taught in Buddhism culminates in Jhana. But the Buddha was not satisfied with mere jhana and mystical experiences; his one and only aim was to attain full enlightenment -Nibbana. Having gained perfect concentrative calm through samatha meditation, he was able to develop vipassana, insight meditation. The word "vipassana" means seeing in an extraordinary way; vipassana therefore means seeing beyond what is ordinary, 'clear vision'. It is not surface seeing or skimming, not seeing mere appearances, but seeing things as they really are. Vipassana or insight meditation, therefore, is an essential, and a typical doctrine of the Buddha.

Types of Buddhist Meditation

In the Majjhima Nikaya, one of the five original collections in Pali containing the discourses of the Buddha, there are two discourses (Nos.61 and 62) that are devoted wholly to instructions on meditation. In discourse No. 62 the Buddha gives seven types of meditation to young Rahula, the novice, who, according to the commentary, was only eighteen years of age when he received them.

Here is an extract from the discourse:

"Develop the meditation on loving kindness (Metta), ill will (Vyapada) is banished.

Develop the meditation on compassion (Karuna), cruelty (Vihesa) is banished.

Develop the meditation on sympathetic joy (Mudita), aversion to meditation (Arati) is banished.

Develop the meditation on equanimity (Upekkha), hatred (Patigha) is banished.

Develop the meditation on repulsiveness (Asubha), lust (Raga) is banished.

Develop the meditation on the perception of impermanence (Anicca sanna), pride of self, or 'I' (Asaminami) is banished.

Develop the concentration of mindfulness on in-and-out-breathing (Anapanasati), in-and-out-breathing with mindfulness, developed and frequently practiced bears much fruit, is of great advantage."

Cure for Psychological Ill Health: Self-mastery and Drugs

The Buddha says: "Though one may conquer in battle a million men, yet he indeed is the noblest victor who conquers himself." This is nothing but self-mastery. It means mastering our minds, or emotions, likes and dislikes and so forth.

From the Buddhist point of view the mind or consciousness is the core of our existence. All our psychological experiences, such as pain and pleasure, sorrow and happiness, good and evil, life and death, are not caused by any external agency. They are the result of our own thoughts and their resultant actions.

There is a mounting feeling of restlessness among the people world over. This feeling is prevalent mostly among the youth who want a quick remedy for the turmoil of the materialistic world. They are in search of peace and tranquility. Young people, who took to narcotic drugs in the belief that they have – the answer to their mental frustration, are now turning to yogic discipline and meditation. Surely narcotic drugs cannot do for us what true meditation can do.

Dr. Herbert Benson, who experimented with meditation for nearly a decade, was mainly interested in finding out how factors that are psychological in nature come to exert physical effects on the heart, blood pressure and other aspects of the circulatory system and its functions. His ideas and research are fully presented in his book,

"The Relaxation Response". Research done at Harvard University, Cambridge, U.S.A. revealed that hundreds of youths who took LSD and smoked marijuana abstained from using them after several months of meditation.

Meditation Cures Pressure

Meditation can help to ease the burden of chaotic cares in life. It can inspire us to discover our own intelligence, richness and natural dignity. Meditation can also stimulate the latent powers of the mind, aid clear thinking, deep understanding, mental balance and tranquility.

In addition, meditation has physical ramifications. Meditation can relax the nerves, control or reduce the blood pressure, make us zestful by stemming the dissipation of energy through tensions, improve our health and keep us fit.

It has now been proved that high blood pressure and other diseases connected with the heart could easily be cured by Buddhist meditation. Dr. Buddhadasa Bodhinayake, Consultant Psychiatrist, Harley Hospital, Essex, UK, and Postgraduate Tutor of the British Medical Federation in charge of doctor's appointments in East London, said that the British Cardiac Society had recently accepted the curative effects of Buddhist meditation. Dr. Bodhinayake stated that over 68,000 British patients were now practicing Anapanasati Meditation.

"It had been scientifically proved through electro-encepholograph EEG readings that Anapanasati Meditation was capable of synchronizing the working of the two sides of the brain. This reduced the patient's oxygen needs, the heartbeat, blood pressure, and the breathing rate. Fifteen minutes of Anapanasati meditation had the effect of three Aldomat tablets 250mg on a high blood pressure patient. Dr. Bodhinayake said that it had also been proved that this meditation could be used to get people out of drug addiction. It also greatly helped brain development, thinking capacity and retentive power.

"A large number of students of Harvard University in the USA are now practising Anapanasati bhavana to get through their exams."

Conclusion

All of our psychological problems are rooted in ignorance, in delusion. Our greed, hates, conceits and a host of other defilements go hand in hand with our ignorance. Only giving up illusions and false concepts and bringing our lives in harmony with reality can solve our real problems. This can be done only through Buddhist meditation.

References

– Piyadassi (1991) The Spectrum of Buddhism, The Corporate Body of Buddha Educational Foundation, Taipei, Taiwan, R.O.C.

– Radha Kumud Mookerji (1993) Ancient Indian Education, (Brahmanical and Buddhist) Motilal Banarsidass, Delhi, Patna, Varanasi.

– Ven matara Sri Nanarama (1993) The seven Stages of Purification and Insight Knowledge, Buddhist Publication Society, Kandy, Sri lanka.

– Visuddacara (2003) Invitation to Insight Meditation, Auspicious Affinity, Malaysia.

❖ ❖ ❖

The Impact of Budhistic Way of Living on Mental Well-being

– *Dr. B. A. Rani*

Indian Psychology accords the pride of place to values. Psychology in India did not originate in wonder but as a practical need arising from presence of moral and physical evil in life. The aim of Indian Psychology is to serve as a practical aid to show the right way of living. Its aim is to discover a way out of misery.

By practicing the Buddhistic teachings, one can get mental health that is urgently required in these days. Mental health can be described as a condition of psychological maturity -a relatively constant and enduring function of personality. It is a condition of personal and social functioning with a maximum of effectiveness and satisfaction. Mental health involves positive feelings and attitudes towards the self and towards others. It is through Buddhism that the youth can be set on the road to the pursuit of the absolute values, truth, righteous conduct, peace, love and non-violence for the development of a balanced personality. Pleasures pass quickly; but the teachings of the Buddha lead to joy, which transcends time, the joy of nirvana. The teachings of the Buddha are like the full moon on a clear night; it shines in the darkness, shedding its light everywhere. Buddhism is one of the most remarkable developments of Indian thought. It is evident that in formulating the four-fold truth Buddha was guided by the medical view of the time in regard to the curing of mental diseases. Buddha the Great Healer, looked upon life with its suffering as a disease and his method was naturally that of a psychologist seeking a remedy for it. Buddha, a teacher par excellence, emphasized on living life of purity, which is based on non-violence,

✍ **Dr. B.A. Rani,** *Librarian, St. Joseph's College of Education for Women, Guntur.*

sacrifice, righteousness, truth, desirelessness, and doing always good to others without caring for returns. Ultimately that one will be bound to reach a 'value' rather than the 'good' itself.

Buddhism- Psychological Aspects

Buddhism is more a psychology of practical life rather than a psychology of ideas and ideals. He carried his teachings into perfect practice. Buddha was the only prophet who said "I do not care to know your various views and theories about God; what is the use of discussing all the subtle doctrines about the soul; do good and be good. And this will take you to freedom, to whatever truth there is" *Mohammad Naqi (2005) p 242.*

He was absolutely without personal motive in his life, the great psychologist preaching the highest psychology of life. Yet, Buddha had the deepest sympathy for the lower animals and never put forth any claim for himself. He is a true lover of mankind.

Buddha recognized diverse ways to reach the Truth. But when the truth is attained the way falls away. One need not think that it is the only way to reach the truth. Buddha gives us the parable of the raft. Any person who wishes to cross a dangerous river having built a raft for this purpose, indeed be a fool when he had crossed if he were to put the raft on his shoulders and take it with him on his journey. The Buddha took up the long and noble work of spreading among the people knowledge of truth, which had brought him illumination and freedom, with sincerity. The feeling which prompted him to such active beneficences very well indicated by a saying which tradition ascribes to him that he would willingly bear the burden of everyone's suffering if he could thereby bring relief to the world. In this work he met with many difficulties, for there were, at the time, several rival doctrines contending for supremacy; but he persevered in his attempt and in the end achieved extraordinary success.

Mind-Value perception- Ultimate truth

Buddhistic philosophy and psychology are revealed in the tri-pitakas. The tri-pitakas are 1. Vinaya pitaka, 2. Sukta pitaka and 3. Abhidamma pitaka. The Dhammapada reveals psychology of Buddhism -the four-fold truth, the nature of man, and the character of the world, the cause his predicament, the way by which man may rise above it and the state of enlightenment or release from subjection to time and the results of his own experience of truth. Buddha shared with men these aspects of his experience, which can be expressed in words. Buddha refused to speculate on the nature of transcendent reality. Each of us has to follow the footsteps of Buddha who blazed the path. Each individual has to attain experience by his own individual effort.

Man himself, the suffering man, is reality. His own desires, and worldly attachments are the cause of his miseries; and this reality has to be faced with true knowledge, so that ignorance is destroyed and man attains salvation and is freed from the miseries. Buddha has given the message to mankind that all miseries come through one's deeds. Therefore each one is responsible for removing his miseries. It should be particularly noted that as per Buddha soul is not reborn. After death the soul of the individual comes to an end, but his deeds continue to remain immortal or imperishable. As a result of these imperishable deeds his second body is formulated and the individual takes rebirth accordingly. Thus Buddha propounds the principle of the theory of Karma.

Ego according to Abhidamma, consists of eight kinds of consciousness; five are related to physical senses and the sixth is mind sense. The seventh sense has the nature of ignorance, cloudiness and confusion. The cloudy mind runs through the sixth sense consciousness so that one does not know exactly what one is doing and this blind consciousness is devoid of precision as well. The eighth consciousness is the common or unconscious ground that makes it possible for all of the other seven to operate. This ground is different from the basic ground, which is oneness.

In simple terms, the cloudy consciousness arises from the eighth consciousness and then the sixth sense consciousness follows it. The basic ground is natural and does not depend on relative situations at all. Energies appear out of this basic ground and those energies are the sources of the development of all relative situations.

Buddha's perception is that mind is the forerunner of all dharma. All follow minds, all are made out of mind seems to be relevant to a wholly different way of valuing and living. The Budha's directions are so simple as to be followed by anyone. His Dhammapada starts with the words,

"Our life is the creation of our minds. If we speak or act with an impure mind suffering will follow. As surely as the chariot follows the animal that draws it .If we speak or act with a pure mind, joy will follow as sure as a shadow follows the person who casts it. Some people look at others and think that person insulted me, that person upset me, that person defeated me, that person cheated me etc.,. Their minds are never free from hate. Hate is never appeased by hate, it is appeased by love, this is an eternal law. Most people do not bear in mind that one day all of us will die. But who do bear this in mind settle their quarrels peacefully." *Robert Van De Weyer (Ed.) (2007) 5 ch /4p*

Buddha describes the nature of mind and its fickle mindedness vividly and urges for the self-control in the following manner:

" The mind is unstable and unsteady. It is difficult to guard and control it. A fish, which has been caught and thrown on dry land, thrashes around, in the same way the mind struggles to free itself from the devil. The mind is flicky and flighty wandering wherever it desires; it is difficult to restrain, yet those who succeed in restraining their minds experience great joy. Those whose minds are calm, who are free from passions and desires and who have transcended good and evil, wise and fearless. As the rain leaks in a house whose thatch is flimsy, passion leaks into a mind whose self-discipline is poor. As a house with strong hatch keep out the rain, a mind whose self-discipline is strong keeps out passions." *Ibid5 ch / 9p*

Some people identify themselves with desires and conflicts, related to a world outside and turn neurotic. The healthy mind does not tend to be selfish, it understands since it sees things as they are because it is so plain, clear and precise. Buddha's abhorrence of luxuries and hypocricy is expressed in the following manner.

"There are many who live only for pleasure, whose senses constantly seek new delights, who eat whatever they want, who are idle and who do not distinguish between virtues and vices. The devil shakes them; just as the monsoon wind shakes a weak tree. There are some who do not live for pleasure, whose senses do not constantly seek new delights, who are careful in what they eat, who work hard, and who can distinguish clearly between virtue and vice; they cannot be shaken by the devil. Just as the monsoon wind cannot shake a mountain. Those who put on the yellow ropes of a monk without having self-control and without purifying the soul of sensuous devices or hypocrites, those who acquire self control and whose souls are pure can, with honesty put on the yellow robes." *Ibid5 ch / 5p.*

Buddhists have their preferences clear. Whether illiterate or learned, simple or refined, all have clarity of ideas and clear vision. Doubt rarely prevails upon them. They follow their faith faithfully. They are seldom weakened. They are free from many abnormalities. Buddha's perception can be seen in these words:

People in fear of their lives flee to mountains or forests, or to sacred trees and shrines. But such places offer no refuge from suffering. He further says:

" Whether a holy person lives in a village or a forest, in a valley or on a hill, that place radiates joy. A holy person can make even the most remote and forbidding place beautiful and appealing. This is because the holy person's joy does not depend on the place but on the mind." *Ibid5 ch /18p*

Buddhism stresses the fact that as human life on this earth is full of pain and grief of various kinds the individual must find a way out. And the way suggested is spiritual development through self-control and right conduct.

Careful consideration, thinking ahead, and thoughtful implementation of definite ideas are boon to Buddhism. Heedful and heedless make a lot of difference in better, greater and prudent ways of living. Buddha through personal example taught carefulness, which has become an integral part of a Buddhist. They are always cautious, watchful, vigilant, attentive and circumspect. In the words of Buddha,

"Those who are always vigilant and never become negligent are like fires; they turn all the obstacles in their path, both great and small. Those who delight in vigilance and fear negligence can never be defeated; they will win the ultimate victory of nirvana" *Ibid5 ch / 8p.*

He further advises "forsake anger; renounce pride; detach yourself from all material possessions. No suffering can befall those who desire nothing. "Those who can exercise perfect control of their actions, speech and mind have acquired true wisdom." *Ibid6 ch /6p.*

Buddhism declared that those who wish to attain the ideal of life shall avoid the two extremes of self-indulgence and self torture because as Buddha said self-indulgence is low, vulgar, ignoble, and harmful, and self-mortification is painful, ignoble, and harmful. Both are profitless. The former retards one's spiritual progress and the latter weakens one's intellect. Thus self-denial is to be understood in a literal sense in Buddhistic ethics. With the negation of self, all selfish impulses necessarily disappear. Since the belief in self-identity, which is the basis of suffering, is false, ignorance becomes the true source of all evil.

Buddha thoroughly describes true nature of man and advises not to care for name and fame:

"People criticize those who are silent; and they criticize those who speak at length; and they criticize those who speak a little. No one can escape criticism in this world. There never was and there never will be and there is not at present, a person who was universally criticized or universally praised". *Ibid6 ch / 7p*

Buddhism is not devoid of personal love but hankers after divine love. Both these aspects of love are charged and interlinked though one cannot be the condition for the other. Both of them are made and maintained as transparent and unconditional. So Buddhists have unconditional love, which is transparent too. They get revelation through their highly charged love and through complete surrender to spirituality and divinity. They maintain it throughout their life. They show utmost compassion without being artificial and imposing.

Buddhism helps us to know and achieve all that is important to human life and spirit. It adds value to our good deeds and fair inventions, it gives meaning to our existence and emotions; it makes the purpose of our birth and living clear and finally it increases the quality of our thinking and prayers. Buddha pondered over general human life and showed the ways and means to bring out the best out of it. Buddhists have an uncanny ability to draw themselves to and from themselves, the exquisite emotions.

Buddha contemplated and declared that all are alike; everything has that celestial power that gives existence and keeps the life element flowing and even growing. That oneness is not very hard to achieve for a Buddhist.

The Buddha said "Out of great suffering comes great peace" The Buddhists wish and try to share the suffering. In this regard their aim is very clear which gives broadness and smoothness to their path. If and when they find obstacles they clear them easily and successfully and moving upward and onward searching bliss and getting blessed. According to Buddha," There is no evil like disharmony. There is no joy like nirvana. Passionate desire is the greatest desire. Disharmony is the greatest sorrow." So they are in harmony with the nature and spirit; with the spirit of nature and the nature of spirit; with the physical and mundane on one hand and with metaphysical and sublime on the other.

They prefer to be independent and work on the theory of co-operation and inter-dependence. Whether they get help or not but they are always ready to help others.

Buddha gave a spiritual value to work. Work must be done. One must keep oneself busy in the work at hand or assist others if he has leisure and is idle. For growth and progress it is an ideal thing to remain busy in one or another type of work.

Content and diligence are two very stable characteristics of Buddhism. Buddhists are always contented but with a difference. They work and strive hard; so they are always confident of growth and progress. They try to be better. They work for betterment. They incessantly try to achieve something greater and to conquer something higher. They are not contented though they are fully satisfied with what they have and are satisfied even with their efforts. They make their place better to live in , live with and live by.

Buddhists are not aggressive in grabbing opportunities but contented with their desires. They feel that whatever they possess at the present moment is enough. They never curse themselves for not being wealthier, healthier or more successful than what they are. So they are a happy lot. Buddhists' insight is powerful enough to keep them moving ahead and their fearlessness gives them enough inner strength to face anything, anywhere -friendly or unfriendly, beneficial or destructive, musical or thundering. With such qualities they are sure to get worldly pleasures and spiritual bliss.

Buddhism stresses on universal salvation also. It teaches that it is not sufficient for a man to attain his own salvation. After achieving his own nirvana he must work for the nirvana of others. This is an ideal of Buddhism; when Buddha was concerned with the sorrows of men he was eager to enter their lives, heal their troubles and spread his message for the good of the many.

Lord Buddha maintained that one can get and feel comfort by comforting others who are in distress by visiting the sick and doing the needful or saying a few soothing words; by cooperating and standing by a mourner whose intense pain has imbalanced his thought, who has a broken and saddened heart. The very presence near such persons lessens their pain and gives much needed relief. Being brotherly is all that is needed and is all that helps others to live well and feel better. Buddhists show utmost compassion without being artificial and imposing.

Buddha stresses on the life of purity by practicing meditation and self-control. In the words of Buddha,

"A peaceful mind is like an empty house. As you enter an empty house, you find silence and stillness. You enter your own mind through meditation; and if your mind is at peace, you will find silence and stillness. A peaceful mind is lit by the light of truth. When you can see this light clearly within your own mind you experience the perfect and eternal bliss of nirvana. Let love guide your actions. Perform your duties to the best of your abilities. Then you will start to tread the path, which leads away from suffering towards perfect joy." *Ibid6 ch /298p*

The Four-fold Truth

It is generally stated that this ignorance is of the four noble truths [arya-satya]- those concerning suffering, its origin, its removal and the way to remove it. We might say that the first three of these truths constitute the theoretical aspect of the teaching and the last its practical. That suffering predominates in life, as we commonly know it was admitted by practically all the Indian psychologists. The peculiar value of Buddhism lies in the explanation it gives of the origin of suffering, in the manner in which it deduces the possibility of its removal and in the means it recommends for doing so.

As per Buddha

- All is transient; when you perceive this you are above suffering; the path is clear
- All is suffering; when you perceive this you are above suffering; the path is clear
- All is unreal; when you perceive this you are above suffering; the path is clear.

The best of all paths is the eight-fold path. The best of all truths are the four noble truths. The following four truths help man to lead life peacefully and joyfully

1. The world is full of miseries.
2. Origin of suffering.
3. Removal of suffering.
4. The way to remove suffering.

Origin of Suffering: Cause and effect principle is controlling and regulating all that happens in the universe and in the life of a human being. Just as it follows from the Buddhistic view of causation that suffering to exist must have been caused, it follows from the same that it must admit of being destroyed. The suffering follows from the belief that whatever is must have had a cause. Buddha found this cause to be ignorance, from ignorance proceeds desire; desire leading to activity brings in its turn rebirth with its fresh desires. This is the vicious circle of samsara.

Removal of Suffering: The path of self-discipline underlying the view, the removal of the cause removes the effect. So when ignorance is dispelled by right knowledge the succeeding links of the chain snap one after another automatically. The process which gives rise to suffering no doubt involves a necessity, as we have stated already is not absolute.

The way to remove suffering: According to Buddhism true knowledge is that which destroys ignorance, which is the cause of human miseries, pain and grief. Nothing happens without a cause and so miseries of life also have a cause and that they can be eliminated by following a particular way of living. Man can attain freedom from life's miseries by not only knowing; for that experience and practice are needed. Apart from this any other knowledge is useless. The true holy seeker is not attached even to the desire of knowledge. "The Salutary knowledge is exclusively the practical illumination by the four great truths of the nature, origin, condition and means of destroying suffering"

The only dependable truth in this world is Dharma, Religious insight {Bodhisatva}. Attainment of this insight is the highest level of the spiritual development and is the ultimate aim of humanity. Buddha suggested an eight-step practical method for achieving spiritual development.

- **Right Insight** (Samyak Drishti): To keep in mind that life is full of misery which has a cause, which can be eliminated and that there are definite ways to achieve this.
- **The Right will Power** (Samyak Sankalp): for observing the four truths.
- **The Right Speech** (Samyak Vak): to be faithful to one's words
- **The Right deeds** (Samyak Karmas): this includes forsaking of violence and stealing observing celibacy and detachment from worldly pleasures.
- **The Right Vocations** (Samyak Aajivika): which means earning one's living by right conduct.

- The Right exercise (Samyak Vyayam) Adopting good ways and to give up bad ideas.
- The Right memory (Samyak Smriti) To remember things correctly
- The Right Meditation (Samyak Samadhi) this is essential for attainment of salvation.

Following above principles one can get freedom from worldly miseries. These principles are generally classified under three heads: a) Morality. b) Meditation. c) Wisdom or Intelligence.

Of these the first two constitute what is called Prajna, the next three constitute what is called Shila and the last three are called Samadhi. For knowledge to become an internal certainty right conduct, and meditation are necessary. There can be no perception of truth without control of thought and action. Shila means right conduct, which includes virtues like veracity, contentment and non-injury or ahimsa. Samadhi is meditation upon the four virtues. It is an aid in securing tranquility of mind and in gaining a clear insight into the truth that has been learnt from others. It is Prajna in the sense of insight or intuition. The outcome of the whole training that will bring heresy. Buddhism also rejected speculation because it would imply an attachment to mundane intellectual knowledge, which is of no use for further perfection.

Buddha insists that his hearers should not borrow their views from him, but should make their own. He often declares that we must accept that we ourselves have realized to be right. In other words, every man should win his own salvation. It is salvation through self-reliance, under the guidance of external authority. Even the guru can only show the way.

These three noble truths sufficiently indicate the scope of Buddhistic discipline.

Importance of Buddhistic Psychology in Education of Mental Well-being

Man is imperfect by nature. His life is a process of development, which tends towards something, which is more perfect.

Education is a deliberate conscious process of modifying the imperfect behaviour.

The techniques of Buddhism provide directions to develop good conduct, which is the essence of a sound system of education. Observance of purity is more important than the observance of rituals. Through education we can impart the preachings of Buddha, which enables full development of child's personality in its physical, mental, emotional, and spiritual aspects. It gives emotional stability, fairness, fearlessness, happiness and cheerfulness, loyality, self-confidence, self-reliance, self-control, silence, social adjustment, consideration for others, honesty, and non-violence. Buddha considered the various miseries of the world as nature of man. If one realizes this truth from the very beginning he will so conduct his life as to ensure his physical, mental, moral and spiritual development. Thus he will become a good citizen.

Eight-fold path as preached by Buddha provides guidance for moral education and peace. This will assist one towards proper behavior with others. After achieving this control one should exercise due restriction over his physical and mental aspirations. Ashtangika Marg is full of very powerful education. Buddha has made man his own destiny maker i.e. master of everything. This pronouncement of Buddha refers to a great educational implication that an individual must not be a fatalist. He should believe in his own efforts and make his life 'sublime'. A kind of despodency is generally seen in the youth of these days. If the teachers of today succeed in imparting in the students the notion that they are makers of their own destinies then the whole society will abound in such well-equipped citizens who will successfully help themselves and others. As a result society will reach the peak of its growth.

Buddha suggests that the mind has a depth far greater than the deepest sea. In its depths, lie untapped, sources of great power. Meditation brings that power out and concentration will be so deep that the student can free the mind of habituation or conditioning and be able to see life in its quality. Naturally, sulkiness, moroseness and irritability are not for them. They may not appear cheerful and pleasant; yet, never try to evade studies.

According to Buddha sin and piety (righteousness) are the outcomes of one's own deeds. The sinner reaps miseries both in this world and in the other beyond and the pious man harvests happiness. Due to one's own efforts someone is rich and the idle one is poor. It is the outcome of one's own deed that one is ill and the other is healthy. One is learned and the other is ignorant. Thus the various peculiarities in this world are not God's creations, but the outcome of some deeds. Thus Buddha has given the message to the mankind that one gets miseries due to his own deeds. Therefore he is quite capable of removing them. Thus the theory of Karma has been propounded very strongly. He firmly believes that god is not the giver of the result of any deed. In fact the deed itself gives its outcome to the doer. Buddha's theory of Karma is pregnant with noble educational meanings. If our educational centers become imbued with the ideals of Karmavad and the parents, teachers and students begin to behave accordingly, all will be "up and doing" and everyone will be the maker of his own destiny. Then no one will curse his fate and sit idle, doing nothing.

According to Buddha meaning of Shunya is freedom from worldly fabrications. The objective of Bodhisatva is to sacrifice one's life for the welfare of others. Thus along with spirituality he is equipped with the cravings for the welfare of all. In short it will not be too much to say that the ultimate purpose of education also should be to make each student a Bodhisatva. If this becomes possible there will be no one miserable in this world. Then others will take up one's miseries as their own and they will try to remove the same. If our education succeeds in achieving this objective this very earth will become a heaven.

Thus the Buddha's teaching is for everyone who would take it -rich or poor, high or low. That is why one quarter of the Earth's people loves him even after twenty-five hundred years.

References

- Mohammad Naqi (2005) "Values of Buddhism"*Modern Value Education.* New Delhi: Anmol Publications Pvt. Ltd.
- Robert Van De Weyer (Ed.) (2007) *36 Readings from Budhism.* Mumbai: Jaico Publishing House.

- Bharadwaj Raj, Tilak (2001) *Education od Human Values.* New Delhi: Mittal Publications.
- Hiriyanna, M. (1973) *Outlines of Indian* Philosophy. Bombay: George Allen & unwin Pvt. Ltd.
- Rudisill, C.A. Kay (2007)" Being a Bodhisatva at Work: Perspectives on the Influence of Budhist practices in Enterpreneurial Organizations." *Journal of Human Values.* 13(1), January-June 2007, pp71-75.
- Vandana Singh (2006) "An observation of Budhist Educational Elements with refeernce to modern age" *National Journal of Education.* 10(1), January 2006.pp43-59.

Holistic Human Development Buddhist View

– *S. Anne Sucharitha*

Development

The term development implies the growth of something, but when used in the sense of a goal, to be pursued by communities and nations the intended growth must be desirable and worthwhile. The term ' development' is used today with a characteristically materialist bias. This is evident when one considers the basis on which countries are described as developed or underdeveloped. The principal criteria adopted for determining whether a nation is developed are the quantity of goods produced and consumed, the gross national produce and the per capita income of the people. All these criteria are monetary or material. Surely, if in any community people die due to starvation, poor health facilities, lack of proper clothing and shelter it would not be proper to call such a community, developed. There are certain basic material needs, without the fulfilment of which, the quality of life of a human being can in no way be conceived as satisfactory. The admission of this fact need not commit us to a purely materialistic conception of development. For, such a concept of development can be said to be based on an inadequate and unexamined evaluative assumption. If people die of starvation in a particular community we will not be inclined to call that community developed. Under such circumstances can we boast of any genuine development?

Need for the Holistic Development

When development is used in the context of human notions it is possible to speak of numerous spheres of development such as economic, technological, political, educational, social, cultural, moral,

✍ **S. Anne Sucharitha,** *M.Ed., Student, A.L.College of Education.*

spiritual and so on, which, though separately conceivable are causally interrelated. Therefore, when development is thought of in general it would be necessary to take into account a desirable harmony and integration of several different areas of human concern. The contradictions and dilemmas that have arisen in connection with the lives of people living in the so-called developed or affluent world makes it imperative that we should consider development in terms of a holistic vision. Such a holistic vision demands a moral foundation for development. In this connection the teachings of Buddhism seem to have something very significant to offer.

Man is getting more alienated, and is being reduced merely to a cogwheel in a machine, created by powers and authorities beyond control, depriving him of the opportunity to develop the real human spiritual potential. The time has reached to reassess this trend and to think of ways and means of holistic development.

Mankind has already begun to feel the effects of the development policy pursued by the so-called developed nations of the present century. The effects of industrialization on the natural environment are drawing the attention of ecologists. The problem of industrial wastes, polluting the water resources, factory fumes and other gases emitted by modern machinery polluting the atmosphere, the damage done to the ozone layer, the poisons introduced in the form of modern agricultural technology affecting all forms of life on earth including human, and numerous other ecological problems are the visible effects of the current development policy which is universally advocated. It is the science of spiritual discipline, the science of self-development, which is advocated in the philosophy of life and the philosophy of development implicit in Buddhism.

Buddhist view of Holistic Development

Buddhism uses the term "bhavaba" which, in meaning is very proximate to the English term development. Since the term has been used primarily in the context of the self or the mind or the spiritual potential of man. In the Buddhist context, development is believed to be desirable first and foremost of man himself, who serves as the very instrument of other forms of development. It is men themselves, who formulate development policy and it is men themselves who implement such policy.

According to Buddhism, development basically stands for the development of man, his character, and personality. In Buddhism, one who has a developed or cultivated personality is referred to as bhavitatta. In the full sense of the term it is a person who is fully enlightened and liberated from the miseries of existence, who is perfectly happy and at ease and who can truly be characterized as a developed personality. The greatness as well as the quality of the life of a human being, according to Buddhism, depends on the wisdom and morality that is perfected in him. The conquest of oneself is better than conquering thousands of men in battle. There is no power in this world that can take away the victory of the person who has conquered himself through self-development. Self-development involves the elimination of the unwholesome traits of mind, the roots of evil behaviour (akusalamual), greed, hatred and confusion of mind. The prescribed method for such development is presented as the Eightfold Path or the Threefold Moral Training consisting of the cultivation of wholesome patterns of behaviour in terms of observing certain norms of conduct (sila), attaining composure of the mind and developing the wisdom which results in a total self- transformation leading to the elimination of all unwholesome traits of mind.

Self-Development as the Basis for the Holistic Development

Self-development should serve as the basis for other kinds of development. As the Dhammapada says: "Irrigators divert water. Fletchers shape the arrow shaft. Carpenters shape wood. The wise ones tame themselves." Any development that is effected outside ourselves, that is in man's material environment, must be directed and controlled by persons with cultivated minds. The Buddhist attempt to attain inner peace (nibbana) through self-development is understood as "an absolutely personal performance of the single individual". Factors of the Nobel Eightfold Path, the threefold scheme of moral development, the four sublime abidings (brahmavihara), and the four grounds of beneficence (sangahavtthu) could be viewed as universally valid schemes for self-development.

In so far as development is conceived as a change in the course of things effected by human intervention, planning, deliberation and effort as a means of overcoming human misery and of promoting human well-being, the proper starting point for such a process of change should be the hearts and minds of men.

Buddhism does not discourage the production of material wealth, and insists that the production of wealth should not overstep morality. There is great inner spiritual wealth, which a person can develop within himself. Such wealth is considered in Buddhism as Noble Wealth (ariyadhana). Noble wealth consists of confidence (saddha), good conduct (sila), sense of shame and fear to do wrong (hiri, ottappa), learning (suta), generosity (caga) and wisdom (panna).

Implications of Buddhist Techniques

Buddhism also teaches universally testable techniques of mind culture (bhavana) which are effective in psychological tension reduction, in the therapy of mental illness, in the treatment of psychological diseases of the body, and above all in the attainment of insight into things as they are (yathabhuatanan) and consequently, in acquiring self-transforming wisdom and attaining inner peace and tranquillity.

The entire techniques of Buddism provide directions to develop good conduct, which is also the essence of a sound system of education. In this materialistic world everybody is facing troubles, stress, violence, misery etc., right from childhood. The teachings of Buddha, such as the Eightfold Path, good moral conduct, meditation etc., can mould the human personality and potency, which is the ultimate aim of education, only when they can be studied in the psychological and moral aspects, more than in the religious aspect.

Conclusion

Buddhism recognizes the importance of the body or man's physical existence as a vehicle through which man can strive for the perfection of human excellence, which consists of nothing but the development of the spiritual aspect of man's being. The essence of the Buddhist teaching on development is that all development must be guided by wisdom. For all development is first and foremost by man and for man. Wisdom can be gained only by self-development.

References

- Altekar A.S. (1943). Education in Ancient India, Motolal Banarassidas, New Delhi.
- Piyadarsi (1991) The Spectrum of Buddhism, The Corporate Body of Buddha Educational Foundation, Taiwan.
- Radha Kumud Mookerji (1969) Ancient Indian Education, Brahanical and Buddhist, Motilal Banarsidass, Delhi.

Explorations of "Sri Rama Krishna Paramahamsa Views on Mental Health"

– *A. Srinivas*

"Mana Eva Manushyanam Karanam Bhamnda Mokshayoh"

(We can make a heaven or hell of own mind)

In the entire creation except man all other creatures struggle only for their existence. Only man struggles to protect not only his life but also his mental peace.

Today the world requires the conditions to live together in a beautiful atmosphere. If the 6 billion people living on this tiny planet go on attacking and killing each other, the whole population will soon collapse. We have to live together in a friendly manner. How to do that? In today's technological age, space has vanished, and though spatial distance has lost it's meaning, the distance between minds has been increasing. Unless this mental distance is removed, even the physical closeness can be dangerous. For immediate relief from physical ailments like fever and headache there are medicines through "Atma Jnana". But for relief from mental sufferings there are more instant medicines. Right now there are only two major problems confronted by the humanity. One is physical i.e. AIDS. The other is psychological that is STRESS.

Only when man is mentally healthy he can see this world, enjoy the beauty of nature and realize the importance of human life, express happiness and also gratitude to the almighty.

Religion ought to promote catholicity. We cannot create or destroy anything in this universe. But only our mind is in our

✍ **A. Srinivas,** *Lecturer in Psychology, BEST College of Education, Tadepalligudem, W.G. Dist. A.P.*

control. Only our thoughts can shape it, mould it, nurture it or destroy; that means only a person's thoughts can determine the entire life of a person.

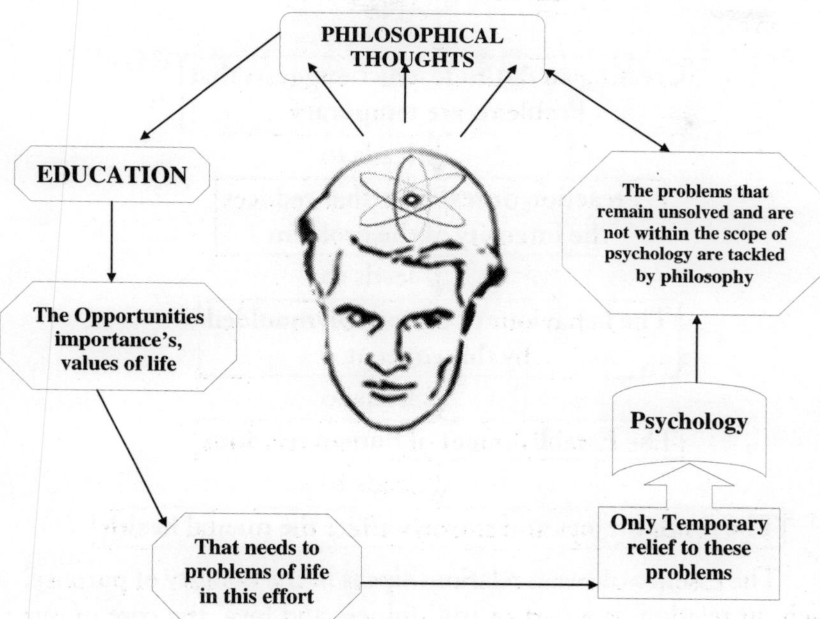

But to promote mental health, a healthy self-concept should be developed. To develop a healthy self-concept there are many factors involved. But in this technological world everything seems to influence mental health. To face such situations man's thinking should be widened. That is possible only through spirituality.

That can be understood on having a look at the following flow chart.

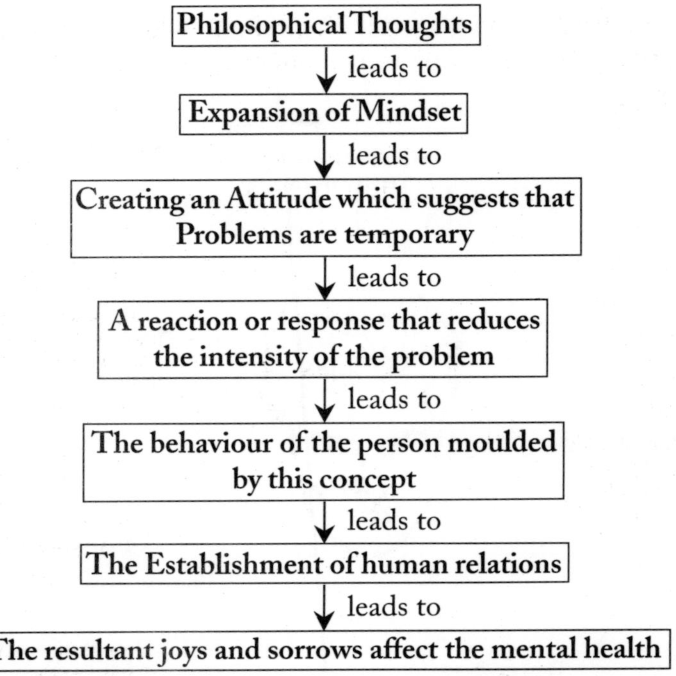

The essence of sweet relationships is in the honesty of purpose, which, in relation, is a part of truthfulness and love, the core of our being – the Divine within. According to Ramakrishna "Godly Nature" gives peace and joy and leads to good relations. The worldly nature brings restlessness and sorrow and leads to bad relations. Hence let us ponder over some of Sri Ramakrishna's teachings on these two aspects of human personality, godliness and worldliness and how they help us to develop good relations.

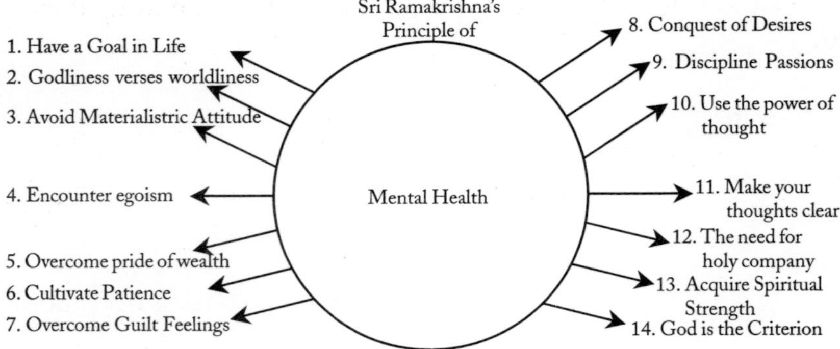

The way to Cultivate Mental Health	*Psychological Importance*
1. Have a Goal in Life	The people who don't have a clear goal of life before them wander away from the useful and serious duties of their life. They forget that life is an invaluable gift and thus waste it away. Many of them turn out to be cynics who belittle the ides about God, after – life and of spiritual enlightment. To such people Ramakrishna advised, "as a lamp cannot burn without oil, so a man cannot live without God".
2. Godliness versus worldliness	Sri Ramakrishna quotes Bhagavadgita and helps to increase our divine qualities. He also said, "whether we are to live in the world or to leave it, depends upon the will of God. Therefore work, leaving everything to him. What else can you do?"
3. Avoid Materia-listic Attitude	Due to materialistic concern we may refuse a friend in dire need a little money which we could easily spare. Such unfriendly behaviour can be avoided by cultivating. Non-attachment. Ramakrishna said "live unattached to this world – to be in the world, but not of it – and at the same time to keep your minds directed to God."
4. Encounter Egoism	The egotism plays havoc in cultivating sweet personal relationship. For example an egoless child has the sweetest relations with all. Sri Ramakrishna says "When this "I" is gone all difficulties vanish. We think – 'I' have done this better than any one". Therefore 'I...' deserve better name and rewards. This is how one's egotism increases.

	Trying to destroy ego is not easy. But Sri Ramakrishna puts it beautifully. "If after all you cannot destroy this 'I', then let it remain as "I" the servant of God. The self that knows itself as the servant and loving God will do little mischief."
5. Overcome pride of wealth	Sri Ramakrishna said "As water flows under a bridge without stagnation so money passes through the hands, but is never hoarded by them. He is a true man to whom money is a servant. Those who have it and do not know how to use it, do not deserve to be called men."
6. Cultivate Patience	Hurry and speed many tmes spoil the mental health. Patience often saves good relations. We receive so many good ideas from others but we spoil our sweet relations by being impractical in putting them to practice. We do not put up hard work which is the only secret of success.
7. Overcome Guilt Feelings	Most people are observed of being sinners. Such people cannot have peaceful minds. What then is the remedy? Sri Ramakrishna said "Why talk of sin and hell – tire all the days of your life? Chant the name of God. Do say but once "I have, O lord, done things that I ought not to have done, and I have left undone things that, ought to have done. O Lord forgive me saying this have faith in Him and soon shall be purged of all sins".
8. Conquest of desires	Desires keep us busy with the worldliness and do not allow us to become Godly. Sri Ramakrishna said "woman and gold", remember, keep men immersed in worldliness and away from God. Ramakrishna used "women" for gross enjoyments of senses and

	"gold" for suitable enjoyments of name, power, position etc. Hence he advised to gradually reduce the selfish desires in order to enjoy the sweet relations.
9. Discipline Passions	It is well known that passions like lust, anger, greed, infatuation and jealousy cause irreparable damage to good health. Then what is the way out? Should we try to eradicate them? Instead, Sri Ramakrishna tells us we should try to "sublimate them". It is like a mighty river in flood, which can deluge large tracks of land and damage crops. But when the river is channeled through building a dam and canals, it can generate hydropower and also irrigate large areas for crops: Ramakrishna said. "The passions need not and cannot be eradicated, but they can be educated and turned into a different channel."
10. Use the power of thought	Very often we feel we are bound, we are not free and thus create lot of frustration to ourselves and damage our relations with others. Sri Ramakrishna has said "The bondage is of the mind, freedom is also of the mind. "I am a free soul I am the son of the God, who can blind me"? A free person is always a happy person."
11. Make your thoughts clear	Sri Ramakrishna advised "one, wish to take pure water from a shallow pond, should not disturb it, but gently take it from the surface. If it is disturbed, the sediment will rise and make the whole water muddy". Therefore we should not ruffle it unnecessarily with erratic thoughts etc. and get confused, confusion is the enemy of mental peace.
12. The need for Holy Company	Our liziness and faithlessness are indeed great obstacles to develop mental health. In order to

	overcome them, we should report to the company of holy people. Ramakrishna said "The company of pious men is like water in which rice has been washed. Spirituality brings all sweet relations with it."
13. Acquire Spiritual Strength	"We can tide over all difficulties if we are strong in our faith in God. Where from is one to get strength in crisis"? "From God" – says Sri Ramakrishna. Listen to him "Where does the strength of an aspirant lie? In his tears. As a mother fulfils any desire of her crying babe, so God vouchsafes to his 'weeping child whatever it cries for:'"
14. God is the criterion	Many times misunderstandings come from superficial judgments of others. We judge merit or sin from outward observations. Sri Ramakrishna remarks "God looks at the working of one's mind. He does not take into account what in particular a person is doing or where he is staying. The Lord recognizes the motive alone. If we also looked at the motives of persons before judgng them our judgements would be fair and save lot of good relations which get damaged by wrong judgments."

The famous prayer – in the Upanishad "Asathoma Sadgamaya" (From evil, lead me to God)

Thamasoma Jyotirgamaya (From darkness lead me to light)

Mrutyorma Amruthangamaya" (From dealth lead me to immotality)

References

– The Vedanta Kesari - December 2006

– NCTE – ANWESHICA - July 2006

– Sri Ramakrishna's Life History - Telugu version.

Concentration: A Priceless Gift

– *Dr. D.Vijaya Bharathi*

The study of mental states is unique to India. 'Ekagrata' or 'One pointedness' that India spoke of was absolutely novel and even incomprehensible to the Western side of the globe in the past, and the same may be said even now. The ancient mental philosophy, now called psychology, housed the concept of Ekagrata, or concentration.

'Dhyana' or 'meditation' is a state of concentration or the nearest approach to spiritual life. It is the one moment in one's daily life that he is not material, but the soul, thinking of itself, free from all matter when one's mind is experiencing such a state, such a feeling, nothing will disturb him. He can accumulate a lot of power in silence and become a dynamo. Without wasting one's energy one can become more energetic through simple concentration.

Energy of the mind and body are essential for all, more for the young who are the future of the country. Swami Vivekananda said, "My faith is in the younger generation, the modern generation, out of them will come my workers. They will work out the whole problem, like lions. I have formulated the idea and given my life to it . . . . . They will spread from centre to centre, until we have covered the whole of India". Vivekananda - Vol. V, p. 223, 1963. The young today are no doubt ambitious, but they are not focussed. They have their fingers dipped in several pies at the same time, unable to take the required and right decisions. Here, it is for the elders to guide them and develop in them the 'shraddha'. They need to be trained to use their mental faculties to the utmost. But the general scenario

✍ ***Dr. D. Vijaya Bharathi,*** *Lecturer, St. Joseph's College of Education for Women, Guntur.*

today is that competition has increased greatly in every field and this has made it very difficult for the young to meet the same speed. In their rush to do many things at the same time they are getting stressed out. They don't find ways and means to overcome this difficult situation. At such times, they should be taught to find peace and strength of mind. This is possible through concentration or meditation or dhyana. This will help them to find their own capacities and direction in life.

To the youth Swami Vivekananda said "Have faith in yourself. You people were once the Vedic Rishis, only, you have come in different forms, that's all. I see it as clear as daylight, that you all have infinite power in you. Rouse that up; arise, arise - apply yourselves heart and soul." Vol. 7, p. 176, Vivekananda, 1963. Such was the faith Swami Vivekananda had in the youth and their capabilities. His suggestions to the youth, to enable them to realise themselves are based on sound philosophy and psychology. Swami Vivekananda could see in the youth the qualities of the ancient rishis, like perservance, patience, tolerance, compassion, love, concern, caring for others etc. Only thing is they need to be surfaced. This surfacing is possible only through Shraddha or concentration. About Shraddha Swami Vivekananda says "What we want is Shraddha, unfortunately it has nearly vanished from India and this is why we are in our present state. What makes the difference between man and man is the difference in this Shraddha and nothing else. What makes one great and another weak and low is this Shraddha." Vivekananda - Vol. III, p. 319. The youth, today, are also becoming weak because of the stress and tension they are experiencing. They could be made to overcome such problems that only make them weak. They need to be advised to develop Shraddha in them, which in turn will develop in them all the necessary qualities of a strong individual with a balanced personality. As long as the mental faculties of an individual are tuned and trained to the desired level there will be no problem with the individual. It is very much possible to mould an individual to be psychologically sound, through the method of concentration or meditation or Shraddha. That is, we need to help the individual to know about his own self, which, in turn will help him to develop himself; after all, development is nothing but forming one's own character, increasing one's strength of mind and expanding one's own intellect by which one can stand on one's own feet.

"Knowledge is inherent in man; no knowledge comes from out side; it is all inside . . . ." Vivekananda, Vol. I, p. 28, 1963. Hence, all we need to do, as teachers, is to help an individual to realise his own potentialities, that is, help him to unfold the perfection that is manifested in him. The library of this Universe is in one's own mind according to Swami Vivekananda. So, let us, teachers, tap the minds of our students, by helping them in concentration or meditation, the very key to knowledge.

Those concerned with education, the planners, the administrators and the teachers would very well agree with Swami Vivekananda who said "To me the very essence of education is concentration of mind, not the collecting of facts. If I had to do my education' over again, and had any voice in the matter, I would not study facts at all. I would develop the power of concentration and detachment and then with a perfect instrument I would collect facts at will." Vivekananda, Vol. VI, p. 38 - 39, 1963.

It is very true and correct that we train the mind of the learner who will then decide for himself what he wants to learn and what he has to learn. Proper orientation and understanding about himself and his personality will help an individual immensely, to grow and develop to the optimum level. When an individual decides for himself and by himself, what he is capable of, then his participation in this world would be more meaningful, satisfying and complete.

Life as of today, especially for the young students, has become very complex, competitive and confusing. The young need a lot of clarity of mind in order to compromise, cooperate and co-exist in the society. This is most important for corporate living. Here, each individual is important and together everybody is important. To be able to live a life of satisfaction and fulfillment, each individual should be complete. This is possible when the mind is undisturbed. The mind could be helped to withstand the many disturbances it faces each day, by making it strong. The way to make the mind strong, stable, open and illumined is through concentration. Through concentration knowledge is acquired ". . . . . . the stronger the power of concentration, the better will that thing be done. This is the one call, the one key which opens the gates of nature, and lets out floods of light" Vivekananda, Vol. II, p. 391, 1963.

It is our mental attitude that makes the world what it is for us. "Our thoughts make things beautiful, our thoughts make things ugly. The whole world is our own mind. Learn to see things in the proper light". Vivekananda, Vol. I, pp. 440-441, 1963.

Whatever one thinks, one will be. If he thinks he is weak, weak he will be. If he thinks he is strong, strong he will be. Strong one will be and feel with the help of one's mind. This mind, with all its faculties is most important for each one of us and it is essential that we train it and mould it. One way to do this is through concentration, a priceless gift that has come to us, as a heritage from our ancestors, the sages and seers of our motherland.

References

– Complete Works of Swami Vivekananda, Vol. I to VII, 1963. Mayavati: Mayavati Memorial edition.

Part-III

Integral Psychology in the Light of Sri Aurobindo

– Kongara Bhaskara Rao

"Our being in God's image be remade
And earthly life become the life divine" - Sri Aurobindo

" ......To Day we see a humanity satiated but not satisfied by victorious analysis of the externalities of Nature preparing to return to its primeval longings. The earliest formula of Wisdom promises to be its last, – God, Light, Freedom, Immortality." [Life Divine - Sri Aurobindo]

As Sri Aurobindo says " You must know the whole before you can know the part". We must know the cosmic psychology in which individual psychology is only a particle.

The Supreme Reality is One and Indivisible and Infinite beside which nothing else really exists.

Brahman (active and inactive): The inactive Brahman and the active Personal Brahman are two aspects of the Divine; in the Supreme these are fused into each other, not separate.

Brahman (sabda): The Brahman is the primal sound-energy. Brahman Consciousness: Brahman Consciousness is sometimes described as a static one, but it has two aspects, static and dynamic, and it is when both are united that it becomes integral. This Consciousness is greater than either that which perceives the Brahmic silence and immobility alone or that which perceives the cosmic existence and action alone.

✍ **Kongara Bhaskara Rao,** *Editor, Divya Deepika, Sri Aurobindo Vidya Kendram, Nazarpet, Tenali .*

Brahman Revelation: Brahman always reveals himself to us in three ways, *within ourselves, above our plane, and around us in the universe.* Within us there are two centers of the Purusha, the inner Soul through which he touches us to our awakening; there is the Purusha in the lotus of the *heart which opens upward all our powers and the Purusha in the thousand -petalled lotus whence descend through the thought and will, opening the third eye in us, the lightenings of vision and the fire of the divine energy.* The bliss of existence may come to us through either one of these centers. When the lotus of the heart breaks open, we feel a divine joy, love and peace expanding in us like a flower of light, which radiates the whole being. They can then unite themselves with their secret source, the Divine in our heart, and adore him as in a temple; they can flow upwards to take possession of the thought and the will and break out upward towards the Transcendent; they stream out in thought and feeling and act towards all that is around us. But so long as our normal being offers any obstacle or is not wholly moulded into a response to this divine influence or an instrument of this divine possession, the experience will be intermittent and we may fall back constantly into our old mortal heart; but by repetition, abhyasa,or by the force of our desire and adoration of the Divine, it will be progressively remoulded until this abnormal experience becomes our natural consciousness.

(Dictionary of Sri Aurobindo's Yoga [P No. 20-21]

Creation

This world was not built with random bricks of chance,
A blind god is not destiny's Architect;
A conscious power has drawn the plan of life,
There is a meaning in each curve and line.
It is an architecture high and grand
By many named and nameless masons built
In which unseeing hands obey the Unseen,
And of its master-builders she is one.

[-Savitri (Page : 460)]

Creation is a misnomer; nothing in this world is created, all are manifested. All exist previously in the mind of knower. Man creates his world because he is the psychic instrument through whom God manifests which he had previously arranged in Himself. In this sense Art can create the past, present and the furure.

All creation proceeds on a basis of oneness and sameness with a superstructure of diversity, and there is the highest creation where is the intensest power of basic unity governed diversity (SABCL V.5-368).

The Universe (Creation) is an objectivisation of the Supreme, as if he had objectivised himself outside of himself in order to see himself, to live himself, to know himself and so that there might be an existence and a consciousness capable of recognizing him as their origin and uniting consciously with him to manifest him in the becoming. There is no other reason for the Universe. (C.W.M.V-9, Page 321-323)

Evolution

There is an ascending evolution in nature which goes from the stone to the plant, from the plant to the animal, from the animal to man. Becaues man is for the moment, the last rung at the summit of the ascending evolution, he considers himself as the final and physical nature; he is yet almost wholly an animal, a thinking and speaking animal, but still an animal in his material habits and instincts. Undoubtedly nature cannot be satisfied with such an imperfect result; she endeavours to bring out a being who will be to man what man is to the animal, a being who will remain as man in its external form, and yet whose consciousness will rise far above the mental and its slavery to ignorance.

Sri Aurobindo came upon earth to teach this truth to men. He told them that man is only a transitional being living in a mental consciousness, but with the possibility of acquiring a new consciousness, the truth -consciousness, and capable of living a life perfectly harmonious, good and beautiful, happy and fully conscious. During the whole of his life upon earth, Sri Aurobindo gave all his time to establish in himself this consciousness what he called Supramental and to help others to realise it.

But why and how this evolution and all that happened is a mystery to the modern mind. Our ancient rishis have already discoverd this secret. In Taithiriyopanished (Chapter 6) the rishis say:

सोऽकामयत। बहु स्यां प्रजायेयेति। स तपोऽतप्यत। स तपस्तप्त्वा। इदं सर्वमसृजत। यदिदं किं च। तत् सृष्ट्वा तदेबानुप्राविश्त्। तदनु-प्रविशय। सच्च त्यच्चाभत्। निरूक्तं चानिरूक्तं च। निलयनं चानिलयनं च। विज्ञान चाविज्ञानं च। सत्यं चानृतं च सत्यमभवत्। यदिदं किं च। तत्सत्यमित्यचक्षते। तदप्येष शलोको भवति॥

The Spirit desired of old " I would be manifold for the birth of people." Therefore He concentrated all Himself in thought, and by the force of His brooding He created all this universe, yea, all whatsoever exists. Now when He had brought it forth, He entered into that He had created, He entering in became the Is here and the May Be there; He became that which is defined and that which has no features; He became this housed thing and that houseless; He became Knowledge and He became Ignorance; He became Truth and He became falsehood. Yea, He became all truth, even whatsoever here exists. Therefore they say of Him that He is Truth. Whereof this is the Scripture.

So the Spirit became Matter for its delight. That ONE wants to become many. Here Matter means, Matter having all the qualities of the Spirit but concealed itself in inconscient Matter. This is involution. This is very essential for evolution through which the One will become many for its delight.

This one is called the Supreme, the Divine, The God, The Trancendent etc. It is having consciousness of its own but the other end of which Matter does't have consciousness of it -self though it is having all the qualities of ONENESS.

Involution

So Involution is a movement opposite to the Evolution. It is infolding of a principle. The involutionary being is from higher worlds, who, when the earth was formed, materialized itself upon earth -it does not come from below, it has come from above.

The being from above which descends into a psychic being is an involutionary Being -a being of the over mind plane or from elsewhere. (C.W.M.-Vol.5; P 329)

If the emergence and growth of consciousness is the central motive of the evolution and the key to its secret purpose, then by the very nature of that evolution this growth must involve not only a wider and wider extent of its capacities but also an ascent to a higher and higher level till it reaches the highest possible. For it starts from a nethermost level of involution in the inconscience which we see at work in Matter creating the Material Universe.

The organs and organisms are in the protoplasm, the leaf, flower, fruit, in the seed and all forms in the ether from which they evolve, in an undifferentiated condition and therefore defy the method of analysis which is confined to the discovery of differences. This is the state called Involution. (SABCL:V.12-P47, V-16, P-16)

According to the Upanishads, the Supreme consionsness is having three important dimensions 1. Sat 2. Chit 3. Anand and in course of involution process

SAT	→	became	→	Matter
CHIT	→	became	→	Life
ANANDA	→	became	→	Psychic
SUPER-MIND	→	became	→	Mind

"The Spirit became Matter and lay in the whirl
A body sleeping without sense or soul." **[-Savitri (Page: 154)]**

Matter and Spirit

Matter reveals itself to the realising thought and to the subtle senses as the figure and body of spirit. Spirit reveals itself through the same consenting agents as the soul, the truth, and the essence of matter. The whole of creation may be said to be a movement between two involutions, spirit in which all is involved and out of which all evolves downward to the other pole of matter. Matter in which also all is evolved and out of which all evolves upwards to the other pole of spirit.(SABCL : V.12-P-47, V-16, P-16)

There Matter is the Spirit's firm density. **[-Savithri (Page: 328)]**

In order to become many the Matter shall reveal the Spirit's face. In the process of the evolution

Matter →	has to transform and reveal the	→	SAT
Life →	has to transform and reveal the	→	CHIT
Psychic →	has to transform and reveal the	→	BLISS

Individual Psychology

Supreme Divine

The Divine is that from which all comes, in which all lives. In its supreme Truth, the Divine is absolute and infinite peace, consciousness, existence, power and Ananda. Indirect connection with the Divine is when one lives in the ordinary consciousness without being able to go up above it and receive influences from above without knowing where they come from or feeling their source.

DIVINE AND FORM. The personal realization of the Divine may be sometimes with form. Without Form, it is the presence of the living Divine Person, felt in everything. With Form, it comes with the image of the One to whom worship is offered. The Divine can always manifest himself in a form to the Bhakta or seeker. One sees him in the form in which one worships or seeks him or in a form suitable to the Divine Personality who is the object of the adoration. Sometimes it is in the heart that the presence with the form is seen, sometimes in any of the other centres, sometimes above and guiding from there, sometimes it is seen outside and to front as if an embodied person. Its advantages are an intimate relation and constant guidance or it is felt or seen within, a very strong and concrete realization of the constant presence. But one must be very sure of the purity of one's adoration and seeking -for the disadvantage of this kind of embodied relation is that other Forces can imitate the Form or counterfeit the voice and the guidance and this gets more force if it is associated with a constructed image which is not the true thing. Several have been misled in this way because pride, vanity or desire was strong in them and robbed them of the fine psychic perception that is not mental.

DIVINE LIFE. A divine life must be first and foremost an inner life. The divine life will reject nothing that is capable of divinisation: all is to be seized, exalted, made utterly perfect. There are always two methods of living in the Supreme. One is to draw away the participation of the consciousness from things altogether and go so much inwards as to be separated from existence and live in contact with that which is beyond it. The other is to get to that which is the true Essence of all things, not allowing oneself to be absorbed and entangled by the external forms.

DIVINE LOVE. Love comes to us in many ways; it may come as an awakening to the beauty of the Lover, by the sight of an ideal face and image of him, by his mysterious hints to us of himself behind the thousand faces of things in the world, by a slow or sudden need of the heart, by a vague thirst in the soul, by the sense of someone near us drawing us or pursuing us with love or of someone blissful and beautiful whom we must discover.

DIVINE WILL. It needs a quiet mind to know the Divine will. In the quiet mind turned towards the Divine the intuition (higher mind) comes of the Divine's will and the right way to do it.

DIVINE WORKING. In all that is done in the universe, the Divine through his Shakthi is behind all action but he is veiled by his Yoga Maya and works through the ego of the jiva in the lower nature (Dictionary of Sri Aurobindo's Yoga by Sri. M.P. Pandit).

Psychoanalyst's Method

Aurobindo says, "I find it difficult to take these pyschoanalysts seriously when they try to scrutinise spiritual experience by the flicker of their torch-lights, yet perhaps one ought to, for half-knowledge is a powerful thing and can be a great obstcale to the coming in front of the true Truth. This new psychology looks to me very much like children learning some summary and not very adequate alphabet, exulting in putting their a-b-c-d of the subconscient and the mysterious underground superego together and imagining that their first book of obscure beginnings (c-a-t cat, t-r-e-e tree) is the very heart of the real knolwledge. They look from down up and explain the higher lights by the lower obscurities; but the foundation of these things is above and not below, *uparibudhna esam.* The superconscient, not the subsconscient, is the true foundation of things. The significance of the lotus is not to be found by analsying the secrets of the mud from which it grows here; its secret is to be found in the heavenly archetype of the lotus that blooms for ever in the Light above. The self-chosen field of these psychologists is besides poor, dark and limited; you must know the whole before you can know the part and the highest before you can truly understand the lowest. That is the promise of the greater psychology awaiting its hour before which these poor gropings will disappear and come to nothing". (SABCL:24-P1608-09)

Sachidananda

Sachihdananda is the manifestation of the higher purusha; its nature of infinite being, consciousness, power and bliss is the higher Nature, *para prakrit.* Mind, life and body are the lower nature, *apara prakrti.*

The state of Sachidananda is the higher half of universal existence, *parardha,* the nature of which is Immortality, *amrtam.* The state of mortal existence in Matter is the lower half, *aparardha,* the nature of which is death, *mrtyu.*

Mind and life in the body are in the state of Death because by ignorance they fail to realise Sachidananda. Realising perfectly Sachchidananda, they can convert themselves, Mind into the nature of the Truth, *vijnana,* Life into the nature of the *caitanya,* Body into the nature of *sat,* that is, into the pure essence.

When this cannot be done perfectly in the body, the soul realises its true state in other forms of existence or worlds, the "sunlit" worlds and states of felicity, and returns upon material existence to complete its evolution in the body.

A progressively perfect realisation in the body is the aim of human evolution.

It is also possible for the soul to withdraw for an indefinable period into the pure state of Sachidananda.

The realisation of the self as Sachidananda is the aim of human existence.

What Consciousness is

Consciousness is a reality inherent in existence. It is there even when it is not acitve on the surface, but silent and immobile; it is there even when it is invisible on the surface, not reacting on outward things or sensible to them, but withdrawn and either active or inactive within; it is there even when it seems to us to be quite absent and the being to our view unconscious and inanimate.

Consciousness is a fundamental thing; the fundamental thing in existence -it is the energy, the motion, the movement of consciousness that creates the unvierse and all that is in it -not only the macrocosm but the microcosm is nothing but consciousness arranging itself. For instance, when consciousness in its movement or rather a certain stress of movement forgets itself in the action it becomes an apparently "unconscious" energy; when it forgets itself in the form it becomes the electron, the atom, the material object. In reality it is still consciousness that works in the energy and determines the form and the evolution of form. When it wants to liberate itself, slowly, evolutionarily, out of Matter, but still in the form, it emerges as life, as animal, as man and it can go on evolving itself still farther out of its involution and become something more than mere man.

Ordinarily we mean by consciousness our first obvious idea of a mental waking consciouness such as is possessed by the human being during the major part of his bodily existence, when he is not asleep, stunned or otherwise deprived of his physicl and superfical methods of sensation. In this sense it is plain enough that consciousness is the exception and not the rule in the order of the material universe. We ourselves do not always posses it. But this vulgar and shallow idea of the nature of consciousness, though it still colours our ordinary thought and associations, must now definitely disappear out of philosophical thinking. For we know that there is something in us, which is conscious when we sleep, when we are stunned or drugged or in a swoon, in all apparently unconscious states of our physical being.

Necessarily, in such a view, the word consciousness changes its meaning. It is no longer synonymous with mentality but indicates a self-aware force of existence of which mentality is a middle term;

below mentality it sinks into vital and material movements, which are for us subconscient; above, it rises into the supramental, which is for us the superconscient. But in all it is one and the same thing organising itself differently. This is .. the Indian conception of Chit which, as energy, creates the worlds.

Consciousness is not only power of awareness of self and things; it is or has also a dynamic and creative energy. It can determine its own reactions or abstain from reactions; it can not only answer to forces, but creates or puts out from itself forces. Consciousness is Chit but also Chit Shakti.

... the origin, the continent, the initial and the ultimate reality of all that is in the cosmos is the triune principle of transcendent and infinite Existence, Consciousness and Bliss which is the nature of divine being. Consciousenss has two aspects, illuminating and effective, state and power of self-awareness and state and power of self force, by which being possesses itself whether in its static condition or in its dynamic movement; for in its creative action it knows by omnipotent self-consciousness all that is latent within it and produces and governs the universe of its potentialities by an omniscient self-energy.

... to the Infinite Consciousness both the static and the dynamic are possible; these are two of its statuses and both can be present simultaneously in the universal awareness, the one witnessing the other and supporting it or not looking at it and yet automatically supporting it; or the silence and status may be there penetrating the activity or throwing it up like an ocean immobile below throwing up a mobility of waves on its surface. This is also the reason why it is possible for us in certain conditions of our being to be aware of several different states of consciousness at the same time. There is a state of being experienced in Yoga in which we become a double consciousness, one on the surface, small, active, ignorant, swayed by thoughts and feelings, grief and joy and all kinds of reactions, the other within calm, vast, equal, observing the surface being with an immovable detachment or indulgence or, it may be, acting upon its agitation to quiet, enlarge, and transfrom it.

Consciousness: A Conscious Force

...The word consciousness... is no longer synonymous with mentality but indicates a self-aware force of existence of which mentality is a middle term; below mentality it sinks into vital and material movements which are for us subconscient; above, it rises into the supramental which is for us the superconscient.... This is... the Indian conception of Chit, which, as energy, creates the world....

We see, for instance, in the animal, operations of a perfect purposefulness and an exact, indeed a scientifically minute knowledge which are quite beyond the capacities of the animal mentality and which man himself can only acquire by long culture and education and even then uses with a much less sure rapidity. We are entitled to see in this general fact the proof of a conscious Force at work in the animal and the insect which is more intelligent, more purposeful, more aware of its intention, its ends, its means, its conditions than the highest mentality yet manifested in any individual form on earth. And in the operations of inanimate nature we find the same pervading characteristic of a supreme hidden ilntelligence, "hidden in the modes of its own working".

The only argument against a conscious and intelligent source for this purposeful work, this work of intelligence, of selection, adaptation and seeking is that large element in nature's operations to which we give the name of waste. But obviously this is an objection based on the limitations of our human intellect which seeks to impose its own particular rationality, good enough for limited human ends, on the general operations of the World- Force. We see only part of Nature's pupose and all that does not subserve that part we call waste. Yet even our own human action is full of an apparent waste, so appearing from the individual point of view, which yet, we may be sure, subserves well enough the large and universal purpose of things. That part of her intention, which we can detect, Nature gets done surely enough in spite of, perhaps really by virtue of her apparent waste. We may well trust to her in the rest, which we do not yet detect.

For the rest, it is impossible to ignore the drive of set purpose, the guidance of apparent blind tendency, the sure eventual or immediate coming to the target sought, which characterise the operations of World-Force in the animal, in the plant, in inanimate things. So long as Matter was Alpha and Omega to the scientific mind, the reluctance to admit intelligence as the mother of intellingence was an honest scruple. But now it is no more than an outworn paradox to affirm the emergence of human consciousness, intelligence and mastery out of an unintelligent, blindly driving unconsciousness in which no form or substance of them previously existed. Man's consciousness can be nothing else than a form of Nature's consciousness. It is there in other involved forms below Mind, it emerges in Mind, it shall ascend into yet superior form beyond mind. For the force that builds the worlds is a conscious Force, the Existence which manifests ltself in them is conscious Being and a perfect emergence of its potentialities in form is the sole object which we can rationally conceive for its manifestation of this world of forms.

Superconscient and subconscient are only relative tems; as we rise into the superconscient we see that it is a consciousness greater than the highest we yet have and therefore in our normal state inaccessible to us and, if we can go down into the subconscient, we find there a consciousness other than our own at its lowest mental limit and therefore ordinarily inaccessible to us. The Inconscient itself is only an involved state of consciousness which like the Tao or Shunya, though in a different way, contains all things suppressed within and all can evolve out of it -" an inert Soul with a somnambulist Force."

Senses

The contact of MIND with its objects creates what we call sense.

The superficial and outward action of the senses is physical and nervous in its character, and they may easily be thought to be merely results of nerve-action; they are sometimes called in the old books pranas, nervous or life activities. But still the essential thing in them is not the nervous excitation, but the consciousness, the action of the chitta, which makes use of the organ and of the nervous impact of which it is the channel. Manas, sense-mind, is the activity, emerging from the basic conciousness, which makes up the whole essentiality of what we call sense.

Sense is in fact the mental contact of the embodied conciousness with its surroundings. This contact is always essentially a mental phenomenon; but in fact it depends chiefly upon the develojpment of certain physical organs of contact with objects and with their properties to whose images it is able by habit to give their mental values. What we call the physical senses have a double element, the physical-nervous impression of the object and the mental-nervous value we give to it, and the two together make up our seeing, hearing, smell, taste, touch with all those varieties of sensation of which they, and the touch chiefly, are the starting-point of first transmitting agency.

What is, not in its functioning, but is in its essence, is the thing we call sense? In its functioning, if we analyse that thoroughly, we see that it is the contact of the mind with an eidolon of Matter, - whether that eidolon be of a vibration of sound, a light image of form, a volley of earth-particles giving the sense of odour, an impression of rasa of sap that gives the sense of taste, or that direct sense of disturbance of our nervous being which we call touch...

The supreme consciousness must not only comprehend and possess in its conscious being the images of things which it creates as its self-expression, but it must place them before it -always in its own being, not externally - and have a certain relation with them by the two terms of apprehensive consciousness. Otherwise the universe would not take the form that it has for us; for we only reflect in the terms our organization the movements of the supreme Energy. But by the very fact that the images of things are there held in front of an apprehending consciosness within the comprehending conscious being and not externalized as our individual mind externalized them, the superme Mind and supreme Sense will be something quite defferent from our mentality and our forms of sensation. They will be terms of an entire knowledge and self-possession and not terms of an ignorance and limitation, which strives to know and possess.

In its essential and general term our sense must reflect and be the creation of this supreme Sense.

"The senses there were outlets of the soul" **(-Savitri P. 398)**

Sight and the other senses are not mere results of the development of our physical organs in the terrestrial evolution. Mind, subconscious in all Matter and evolving in Matter, has developed these physical organs in order to apply its inherent capacities and not dependent on the curcumstance of terrestrial evolution and they can be employed without the use of the physical eye, ear, skin, palate. Supposing there are psychical senses which act through a psychical body, and we thus explain these psychical phenomena, still that action also is only an organization of the inherent functioning of the essential sense, the Sanjnana, which in itself can operate without bodily organs. This essential sense is the original capacity of consciousness to feel essential properties and operations of that which has form, whether represented materially by vibration of sound or images of light or any other physical symbol. (SABCL V. 21 & V. 12)

Psychic Being

With regard to the evolution upwards, it is more correct to speak of the psychic presence than the psychic being, for it is the psychic presence, which little by little becomes the psychic being. In each evolving form, there is this presence, but it is not individualised. It is something, which is capable of growth and follows the movement of the evolution. It is not a descent of the involution from above. It is formed progressively round the spark of Divine consciousness which is meant to be the centre of a growing being which becomes the psychic being when it is at last individualised. It is this spark that is permanent and gathers round itself all sorts of elements for the formation of that individuality. The true psycihc being is formed only when the psychic pertsonality is fully grown, fully built up round the eternal Divine spark; it attains culmination, its total fulfillment if and when it unites with a being or personality from above. (C.W.M. V-3, P 150). For further studies on this subject the reader may refer to [CWM V4, p150-151, 184-185, 196 V-11, P 290-292, V-12, P 430, V-14, P 248, V-15, P-265, 310, 323, 339, 357-358]. The psychic being is the soul developing in the Evolution. The Psychic being is especially the soul of the individual evolving in the manifestation, the individual prakriti and taking part in the evolution. It is that spark of the Divine Fire that grows beyond the mind, vital and physical as the psychic being until it is able to transform the Prakriti of Ignorance into Prakriti of knowledge. (SABCL V.22 301, 291). For further detailed studies on this subject the reader may refer to (SABCL V-18, P-225-228,610, V-19, P797, 893-96).

Now the evolution in its process has reached upto mind and its effect is emergence in man is only a transitional being.

All the world's possibilities in man
Are waiting as the tree waits in its seed: **[-Savitri (Page: 482)]**

The mind is having so many gradations and they have to be manifested and the corresponding beings will also come into existence.

Meanwhile the -

Mind is the author, spectator, actor, stage:
Mind only is and what it thinks is seen.
If Mind is all, renounce the hope of bliss;
If Mind is all, renounce the hope of Turth.
For Mind can never touch the body of Truth
And Mind can never see the soul of God;
Only his shadow it gropes nor hears his laugh
As it turns from him to the vain seeming of things.
Mind is a tissue woven of light and shade
Where right and wrong have sewn their mingled parts;
Or Mind is Nature's marriage of covenance
Between truth and falsehood, between joy and pain:
This stuggling pair no court can separate.

[-Savitri (Page : 645)]

Grades of Consciousness

A progressive evolution of the visible and invisible instruments of the Spirit is the whole law of the earth nature; that too is the fundamental value, which underlies all the other values of its existence and its process and gives them their significance.

Spirit has concealed itself in inconscient matter. It evolves, for itself first of all and as if that were its only preoccupation, forms of matter by the working of matter forces. It is only when this has been sufficiently done, that it thinks of life.

And yet a Sub-conscient life and its imprisoned forces were there all the time in matter and its forces and are there even in its mass apparently inanimate to forms...

Afterwards came an evolution of mind in many forms by the working of liberated mind-forces in those life-forces in matter and even in the very substance of matter mind was latent. An evolution of mind in the living forms by a working of liberated mind-forces was the third chapter of the story. The third chapter is not completed; neither will it be the end of the narrative.

Matter, life mind, supermind or gnosis, and beyond these a supreme being consciousness Force - Bliss: these are the grades of the evolutionary ascent from conscience to the superconscience.

This is the stupendous hierachy of the grades of consciousness between the darkest matter and the most luminous spirit. Consciousness in matter has to go on climbing to the very top of the series and return with all it has to give up before the evolution can uttrely fulfil its purpose. (SABCL. Vol 17, Page 16-17)

From the viewpoint of Sri Aurobindo, the fundamental limitation of modern psychology in delineating the nature of what it calls the unconscious stems from the mistake of describing the whole of a vast and complex reality in terms of a minuscule part, very much like the groping blind men of the well-known parable who, having each grasped a particular part of an elephant, depicted the whole elephant in terms of the particular part of the elephant's body which he happened to grasp and palpate. Sri Aurobindo has pointed out this error on more than one occasion.

Sri Aurobindo's remark that *"you must know the whole before you can know the part"* finds elucidation in his description of the various parts of the being: - (SABCL. Vol 24 Page: 1609)

By knowing too much they missed the whole to be known:
The fathomless heart of the world was left unguessed
And the Transcendent kept its secrecy.

[-Savithri P. 271]

Totality of Man's Being

Broadly speaking, Sri Aurobindo distinguishes four elements which make up the totality of man's being:

a) The surface or outer being,

b) The subconscient,

c) The subliminal and

d) The superconscient.

In order to understand the nature of this fourfold constitution of the being, certain fundamental views of Sri Aurobindo's philosophy need to be grasped. First, *man's being is part of the being of the universe, man being a microsm of the macrocosm;* therefore the psychological nature of man is intimately related to the metaphysical nature of the universe. Secondly, all of the universe is a manifestation of consciousness which has been evolving from the nethermost level - the Inconscient - towards the highest levels of the superconscient; thus *"the emergence and growth of consciousness is the central motive of the evolution and the key to its secret purpose"*. (SABCL. Vol. 16. Page: 6)

Thirdly, the evolution of consciousness is preceded by its involution; therefore the Inconscient is a concealed consciousness and "an inverse reproduction of the supreme superconscience"; evolution thus is a process of the return of Inconscience to the supreme Consciousness. Implicit in these fundamental propositions is the view that nothing is truly unconscious or totally devoid of consciousness; therefore the unconscious spoken of in psychology is a misnomer; what is called the unconscious is simply that which lies outside the surface conscious awareness and of which the mind in its ordinary states is not conscious.

In the evolutionary process, the first emergence from the Inconscient is Matter from which the human body is evolved. Regarding the workings of the Inconscient in Matter and the body,

Sri Aurobindo states:

"The body ... is a creation of the Inconscient and itself inconscient or at least subconscient in parts of itself and much of its hidden action ; but what we call the Inconscient is an appearance, a dwelling place, an instrument of a secret Consciousness or a Superconscient which has created the miracle we call the universe. Matter is the field and the creation of the Inconscient and the perfection of the operations of inconscient Matter, their perfect adaptation of means to an aim and end, the wonders they perform and the marvels of beauty they create, testify, in spite of all the ignorant denial we can oppose, to the presence and power of consciousness of this Superconscience in every part and movement of the material universe. It is there in the body, has made it and its emergence in our consciousness is the secret aim of evolution and the key to the mystery of our existence. " (SABCL.Vol. 16 Page : 16)

From the seemingly inconscient Matter emerge successively life and Mind. Explaining the nature and function of Life as is a middle term between Mind and Matter, Sri Aurobindo writes:

"Life then reveals itself as essentially the same every where from the atom to man, the atom containing the subconscious stuff and movement of being which are released in consciousness in the animal, with plant life as a midway stage in the evloution. Life is really a universal operation of Conscious-Force acting subconsciently on and in Matter; it is the operation that creates, maintains, destroys and recreates forms or bodies and attempts by play of nerve-force, that is to say, by currents of interchange of stimulating energy to awake conscious sensation in those bodies. In this operation there are three stages; the lowest is that in which the vibration is still in the sleep of Matter, entirely subconscious so as to seem wholly mechanical; the middle stage is that in which it becomes capable of a response still submental but on the verge of what we know as consciousness; the highest is that in which life develops conscious mentality in the form of a mentally perceptible sensation which in this transition becomes the basis for the development of sense-mind and intelligence. It is in the middle stage that we catch the idea of Life as distinguished from Matter and Mind, but in reality it is the same in all the stages and always a middle term between Mind and Matter, constituent of the latter and instinct with the former. " (SABCL Vol. 18. P186)

The Surface Being

To return to Sri Aurobindo's fourfold classification of the human constitution, man's surface consciousness, derived from the three universal principles just mentioned, is composed of mind, life (generally referred to by Sri Aurobindo as the vital) and body consciousness. Sri Aurobindo states that the term "mind", which has been used indiscriminately to cover the whole surface consciousness, connotes in the language of his yoga that part of the being which is related to cognitive elements and functions, such as ideas and thoughts, intelligence, thinking and reasoning. He distinguishes mind from the other two elements of the surface nature, namely, the vital and the body-consciousness, which are mixed up with mind on the surface. The vital is the Life-Nature made up of sensations, energies of action, instincts, impulses, desires, feelings and emotions. The body, says Sri Aurobindo, "is not mere unconscious Matter: it is a structure of a secretly conscious Energy that has taken form in it. Itself occultly conscious, it is, at the same time, the vehicle of expression of an overt Consciousness that has emerged and is self-aware in our physical energy-substance. (SABCL. Ibid P. 305) Regarding the confounding of the vital and the body-consciousness with mind, Sri Aurobindo explains:

"Mind identifies itself to a certain extent with the movements proper to physical life and body and annexes them to its mentality, so that all consciousness seems to us to be mental. But if we draw back, if we separate the mind as witness from these parts of us, we can discover that life and body,- even the most physical parts of life,- have a consciousness of their own, a consciousness proper to an obscurer vital and to a bodily being, even such an elemental awareness as primitive animal forms may have, but in us partly taken up by the mind and to that extent mentalised. Yet it has not, in its independent motion, the mental awareness which we enjoy; if there is mind in it, it is mind involved and implicit in the body and in the physical life: there is no organized self-consciousness, but only a sense of action and reaction, movement, impulse and desire, need, necessary activities imposed by nature, hunger, instinct, pain, insensibility and pleasure. Although thus inferior, it has this awareness obscure, limited and automatic;.... When we stand back from it, when we can separate our mind from its sensations, we perceive that this is a nervous, sensational and automatically dynamic mode of consciousness, a gradation of awareness different from the mind: it has its own separate reaction to contacts and is sensitive to them in its own power of feeling; it does not depend for that on the mind's perception and response." (Ibid. P.558)

The Subconscient and the Inconscient

Sri Aurobindo defines the subconscient as follows:

The subconscious in us is the extreme border of our secret inner existence where it meets the Inconscient, it is a degree of our being in which the Inconscient struggles into a half consciousness;.... Or, from another viewpoint, this nether part of us may be described as the antechamber of the Inconscient.(Ibid.P 422)

An important distinction to be made for understanding the nature of the subconscient is between the submental and the subconscient. The former refers to that, which, from the evolutionary point of view, is lower than or inferior to mind. The physical conciouness of the body and that of the vital are in this sense submental, but they are not entirely subconscient, for in them consciousness has already evolved a certain degree of its formulation and expression, though for the most part the operations of consciousness in the physical and vital parts of our being are subconscious to the mind and would therefore be regarded in modern psychology as part of the unconscious. "The true subconscious", says Sri Aurobindo, "is other than this vital or physical substratum; it is the Inconscient vibrating on the borders of consciousness..."In other words, whereas the submental is that which is below mind, the subconscient is what lies below even the physical and body-consciousness. (Ibid. P. 559)

Sri Aurobindo elaborates the description of the subconscient in the following extracts, which reiterate some of its basic characteristics:

"The subconscient is universal as well as individual like all the other main parts of the Nature. But there are different parts or planes of the subconscient. All upon earth is based on the Inconscient as it is called, though it is not really inconscient at all, but rather a complete "sub" -conscience, a suppressed or involved consciousness, in which there is everything but nothing is formulated or expressed. The subconscient lies between - this Inconscient and the conscious mind, life and body. It contains the potentiality of all the primitive reactions to life, which struggle out to the surface from the dull and inert strands of Matter and form by a constant development a slowly evolving and self-formulating consciousness; it contains them not as ideas, perceptions or conscious reactions but as the fluid substance of these things. But also all that is consciously experienced sinks down into the subconscient, not as precise though submerged memories but as obscure yet obstinate impressions of experience, and these can come up at any time as dreams, as mechanical repetitions of past thought, feelings, action, etc., as "complexes" exploding into action and event, etc., etc. The subconscient is the main cause why all things repeat themselves and nothing ever gets changed except in appearance. It is the cause why people say character cannot be changed, the cause also of the constant return of things one hoped to have got rid of forever." (Letters on Yoga P. 354. vol. 22)

"In our yoga we mean by the subconscient that quiet submerged part of our being in which there is no wakingly conscious and coherent thought, will or feeling or organized reaction, but which yet receives obscurely the impressions of all things and stores them up in itself and from it too, all sorts of stimuli, of persistent habitual movements, crudely repeated or disguised in strange forms can surge up into dream or into the waking nature. For if these impressions rise up most in dream in an incoherent and disorganized manner, they can also and do rise up into our waking consciousness as a mechanical repetition of old thoughts, old mental, vital and physical habits or an obscure stimulus to sensations, actions, emotions which do not originate in or from our conscious thought or will and are even often opposed to its perceptions, choice or dictates. In the subconscient there is an obscure mind full of obstinate Sanskaras, impressions, associations, fixed notions, habitual reactions formed by our past, an obscure vital full of the seeds of habitual desires, sensations and nervous reactions, a most obscure material which governs much that has to do with the condition of the body. It is largely responsible for our illnesses; chronic or repeated illnesses are indeed mainly due to the subconscient and its obstinate memory and habit of repetition of whatever has impressed itself upon the body-consciousness." (Ibid P. 353)

"It is a known psychological law that whatever is suppressed in the conscious mind remains in the subconscient being and recurs either in the waking state when the control is removed or else in sleep. Mental control by itself cannot eradicate anything entirely out of the being. The subconscient in the ordinary man includes the larger part of the vital being and the physical mind and also the secret body-consciousness." (Vol. 23 P. 898)

"When something is thrown out of the vital or physical, it very usually goes down into the subconscient and remains there as if in seed and comes up again when it can. That is the reason why it is so difficult to get rid of habitual vital movements or to change the character; for, supported or refreshed from this source, preserved in this matrix your vital movements, even when suppressed or repressed, surge up again and recur." (Vol. 22. P. 357)

"That part of us which we can strictly call subconscient because it is below the level of mind and conscious life, inferior and obscure, covers the purely physical and vital elements of our constitution of bodily being, unmentalised, unobserved by the mind, uncontrolled by it in their action. It can be held to include the dumb occult consciousness, dynamic but not sensed by us, which operates in the cells and nerves and all the corporeal stuff and adjusts their life process and automatic responses. It covers also those lowest functioning of submerged sensemind, which are more operative in the animal and in plant life." (Vol. 19-P. 733)

The Subliminal

"Subliminal is a general term used for all parts of the being which are not on the waking surface. Subconscient is very often used in the same sense by European psychologists because they do not know the difference. But when I use the word [subconscient], I mean always what is below the ordinary physical consciousness, not what is behind it." (Vol. 22 - P. 354)

Sri Aurobindo has occasionally used "subliminal" as a general term to denote all parts of the being which are not on the waking surface consciousness, "so conceiving it as to include in it our lower subconscient and upper superconscient ends." (Life divine 18 P. 557)

However, for the most part he distinguishes three parts of the being, which are outside the surface consciousness: that which lies below (the subconscient), that which lies behind (the subliminal), and that which is high above (the superconscient). Regarding the distinction between the subconscient and the subliminal, Sri Aurobindo states:

"The real subconscious is a nether diminished consciousness close to the Inconscient; the subliminal is a consciousness larger than our surface existence. But both belong to the inner realm of our being of which our surface is unaware, so both are jumbled together in our common conception and parlance." (SABCL Vol. 18 - P. 223)

"When we say subconscious, we think readily of an obscure unconsciousness or half-consciousness or else a submerged consciousness below and in a way inferior to and less than our organised waking awareness or, at least, less in possession of itself. But we find, when we go within, that somewhere in our subliminal part, ...though not co-extensive with it since it has also obscure and ignorant regions, ...there is a consciousness much wider, more luminous, more in possession of itself and things than that which wakes upon our surface and is the percipient of our daily hours; that is our inner being, and it is this which we must regard as our subliminal self and set apart the subconscient as an inferior, a lowest occult province of our nature." (Ibid .P. 557)

Sri Aurobindo states further the nature of the subliminal self as follows:

"The subliminal self stands behind and supports the whole superficial man; it has in it a larger and more efficient mind behind the surface mind, a larger and more powerful vital behind the surface vital, a subtler and freer physical consciousness behind the surface bodily existence. And above them it opens to higher superconscient as well as below them to lower subconscient ranges." (Vol. 24 P. 1606)

There is a "subliminal" self behind our superficial waking mind, not inconscient but conscient, greater than the waking mind, endowed with surprising faculties and capable of a much surer action and experience, conscient of the superficial mind, though of it the superficial mind is inconscient. (Vol. 16. P. 261)

Our subliminal self is not, like our surface physical being, an outcome of the energy of the Inconscient; it is a meeting-place of the consciousness that emerges from below by evolution and the consciousness that has descended from above for involution. There is in it an inner mind, an inner vital being of ourselves, an inner or subtle-physical being larger than our outer being and nature. ... There is here a consciousness, which has a power of direct contact with the universal. Unlike the mostly indirect contacts which our surface being maintains with the universe through the sense-mind and the senses. There are here inner senses, a subliminal sight, touch, hearing; but these subtle senses are rather channels of the inner being's direct consciousness of things than its informants: the subliminal is not dependent on its senses for its knowledge, they only give a form to its direct experience of objects; they do not, so much as in waking mind, convey forms of objects for the mind's documentation or as the starting-point or basis for an indirect constructive experience. The subliminal has the right of entry into the mental and vital and subtle-physical planes of the universal consciousness.

"It is not confined to the material plane and the physical world; it possesses a means of communication with the worlds of being which the descent towards involution created in its passage and with all corresponding planes or worlds that may have arisen or been constructed to serve the purpose of the re-ascent from Inconscience to Superconscience. It is into this large realm of interior existence that our mind and vital being retire when they withdraw from the surface activities whether by sleep or inward-drawn concentration or by the inner plunge of trance." (Life Divine P. 425)

Sri Aurobindo has called the subliminal self the inner being as distinguished from the outer or surface being. Thus he states:

"There are, we might say, two beings in us, one on the surface, our ordinary exterior mind, life, body consciouness, another behind the veil, an inner mind, an inner life, an inner physical consciousness constituting another or inner self." (SABCL . Vol. 23 - P. 1020 - 21)

The outer being is connected with the subliminal and, though unaware of it, receives from the subliminal its inspirations, intuitions, etc. As Sri Aurobindo states:

"It [the subliminal] is, according to our psychology, connected with the small outer personality by certain centres of consciousness of which we become aware by yoga. Only a little of the inner being escapes through these centres into the outer life, but that little is the best part of ourselves and responsible for our art, poetry, philosophy, ideals, religious aspirations, efforts at knowledge and perfection." (SABCl. Vol. 24 - P. 1164 - 65)

Thus though the surface being of the average individual is largely influenced by the subconscient it is also influenced to a significant extent by the subliminal.

The Superconscient

As stated previously, the superconscient is the starting point of the involution of consciousness and the ultimate goal of its evolution. Regarding the superconscient, Sri Aurobindo writes:

"If the subliminal and subconscient may be compared to a sea which throws up the waves of our surface mental existence, the superconscience may be compared to an ether which constitutes, contains, over roofs, inhabits and determines the movements of the sea and its waves. It is there, in this higher ether, that we are inherently and intrinsically conscious of our self and spirit, not as here below by a reflection in silent mind or by acquisition of the knowledge of a hidden Being within us; it is through it, through that ether of superconscience, that we can pass to a supreme status, knowledge, experience. Of this superconscient existence through which we can arrive at the highest status of our real, our supreme self, we are normally even more ignorant than of the rest of our being; yet is it into the knowledge of it that our being emerging out of the involution in Inconscience is struggling to evolve." (Life Divine P. 561)

In the superconscience beyond our present level of awareness are included the higher planes of mental being as well as the native heights of supramental and pure spiritual being. Among the higher planes of mental being, Sri Aurobindo distinguishes various distinct levels, which he terms

a) Higher Mind,
b) IIlumined Mind,
c) Intuitive Mind and
d) Over mind, culminating in what Sri Aurobindo calls
e) Super mind or the Truth-Consciousness, which secretly supports all the universe and leads all towards itself, through the evolutionary process.

Sri Aurobindo points out that the mind, because of its inherent limitations, is incapable of knowing anything in its essential nature... ... ...

Parts of the Mind

The mind proper is divided into three parts -thinking Mind, dynamic Mind, externalising Mind -the former concerned with ideas and knowledge in thier own right, the second with the putting out of mental forces for realisation of the idea, the third with the expression of them in life (not only by speech, but by any form it can give).

Vital Mind proper is a sort of a mediator between vital emotion, desire, impulsion, etc. and the mental proper. It expresses the desires, feelings, emotions, passions, ambitions, and possessive and acitve tendencies of the vital and throws them into mental forms (the pure imaginations or dreams of greatness, happiness, etc. in which men indulge, are one peculiar form of the vital - mind activity). There is still a lower stage of the mental in the vital which merely expresses the vital stuff without subjecting it to any play of intelligence. It is through this mental vital that the vital passions, impulses, desires, rise up and get into the Buddhi and either cloud or distort it.

As the vital Mind is limited by the vital view and feeling of things (while the dynamic Intelligence is not, for it acts by the idea and reason), so the mind in the physical or mental physical is limited by the physical view and experience of things, it mentalises the experiences brought by the contacts of outward life and things, and does not go beyond that (though it can do that much very cleverly), unlike the externalising mind which deals with them more from the reason and its higher intelligence. But in practice these two usually get mixed together. The mechanical mind is a much lower action of the mental physical, which, left to itself, would only repeat customary ideas and record the natural reflexes of the physcial consciousness to the contacts of outward life and things.

The physical mind is that part of the mind which is concerned with the physical things only - it depends on the sense-mind, sees only objects, external actions, draws its ideas from the data given by external things, infers from them only and knows no other Truth until it is enlightened from above.

That is the nature of the mental physical to go on repeating without use, the movement that has happened. It is what we call the mechanical mind - it is strong in childhood because the thinking mind is not developed and has besides a narrow range of interests. Afterwards it becomes an undercurrent in the mental activities.

Mind in its essence is a consciousness, which measures, limits, cuts out forms of things from the indivisible whole and contains them as if each were a separate integer.

Mind is an instrument of analysis and synthesis, but not of essential knowledge. Its function is to cut out something vaguely from the unknown thing itself and call this measurement or delimitation of it the whole, and again to analyse the whole into its parts, which it regards as separate mental objects.

Because of the intrinsic limitations of the mind as stated above, the method employed for understanding the unconscious, consisting in a mental analysis of what are believed to be the products of the unconscious, namely, dreams, free-associations, etc., has yielded only fragmentary and relatively superficial insights into the so-called unconscious. From these limited insights the mind has sought to construct the total reality of that which lies below, behind and beyond mind.

According to Sri Aurobindo, in order to know what lies outside mental awareness and be able to distinguish between the subconscient, the subliminal and the superconscient, it is necessary to break the walls that separate the surface consciousness from what lies behind and beyond it so as to emerge into the subliminal and the superconscient. As he states:

"A descent into the subconscient would not help us to explore this region, for it would plunge us into incoherence or into sleep or a dull trance or a comatose torpor. A mental scrutiny or insight can give us some indirect and constructive idea of these hidden activities; but it is only by drawing back into the subliminal or by ascending into superconscient and from there looking down or extending ourselves into these obscure depths that we can become directly and totally aware and in control of the secrets of our subconscient physical, vital and mental nature." (Life divine P. 734)

"..... though large parts of it [the subliminal] can be thus known by a penetration and looking within or a freer communication, it is only by going inward behind the veil of superficial mind and living within, in an inner mind, an inner life, an inmost soul of our being that we can be fully self -aware- by this and by rising to a higher plane of mind than that which our waking consciousness inhabits. An enlargement and completion of our present evolutionary status, now still so hampered and truncated, would be the result of such an inward living; but an evolution beyond it can come only by our becoming conscious in what is now superconscient to us, by an ascension to the native heights of the Spirit." (Life divine P. 736)

Gradations between Mind and Supermind

Higher Mind

Our first decisive step out of our human intelligence, our normal mentality, is an ascent into a higher Mind, a mind no longer of mingled light and obscurity or half - light, but a large clartiy of the spirit. Its basic substance is a unitarian sense of being with a powerful multiple dynamisation capable of the formation of a multitude of aspects of knowledge, ways of action, forms and significances of becoming, all of which there is a spontaneous inherent knowledge. It is therefore power that has proceeded from the Overmind, - but with the Supermind as its ulterior origin, - as all these greater powers have proceeded: but its special character, its activity of consciousness is dominated by Thought; it is a luminous thought-mind, a mind of Spirit-born conceptual knowledge. An all-awareness emerging from the original identity, carrying the truths, the identity held in itself, conceiving swiftly, victoriously, multitudinously, formulating and by self-power of the Idea effectually realising its conceptions, is the character of this greater mind of knowledge.

Illumined Mind

This greater Force [than the higher Mind] is that of the Illumined Mind, a Mind no longer of higher Thought, but of sprititual light. Here the clarity of the spiritual intelligence, its tranquil daylight, gives place or subordinates itself to an intense lustre, a splendour and illumination of the Spirit: a play of lightenings of spiritual truth and power breaks from above into the consciousness and adds to the calm and wide enlightenment and the vast descent of peace which characterise or accompany the action of the larger conceptual-spiritual principle, a fiery ardour of realisation and a rapturous ecstasy of knowledge.

Intuition

But these two stages of the ascent [Higher Mind and Illumined Mind] enjoy their authority and can get their own united completeness only by a reference to a third level; for it is from the higher summits, where dwells the intuitional being, that they derive the knowledge which they turn into thought or sight and bring down to us for the mind's transmutation. Intuition is a power of consciousness nearer and more intimate to the original knowledge by identity; for it is always something that leaps out direct from a concealed identitiy. It is when the consciousness of the subject meets with the consciousness in the object, penetrates it and sees, feels or vibrates with the truth of what it contacts, that the intuition leaps out like a spark or lightning-flash from the shock of the meeting, looks into itself and feels directly and intimately the truth or the truths that are there or so contacts the hidden forces behind appearances, then also there is the outbreak of an intuitive light; or, again, when the consciousness meets the Supreme Reality or the spiritual reality of things and beings and has a contactual union with it, then the spark, the flash or the blaze of intimate truth-perception is lit in its depths. This close perception is more than sight, more than conception: it is the result of a penetrating and revealing touch which carries in it, sight and conception as part of itself or as its natural consequence. A concealed or slumbering identity, not yet recovering itself, still remembers or conveys by the intution its own contents and the intimacy of its self-feeling and self-vision of things, its light of truth, its overwhelming and automatic certitude.

Overmind

The overmind is the highest of these ranges; it is full of lights and powers; but from the point of view of what is above it, it is the line of the soul's turning away from the complete and indivisible knowledge and its decent towards the ignorance. For although it draws from the Truth, it is here that begins the separation of aspects of the Truth, the forces and their working out as if they were independent truths and this is a process that ends, as one descends to ordinary Mind, Life and Matter, in a complete division, fragmentation, separation from the indivisible Truth above. There is no longer the essential, total, perfectly harmonising and unifying knowledge, or rather knowledge for ever harmonious because for ever one, which is the character of supermind.

The supermind is the One Truth deploying and determining the manifestation of its Powers -all these Powers working as multiple Oneness, in harmony, without opposition or collision, according to the One Will inherent in all. The overmind takes these Truths and Powers and sets each working as a force in itself with its necessary consequences -there can be harmony in their action, but it is rather synthetic and mostly partial than inherent and inevitable and as one descends from the highest overmind, separation, collision and conflict of forces increase, separability dominates, ignorance grows, existence becomes a clash of possibilities, a mixture of conflicting half-truths, an unsolved and apparently unsolvable riddle and puzzle.

The Supermind is the total Truth Consciousness; the Overmind draws down the truths separtely and gives them a separate activity - e.g. in the Supermind the Divine Peace and Power, Knowledge and Will are one. In the Overmind each of these becomes a separate aspect, which can exist or act on its own lines apart from the others. When it comes down to Mind they turn into an ignorance and incapacity - because Knowledge can come without a will to support it or peace can be disturbed by the action of Power etc.

The Indian systems did not distinguish between two quite different powers and levels of consciousness, one, which we can call overmind and the other the true supermind, or Divine Gnosis. That is the reason why they got confused about Maya (overmind - Force or Vidya-Avidya), and took it for the supreme creative power. In so stopping short at what was still a half-light they lost the secret of transformation - even though the Vaishnava and Tantra yogas groped to find it agian and were sometimes on the verge of success. For the rest, this, I think, has been the stumbling-block of all attempts at the discovery of the dynamic divine Truth; I know of none that has not imagined, as soon as it felt the overmind lustres descending, that this was the true illumination, the Gnosis, with the result that they either stopped short there and could get no farther, or else concluded that this too was only Maya or Lila and that the one thing to do was to get beyond it into some immovable and inactive silence of the Supreme.

Supermind

By the supermind is meant the full Truth-Consciousness of the Divine Nature in which there can be no place for the principle of division and ignorance; it is always a full light and knowledge superior to all mental substance or mental movement. Between the supermind and the human mind are a number of ranges, planes or layers of consciousness -one can regard it in various ways -in which the element or substance of mind and consequently its movements also become more and more illumined and powerful and wide.

AIM OF LIFE

The true aim of human life is to discover the Divine and to manifest it. Naturally this discovery leads to happiness; but this happiness is a consequence, not an aim in itself. And it is this mistake of taking a mere consequence for aim of life that has been the cause of most of the miseries, which are affecting human life.

(C.W.M.V-12 Page - 312).

Before we examine the principles and process of the evolutionary ascent of consciousness, it is necessary to restate what our theory of integral knowledge affirms.

Our imperfection is the sign of a transitional state, a growth not yet complete; an effort that is finding its way. Such a progression here can only have for its aim a self-fulfilment.

To maintain existence is, indeed, our first occupation and necessity, but it is only a starting point: for the mere maintenance of an imperfect existence chequered with suffering, cannot be sufficient as an aim of our being. (SABCL V-19, Page 667, 682, 981).

The instinctive will of existence, the pleasure of existence, which is all that the Ignorance can make out of the secret underlying Power and Ananda, has to be supplemented by the need to do and become.

On Nature's luminous tops, on the Spirit's ground
The superman shall reign as king of life,
Make earth almost the mate and peer of heaven
And lead towards God and truth man's ignorant earth
And lift towards godhead his mortality.

– Sri Aurobindo - Savitri - 707

Other References

- Dalal A.S. 'Psychology, Mental Health and Yoga'. Pondicherry: Sri Aurobindo Ashram.
- Aurobindo Sri 'Eight Upanishads'. Pondicherry: Sri Aurobindo Ashram.
- Indra Sen 'Integral Psychology'. Pondicherry: Sri Aurobindo International Centre of Education.
- Aurobindo Sri (1993): 'The Life Divine'. Sri Aurobindo Ashram, Pondicherry.
- Aurobindo Sri (1971): SABCL. Vol I to 24, Sri Aurobindo Ashram, Pondicherry.
- Mother ( ) CWA, Sri Aurobindo Ashram, Pondicherry.
- Aurobindo Sri ( ) 'Savitri', Sri Aurobindo Ashram, Pondicherry.
- Aurobindo Sri ( ) 'Letters on Yoga', Sri Aurobindo Ashram, Pondicherry.

❖ ❖ ❖

Does Sri Aurobindo Offer an Alternative for Humankind?

– Jacksan Judan Fernandes,
Sadasiva Rao

Introduction

To say that Sri Aurobindo is not easy to comprehend would be a huge understatement, if nothing else. While that can dissuade a number of people from going any further, it can motivate a number of others to study that, much more closely.

Humanity today is indeed passing through numerous crises and yet surviving. While we all no doubt wish to continue to evolve through all this survival (hopefully even reaching the supramental state promised by the great seer of Pondicherry), our concerns here are a little more pedestrian. We propose to look into some of the problems of contemporary man as an individual, a member of society, a citizen of his country, a component of this world, and of nature itself.

Some concepts like Science, Nature, Matter, Mental Being, Nation-ego and Nation-soul, True and False Subjectivism, World-state and World-union, and The Religion of Humanism will be the focus of this paper. Well, why not the rest, you may ask? Well, why not. Not that the others are not important. But we believe these deserve our focus here, and today, as humanity finds itself at the crossroads, and gropes around rather gingerly for some tentative answers, which may hopefully translate into permanent solutions.

✍ ***Jacksan Judan Fernandes,*** *Faculty and Research Scholar, Institute for Human Science and Service. Visakhapatnam, India.*

✍ ***Sadasiva Rao,*** *Research Scholar, Centre for Mahayana Buddhist Studies, ANU.*

Science, Matter and Nature

While Science is engaged in highlighting the distinguishing characters, the "discontinuities and discreteness of the elements of Nature," and with ample justification, "there is a level of reality which is continuous and yet to be grasped by the physical sense and science" (Chatopadhyayya 1998 p)

What is this level of reality, which is continuous? It is to understand that nature has immense potentialities. It is like a sleeping God. If awakened, it can raise all the elements that constitute it, including man, through the different levels of existence - material, vital, mental, and to the beyond -which is the supramental. This is possible only if we first of all realize that beneath the diversity and uniqueness of the different elements in Nature, there is an essential unity that not only allows this diversity but also supports it. Which means if the diversity of elements in nature is fundamental, equally fundamental is the unity that runs through these diverse elements. One of the important assignments for the scientific man of today would be to engage in tracing out this unity, while he is justifiably busy engaged in his methods of categorizing, classifying, differentiating etc. Otherwise it is in danger of remaining just a mass of formulae, ignorant of the foundation of being, and a poor instrument to perfect our nature, or our life:

" …our science itself is a construction, a mass, of formulas and devices; masterful in knowledge of processes and in the creation of apt machinery, but ignorant of the foundations of the being and of world-being, it cannot perfect our nature and therefore cannot perfect our life" (Sri Aurobindo 1993, p.1034)

The larger problem remains: whether Science will arrive at *the* ultimate truth, or *any* ultimate truth. To this too Sri Aurobindo has a rather insightful remark:

"… one might ask whether science has arrived at any ultimate truth; on the contrary, ultimate truth even on the physical plane seems to recede as science advances" (Sri Aurobindo 1972, p. 12)

Which makes us remember the astute remark of George Bernard Shaw: "Every true scientist is a metaphysician", and the other, of Albert Einstein: "Science without religion is lame; religion without science is blind" (Cohen and Cohen, 1986). And by religion, may we add, Einstein most probably meant spirituality and the ennobling aspects of religion, not its dogmatic and fanatical manifestations.

Science, its methods and approach, is the favourite whipping boy of most philosophers (Singh and Singh, 2004 p 59-64). So much so, I suspect it is in danger of becoming immune to even philosophy's legitimate pleas. However, a happy meeting ground would be a realization of each other's limitations, and more important, working together in an atmosphere of intellectual integration wherein the insights of philosophy could become heuristic and algorithmic models for scientific experimentation. For, let's face it, if science cannot lay claims to being the sole guardian of humanity, neither can philosophy.

This challenge and realisation have to be accepted by both sides for the welfare of society, if nothing else.

Nature: The forces of Nature have exercised a fascinating influence on human beings. While we know that so many of these forces are promotive to existence, we also know that a number of them are far from being so. Earthquakes, cyclones, floods, natural calamities in various forms have a devastating effect on the constituents of nature. In what sense, then, can the following statement have meaning: " the forces of Nature expressed through laws are not destructive, rather expressive and promotive, of the human mind, its thought and action, and their freedom" (Chatopadhyayya 1998).

How can the forces of Nature which cause natural calamities like the recent *tsunami* disaster, and the multiple earthquakes, and cyclones, and famines, which have ravaged this country, as also a number of others all over the world –how can such forces of nature not be destructive, rather be expressive and promotive? Of course we can find a convenient escape route by saying that what we refer to here are not the forces of nature as such, but as they are expressed through the fundamental laws. In which case we are not concentrating on certain events but on the laws, which govern them.

And we can very well say that such laws are expressive and promotive at a deeper level, which is not comprehensible to our superficial and distressed awareness. And maybe it is so. For, the justification for natural disaster as a means to bring about population control, or reduce the evil in society, has been advanced by a number of thinkers even earlier, Gandhi being not the least of them when he talked of the justification for the Bihar earthquake of 1934. Such reasoning defies comprehension to the mind acutely aware of the tragedy that surrounds it. And while it may be convenient to accept that behind every action manifest in Nature the Supreme is trying to arouse and guide us to perfection, let us fervently hope that none of those who were on that path were a part of that disaster. And they continue to remain so "protected".

Strange and incomprehensible are the ways of nature. Equally strange and incomprehensible can be the ways man can justify the vagaries of nature.

Having said that, however, even expression of the destructive forces of nature can be " "expressive and promotive, of the human mind, its thought and action, and their freedom" (Chatopadhyayya 1998), in at least one way. It has made a number of people express their solidarity towards the disaster affected victims, and it has helped promote the feeling of care and compassion for the disadvantaged in the more privileged and fortunate sections of the world. Well, every cloud has a silver lining. Only here the cloud seems to be enormous, and the silver lining appears to be far too thin.

Nature: Let us come to an interesting aspect of Sri Aurobindo's philosophy, and that is his acceptance of the reality of matter while highlighting its inadequacies. "Sri Aurobindo is a naturalist in a special sense. He affirms the reality of matter and at the same time highlights its imperfection. He affirms the reality of life-world and points out its imperfection and even distortion. He analyses the rich complexity of the human mind and also shows its inadequacy to grasp the integrality of reality as a whole," (Chatopadhyayya 1998).

Do we now, here, have an answer? That matter exists and it is imperfect. The world exists, but it is imperfect, even distorted. Hence it is subject to calamities and disasters. That the human mind is rich and complex, all right. But it may not be able "to grasp the integrality of reality as a whole" (chatopadhyayya 1998). Which means even when things go drastically wrong in nature, or in man, we should be able to understand that there is integrality even in such a reality, which only a holistic approach will make obvious. This is because the human mind, howsoever rich and complex in its ability, is still inadequate in its grasp of the integral nature of phenomena as they express themselves in nature outside, and in its nature within as well.

To understand the mysteries of events and happenings around us, we must, besides helping correct the situation outside, look within ourselves and examine the *tsunamis* and earthquakes and cyclones and floods and droughts that afflict us within. The *tsunamis* of our desires devastate our rationalities, the floods of greed rampage our morality, the droughts of compassion dwarf our sense of fraternity, and the earthquakes of our personal tragedies break down the edifices of our beliefs. And, to that extent, all such tragedies and events in nature do have ostensibly a destructive but fundamentally an expressive and promotive effect on human nature.

All the laws of nature is a thing precise in its necessities of process, but is yet in the cause of that necessity and of its constancy of rule, measure, combination, adaptation, result a thing inexplicable, meeting us at every step with a mystery and a miracle, and this must be either because it is irrational and accidental even in its regularities or because it is supraratational, because the truth of it belongs to a principle greater than that of our intelligence. That principle is the supramental; that is to say, the hidden secret of Nature in the organization of something out of the infinite potentialities of the self-existent truth of the spirit the nature of which is wholly evident only to an original knowledge born of and proceeding by a fundamental identity, the spirit's constant self-perception… All these processes are actually spiritual and supramental in their secret government, but mental, vital and physical in their overt process (Sri Aurobindo 1972, p 754-768).

While every disaster is heart rendering, it is also an occasion, and an invitation, to human growth. This of course is not in any way to reduce the impact such tragedies have on our brethren, or to trivialise the issue by offering smart intellectual justification for events around. But in some special sense, the ill-understood and inexorable ways of nature, and the forces that move it, are guiding man's destiny, and hopefully, his actions in the direction of not just a survival, but of an integral evolution. We pray that this hope becomes a conviction, which furthers man's self-actualisation rather than remaining only an excuse to quieten internal disturbances.

If mankind can quieten the *tsunamis* and cyclones and droughts and earthquakes that rage within, and behave with care and compassion towards Nature, not exploiting or denuding or denigrating it, there is a strong possibility that Nature too will behave with equal care and compassion towards man, and spare him the natural calamities than render him asunder. This is the lesson of the *tsunami* tragedy that engulfed us recently, and of all such tragedies that have ravaged mankind from times immemorial.

This realisation may be considered one manifestation of how human consciousness, which is in the "twilight zone of reality...is being increasingly brightened by the light beyond the super - mind" (Chatopadhyayya 1998). And only the descent of the supra-mental consciousness on the earth could rid humanity of the "poverty of the powers of consciousness besieged by maladies of various kinds" (J.Krishnamurti, 1998).

Man and his Relation with Nature

In Man two ends of Nature, the growing animal sector and the arc above, meet and interact, supplementing and complementing each other (Chatopadhyayya 1998).

What is the essence of being a Man? Firstly, that he is an animal, and secondly, that he is capable of evolving because of "the arc above", which finds a resonating cord in his inner-being. If the cord is well tuned, it will vibrate in harmony with the symphony from above. And it makes sense to say that the major part of our energies must be directed to such self-tuning. This is one important task before mankind today. But it must be supplemented by the knowledge that the two forces of Nature working on him interact in him not to contradict each other or to disturb his fundamental equilibrium, (although it may disturb his superficial equilibrium to an extent), but in a manner which supplements, that is adds on to, and complements, that is completes, the work of these two forces in their attempt to bring about man's evolution. To that extent, Nature is both a benefactor and a force: a benefactor, because it acts to carry out the evolution of mankind; a force, because it also supplies the necessary energy and momentum to achieve it. In this way, it is both the visionary and the executor. And, as it is guided by and acted upon by "the arc above", it fulfills its role in mankind's evolution much more integrally. The task before the thinking mind of today is to realize this happening, to be receptive to the changes and modifications it brings about in him, and to allow for the actions that spontaneously and inevitably spring therefrom.

Purusha, Nation - Soul and World Unity

Let us come to the concepts of *mana-purusa, prana-purusa* and *citta- purusa*[14]:

The mental being *(mana-purusa)* has a frontal formation *(prana-purusa)* and transcendental psychic formation *(citta-purusa)*[15].

We must also understand these concepts in the light of what Sri Aurobindo considers false subjectivism and true subjectivism[16].

The *mana-purusa* is acted upon by the *prana-purusa,* which is the vital being, and the *citta-purusa,* which is the psychic formation. The *prana-purusa* can give rise to obsessive vital cravings, which can be a drag on the *mana-purusa*; while the *citta-purusa,* which is subliminal and transcendental, uplifts him to function at a higher plane. The *mana-purusa,* while it cannot avoid the legitimate needs of his *prana-purusa,* must not get obsessively preoccupied with it. Because that would lead to man becoming unduly pragmatic making "our political interests also perniciously narrow"[17].

This is exactly what happens in man of today who is obsessively preoccupied with satisfying his physical needs and emotional desires at the cost of his spiritual development. The ills of hyper-consumerism are a manifestation of this obsessive need to satisfy his *prana-purusa.* And the consequent deviance, psychopathology and social strife that we see around us, is a manifestation of the frustration that results due to such dissatisfaction. However, if the *mana-purusa* were to *log on* to the *citta-purusa*, without necessarily *logging off* from the *prana-purusa*, it may help quieten the turbulences within, which may be a prelude to quietening the disturbances without, whether it be wars, terrorism, ethnic conflicts, communal riots, and other such social maladies that afflict mankind today.

To *log on* to the *citta-purusa* means to *log on* to the unity that underlies the diversity within human beings. And, somewhere down the line, it also means to *log on* to the integrity that underlies all existence. This would amount to being the true subjectivism of Sri Aurobindo, and help get rid of the false subjectivism that binds contemporary man's *mana-purusa* unhealthily and obsessively with his *prana-purusa.* In other words, the first halting steps on the journey to true subjectivism must be taken in this manner by the man of today.

A related concept for us in these times is that of Nation-ego and Nation-soul given by Sri Aurobindo. He considers Nation-ego an example of false subjectivism, in which national identity and pride are stressed upon to prove one's superiority and suppress or exploit the rest. The example he quotes frequently is that of Nazism of Germany, obviously because he was living during that period.

She (Nazi Germany) had mistaken her vital ego for herself; she had sought for her soul and found only her force. For she had said, like the Asura, "I am my body, my life, my mind, my temperament," and became attached with a Titanic force to these; especially she had said, "I am my life and body", and that there can be no greater mistake for man and nation. The soul of a man or nation is something more and diviner than that; it is greater than its instruments and cannot be shut up in a physical, a vital, a mental or a temperamental formula....It is evident that there is a false as well as a true subjectivism and the errors to which the subjective trend may be liable are as great as its possibilities and may well lead to capital disasters. This distinction must be clearly grasped if the road of this stage of social evolution is to be made safe for the human race[18].

For us today, it is necessary to analyse and place in perspective such fascist and fundamentalist ideologies and forces which not only raise their ugly heads once in a while, but attempt to capture the social consciousness of communities. The implications of this statement for India should be obvious. But if some people feel like implicating the extreme Right here, let us not forget that the extreme Left can be equally so. For, dogmatism and fanaticism have the curious ability to cut across ideological boundaries.

As distinct from the Nation-ego is the concept of Nation-soul. The Nation-soul is an attempt to capture one's traditional heritage and values in its pristine form, not as a reaction to hurts and angers, or due to real or imagined injuries or indignities of the past. For, an ideology or organization, or even a movement, which is based wholly or even mainly on anger or the desire for retribution, can only breed discord, further strife, clashes and enmity between groups and peoples. This is at the source of the various ethnic conflicts from times immemorial, and which continue to plague mankind even today.

More germane to the issue for us in India today is whether concepts like *hindutva* are manifestation of Nation-ego or Nation-soul. While the protagonists would immediately jump and exclaim that it is a manifestation of the Nation-soul, the opponents would be equally insistent it is a perfect manifestation of the Nation-ego. And a puerile manifestation, if ever there was one.

Now our purpose here is not to take sides, or even act the arbiters, or incite passions, which is easy even in gatherings like these. For the *prana-purusa,* whether we like it or not, continues to exercise a great hold even here. Be that as it may. If the votaries of *hindutva* propagate their ideal, not only as an affirmation of cultural and civilizational underpinnings of this nation's great heritage, but utilize it as a convenient handle to intimidate and suppress minorities, then it would be akin to the Nazi's attitude towards the Jews. However, if it is not exclusivist and is a careful and compassionate assertion of the tradition, the heritage bequeathed and the values eternally followed and universally applicable, such a *hindutva* need have no difficulty becoming a true subjectivism, and ideology, fit for the Nation-soul.

In this there is a challenge and an opportunity, as much for the votaries of this concept as its opponents: for the votaries to keep it a concept of Nation-soul, and never to allow it to become a concept to justify Nation-ego; for the opponents of today to be vigilant that it does not so happen. But at the same time not to cry wolf, or get unduly alarmed at a genuine affirmation of all that was noble and sublime in Indian tradition, which needs a careful reappraisal and rejuvenation as much by the votaries as by the adversaries of today. for, this is what a true subjectivism teaches us; First, that we are a higher self than our ego or our members, secondly, that we are in our life and being not only ourselves but all others; for there is a secret solidarity which our egoism may kick at and strive against, but from which we cannot escape[19].

The larger context in this connection should not also be forgotten. For in our narrow preoccupations we may forget that India may indeed have a larger role to play in the world.

Another point very important to remember is that Sri Aurobindo always placed India's freedom in the larger context of the destiny of the human race. This fact is most remarkable because revolutionaries talk only about their own country. However, Sri Aurobindo always had a deeper vision of what India should do for humanity[20].

Let us now come to another important distinction made by Sri Aurobindo which is equally important today, the distinction between World-state and World-union:

To that reason two alternative possibilities and therefore two ideals present themselves, a World- State founded upon the principle of centralization and uniformity, a mechanical and formal unity, or a world-union founded upon the principle of liberty and variation in a free and intelligent unity[21].

This is a logical extension of his distinction between Nation-ego and Nation-soul. Just like his spiritualism does not negate matter, his idea of global unity does not negate the idea of National freedom. Nations bring their own civilizational diversities and need to preserve their cultural autonomy even whilst coming together and thinking in terms of global issues:

A free world-union must in its very nature be a complex unity based on a diversity and that diversity must be based on free self-determination[22].

The concept of a World-state, on the other hand, is a false subjectivism according to him, because it would result in bringing about forced and imposed uniformity.

The ideal of uniformity, like the cult of state, is tainted by antilibertarianism. It amounts to the denial of basic principle of human unity amidst civilizational diversity and cultural autonomy. He (Sri Aurobindo) thinks that our experiments with the *Ideal of One World* must be free from misplaced commitment to barren uniformism and hegemonism[23].

The very movement towards uniformism is fundamentally flawed. It is a misplaced extension of the scientific attitude of finding out only commonalities in peoples and phenomena. Even if two human beings are similar, in so far as they are human beings, there is so much diversity in them. Part of the movement towards human self-actualisation lies in the fact that this diversity should not be forcibly curbed, as also the realization that beneath all that appears disparate, there is an essential unity. To stress on that disparateness which leads to the growth of human and national potential, while at the same time not forgetting to accent on the essential unity of all mankind, is a true and genuine affirmation of the ideal of World-union, as distinct from a narrow, mechanistic and constricting ideal that the concept of a World-state represents. In other words, all such movements toward Internationalism, which stifle the genuine cultural, civilizational and patriotic aspirations of its member states, will always be a failure. While those that accept and respect their cultural and ideological diversity, and yet help them to come together on broad consensual issues alone, will succeed in forging true Internationalism and world-unity. And what is applicable to the member nations of the world is equally applicable to the member states of the Indian union.

Religion of Man and Religion of Humanity

What can be the religion of the Man of today, besieged as he is by the numerous pulls and pressures of creeds, dogmas and religious ideologies, ritualized and fossilized beyond recognition by dogmatic followers, and adept at offering glib rationalizations for the sufferings of mankind?

"...the orthodox religions looked with eyes of pious sorrow and gloom on the earthly life of man and were ready to bid him bear peacefully and contentedly, even to welcome its crudities, cruelties, oppressions, tribulations as a means for learning to appreciate and for earning the better life which will be given us hereafter[24].

Sri Aurobindo is quite categorical in emphasizing that neither an " idol, nor the nation, the State, the family nor anything else ought to take (the) place (of)... The fundamental idea that mankind is the godhead to be worshipped and served by man"[25]. For that alone will ensure that the body of man, the life of man, the heart of man and the mind of man develop in their quest for divinity.

Man must be sacred to man regardless of all distinctions of race, creed, colour, nationality, status, political or social advancement. The body of man is to be respected, made immune from violence and outrage, fortified by science against disease and preventable death. The life of man is to be held sacred, preserved, strengthened, ennobled, uplifted. The heart of man is to be held sacred also, given scope, protected from violation, from suppression, from mechanization, freed from belittling influences. The mind of man is to be released from all bonds, allowed freedom and range and opportunity, given all its means of self-training and self-development and organized in the play of its powers for the service of humanity[26].

The challenge that Sri Aurobindo throws to orthodox or organized religion is but appropriate. For, in sustaining and perpetuating the outer symbols and structures of religion, man may forget to resurrect the inner spiritual symbols and structures, which alone can sustain true religiosity. And any religion which neglects the advancement of man's spiritual quest so as to sustain its dogmas, rituals and blind obedience, will, in the final analysis, turn out to be a false God. His accent on the religion of humanity is to make organized religion beware of the dangers of fossilization and make us aware once again of the fundamental tenet of humanism that:

Man is the measure of all things[27].

Which reminds us of another great contemporary of Sri Aurobindo, Gandhi, and what he said about the practical aspect of religion:

Religion, which takes no account of practical affairs and does not help to solve them, is no religion[28].

Coming back to Sri Aurobindo, we cannot but be impressed with the breadth of his expanse and the invitation he offers us to change and evolve. And that brings home the insightful comment of another keen Aurobindo researcher:

If we make a serious study of Sri Aurobindo, we shall find ourselves to be a participant of that adventure of consciousness which invites us to collaborate with that wide-ranging Yoga that can liberate us from the fetters of dogmas and preconceptions and inspire us to realise the highest and the best not only for ourselves but for the entire humanity[29].

Concluding Remarks

We have taken a rather brisk but eventful journey through the fascinating lanes and bylanes of Sri Aurobindo's thoughts. As humanity stands at the crossroads today, we find that one road leads to disaster, which is paved by the misadventures of science coupled with the ulterior motives of man, the other leads to despair, because of the pessimism and cynicism of the uglinesses of modern life. The third is lit by hope, based on the wonderful advancements of science and technology and the last pathway is lit brilliantly, and that is by a mankind rooted in matter but soaring towards the spirit.

Humanity, thou art afoot. Take what course thou wilt.

References

- Chattopadhyaya, D. P. (1998), Sri Aurobindo, India and the World, In *Seminar: Sri Aurobindo and the World and Education for Tomorrow in the Light of Sri Aurobindo* , 21 and 22 Nov 1998, New Delhi.
- Sri Aurobindo (1993), The Divine Life. In: *The Life Divine*, Sri Aurobindo Ashram, Pondicherry, First Edn. 1939 - 40, Tenth impression 1993, p 1034.
- Sri Aurobindo and the Mother (1972), Drawbacks and Limitations. In: *On Science*, Sri Aurobindo Ashram, Pondicherry, p 12.
- Cohen, J.M., Cohen, M.J. (1986), *The Penguin Dictionary of Modern Quotations,* II Ed. Middlesex.
- Singh, A. R., Singh, S. A. (2004*),* Replicative Nature of Indian Research, Essence of Scientific Temper, and Future of Scientific Progress. In: *Psychiatry, Science, Religion and Health,* Mens Sana Monographs Annual 2004, II, 1-3, p 57-69. This is our recent attempt to correct the situation, act the arbiters, and douse the fires. Well, hopefully. New conflagarations, however, are guaranteed.
- Chattopadhyaya, *op. cit.*
- *Ibid.*
- *Ibid.*
- *Ibid.*
- Sri Aurobindo (1971) Yoga of Self-Perfection. Chapter XIX: The Nature of Supermind (Arya-July 1920). In: *The Synthesis of Yoga-Part 4: The Yoga of Self Perfection, SABCL,* Vol. XXI, Sri Aurobindo Ashram, Pondicherry, p 754-768.
- Chattopadhyaya, *op. cit.*
- Joshi, Kireet (1998), Sri Aurobindo, In Seminar: *Sri Aurobindo and the World and Education for Tomorrow in the Light of Sri Aurobindo,* 21 and 22 Nov.,1998.
- Chattopadhyaya, *op. cit.*
- This is Prof. Chattopadhyaya's formulation, an interesting one, but not presented in this manner in Sri Aurobindo's writings. The latter talks of *Manomaya purusa* (mental person, the mental being), and *pranamaya purusa* (the true, vital being; soul in life), and *citta (not citta purusa; citta* meaning basic consciousness; mind stuff, the general stuff of mental consciousness. He also talks of *cittakasa, cittapramatha, cittasakti, cittashuddhi, cittavrtti, cittavrttinirodha, citti, citti acitti, cittim acittim cinavan vi vidvan etc.* However, that need not detract us from the burden of the argument Prof. Chattopadhyaya forwards.

– Chattopadhyaya, *op. cit.*

– Sri Aurobindo (1971), True and False Subjectivism. In: *The Human Cycle,* Ch V; In:*Social and Political Thought: The Human Cycle- The Ideal of Human Unity War and Self-determination, Vol 15, SABCL*, Sri Aurobindo Ashram, Pondicherry, p37-47.

– Chattopadhyaya, *op. cit.*

– Sri Aurobindo (1971), The Discovery of the Nation-Soul. In: *The Human Cycle,* Ch IV; In: *Social and Political Thought: The Human Cycle- The Ideal of Human Unity War and Self-determination, Vol 15, SABCL*, Sri Aurobindo Ashram, Pondicherry, p36. Parenthesis added.

– Sri Aurobindo, cfr.16 above, p40.

– Singh Karan, The Message of Sri Aurobindo, Mandala of Indic Tradition, *infinityfoundation.com*

– Sri Aurobindo (1971), World-Union or World-State. In: *The Ideal of Human Unity,* Ch XXII, In *Social and Political Thought: The Human Cycle- The Ideal of Human Unity War and Self-determination, Vol 15, SABCL*, Sri Aurobindo Ashram, Pondicherry, p441-442.

– Sri Aurobindo (1971), The Conditions of a Free World-Union. In: *The Ideal of Human Unity,* Ch XXXI, In *Social and Political Thought: The Human Cycle- The Ideal of Human Unity War and Self-determination, Vol 15, SABCL*, Sri Aurobindo Ashram, Pondicherry, p517.

– Chattopadhyaya, *op. cit.* Parenthesis added.

– Sri Aurobindo (1971), The Religion of Humanity. In: *The Ideal of Human Unity,* Ch XXXIV, In *Social and Political Thought: The Human Cycle- The Ideal of Human Unity War and Self-determination, Vol 15, SABCL*, Sri Aurobindo Ashram, Pondicherry, p543.

– Ibid, p542. Parenthesis added.

– Ibid, p542.

– Singh, S.A. (2000), Relevance of Renaissance Humanism for Man in the Third Millennium, Dr. K.M.A. Hay Lecture on Humanism. *The Proceedings of the 74th Session of Indian Philosophical Congress*, Dec 28-30, 1999. Bodh-Gaya. Published 2000 (ed. Shukla Sinha), p215-226.

– *Young India,* 07.05.25. See also Singh, A. R., and Singh, S. A. (2004), Gandhi on Religion, Faith and Conversion: Secular Blueprint Relevant Today. In: *Psychiatry, Science, Religion and Health*, Mens Sana Monographs Annual 2004, II, 1-3, p79-87. This is a recent attempt to find practical correlates in Gandhi's thought on religion and secularism of relevance to the man and times of today.

– Joshi, Kireet *op. cit.*

Personality Development Manifesting the Divinity Within

– Dasapathi Rao

Personality is generally understood as the organised, consistent and general pattern of behaviour of a person across situations, which helps us to understand his or her behaviour as an individual. Personality is also termed as the sum total of the characteristics of a person. The term personality explains the integration of different behavioural processes resulting in meaningful behaviour in such a way as to make one person different from others.

Modern psychology, in the words of Sri Aurobindo "is an infant science at once rash, fumbling and crude."

"It takes a partial truth for the total truth and hastens to explain the whole of Reality in its narrow terms. It is necessary therefore to look for the whole truth behind the surface phenomena."

Sri Aurobindo says that the present psychological methods are quite inadequate to understand and assess the real personality. It is mostly a partial truth. The Indian concept of personality and personalty development take a different view. The real personality of a person is the expression of her/his infinite self. It is also termed as manifestation of the divinity within.

Swami Vivekanda also deals with personality and personality development at length in his speeches and writings. Vivekananda says personality is not merely what a person appears to be, speaks, thinks but it is his real being. He says, "words, even thoughts, contribute only one-third of influence in making an impression, the man, two-thirds. What you call the personal magnetism of the man - that is what goes out and impresses you." He further says, "Now to take a

✍ **Dasapathi Rao,** *Lecturer, IASE, Nellore.*

concrete example a man comes; you know he is very learned, his language is beautiful and he speaks to you by the hour -but he does not make any impression. Another man comes, and he speaks a few words, not well arranged, ungrammatical perhaps; all the same, he makes an immense impression. *(Vivekanda, Vol. I, P. 13)*

The Indian approach to personality is more holistic in nature. It goes beyond the outward approach and traits, resulting in the unfolding of the inner self. The external self is nothing but the expression of the inner self.

Vivekanda further says, "Now we see that though this is a fact, no physical laws that we know will explain this. How can we explain it by chemical and physical knowledge? How much oxygen, hydrogen, carbon -how many molecules in different positions and how many cells etc. can explain the mysterious personality? ... Compare the great teachers of religion with the great philosophers. The philosophers scarcely influenced anybody's the human, and yet wrote most marvellous books. The religious teachers, on the otherhand, moved countries in their lifetime. The difference was made by personality. In the philosopher it is a faint personality that influences, in the great prophet it is tremendous. In the former we touch the intellect, in the latter we touch life. In the one case, it is simply a chemical process, putting certain chemical ingredients together which may gradually combine under proper circumstances bring out a flesh of light or may fail. In the other, it is like a torch that goes round quickly, lighting other." *(Vivekanda Vol. 2, P. 15)*

The goal of human life as per the Indian ethos and spiritual literature has been self-realisation. Put in the other way, it means experiencing the oneness in the universe or to experience a higher level of consciousness.

"Man's personality is a composition of Prakriti, made up of mind, life and body. The three fundamental qualities of Prakriti - Sattwa, Rajas and Tamas, determine the nature of his personality; the unequal working of these modes is the constitutional force of his active nature and his temperament. The predominance of one or the other determines the dominant tendencies, qualities or capacities of the individual. It is these personality characteristics that constitute outword by the psychological types, which, in essence are the soul force of Prakriti." *(Madhusudan Reddy, P.91)*

It seeks the integration of all the planes and parts of human personality - physical, vital, mental, psychical and spiritual as well as the integral personality growth leading to perfect self-actualisation. Self-transcendence, authentic self-awareness and self-transformation are part of its creative process leading to joyous self-expression and self-manifestation of the Divine. Man is conceived as an evolving phenomenon -evolving towards the realisation of his higher nature, his infinite potentialities and capacities.

The scope of Integral Yoga psychology, as envisaged by Sri Aurobindo, is indicated in the following passage. "It is not enough to observe and know the moments of our surface nature and superficial nature of other living creatures ... a whole world of occult phenomena have to be laid bare and brought under control before the psychologist can hope to be master of his province."

In his Integral Yoga psychology, Aurobindo speaks more about the holistic approach to psychology. He says personality is viewed mostly from the mental and emotional points of view, but in fact its dimensions are much wider. But it is a psycho-spiritual and a dynamic approach and it is multidimensional. He says, "While the traditional Western psychology deals with mental and emotional aspects of personality in the larger context of society, and modern psychology focuses on issues in the humanistic and transpersonal spheres. Integral Yoga postulates an evolutionary integral approach, which includes man's uniqueness, his transpersonal depth dimension, his transcendental, evolutionary and creative aspects. It is a psycho-spiritual and dynamic approach to the total phenomenon of man, to the multidimensional personality of man in the context of the universe and that which includes and transcends the universe." *(Madhusudana Reddy, p. 137)*

Western psychology neglects this ontological dimension of man, his creative psyche, and blows out of proportion the existential aspect. It includes man's social, mental and cultural dimensions as well as his transpersonal self.

It is the spiritual that is the perennial source and reason of man's growth process and his urge for wholeness.

Indian psychological approach takes us altogether to a new plane and form of consciousness, which is capable of synthesising all the demands of psychology. For Aurobindo "psychology is the science of consciousness and its states and operations in Nature and, if that be glimpsed or experienced, its status and operations beyond what we know as Nature." *(Sri Aurobindo. The Hour of God. Vol 17. P. 21)*

Also, for him, the science of consciousness is not the same, as it is normally understood in the West.

"Consciousness is usually identified with mind, but mental consciousness is only the human range which no more exhausts all the gradations of colour or human hearing all the gradations of sound - for there is much above or below that is to man invisible and inaudible." *(Sir Aurobindo: Letters on Yoga. Vol. 22, P. 234)*

Our observable consciousness, which we call ourselves, is only the little visible part of our being. It is a small field below, which are depths and farther depths and widths and ever wider widths which support and supply it but to which it has no visible access. All that is ourself, our being; what we see at the top is only our ego and its visible nature ...

"Far below this conscient nature is the vast Inconscient out of which we come. The Inconscient is greater, deeper, more original, more potent to shape and govern what we are and do than our little, derivative conscient nature."

(Sri Aurobindo. The Hour of God. Vol. 17, P. 21-22)

Aurobindo further feels that the so-called depth psychology cannot explain human behaviour in terms of the subconscious or the unconscious. It miserably fails to reach the core of the truth of human personality. Sri Aurobindo significantly observes "This new psychology looks to me very much like children learning some summary and not very adequate alphabet, exulting in putting their a-b-c-d of the subconscient and mysterious underground super-ego together..... **The super conscient, not the subconscient, is the true foundation of things.** The significance of the lotus is not to be found by analysing the secrets of the mud from which it grows here; its secret is to be found in the heavenly archetype of the lotus that blooms for even in the light above ...... **you must know the whole before you can know the part and the highest before you can truly understand the lowest.** That is the promise of the greater psychology awaiting its hour before which these poor groupings will disappear and come to nothing."

(Sri Aurobindo Letters on Yoga, Vol. 24, P. 1608-09)

The Science of Yoga claims that it has discovered the laws, which develop this personality, and by proper attention to these laws and methods, each one can grow and strengthen his personality. It is to move to the finer i.e., from body; from action to thought. If we can get hold of thought at the root, before it has become thought, before it has become action, then it would be possible for us to control the whole .... A pure, moral man has control of himself. And all minds are the same, different parts of one mind ... He who knows and controls his own mind knows the secret of every mind and has power over every mind. This control brings out the perfect man.

He further says that the secret of personality development is unfolding the strength within. "Each soul is potentially divine. The goal is to manifest this divinity within by controlling nature, external and internal. Do this either by work, or worshping, or psychic control, or philosophy -by one or more, or all of these -and be free". *(Vol. I, P. 257)*

Swami Vivekananda talked about the principles and laws that make the personality of the individual.

"Truth, purity and unselfishness -wherever these are present, there is no power below or above the sun to crush the possessor there of. Equipped with these, one individual is able to face the whole universe in opposition." *(Vol. IV, P. 279)*

"Every successful man must have behind him somewhere, tremendous integrity, tremendous sincerity, and that is the cause of his success in life. He may not have been perfectly unselfish, yet he was tending towards its .... The degree of unselfishness marks the degree of success everywhere."

"The History of the world is the history of persons like Budha and Jesus. The passionless and unattached do most for the world. *(Vol. VIII, P. 226)*

"The good live for others alone. The wise man should sacrifice himself for others. I can secure my own good only by doing your good. There is no otherway, none what so ever. *(Vol. VI, P. 317)*

"When there is a conflict between the heart and the brain, let the heart be followed, because intellect has only one status, reason and within that it works and cannot go beyond. It is the heart which takes one to the highest plane, which intellect can never reach., it goes beyond intellect, and reaches to what is called inspiration." *(Vol. I, P. 412-13)*

Educational Implications

Hence, it is said that the goal of education, all training, should be man-making. The end and aim of all training is to make man grow. Education should aim at bringing under control the current expression of will and touch the hearts of everybeing.

The educational system must concentrate more on character building process. The personality development process must be paid more attention than mere giving knowledge and skill only.

We talk more about the methods, but the person behind it is more important.

Yoga, meditation, introspection as techniques of personality development should be given importance.

References

- Complete Works of Swamy Vivekananda. Vol. I to VII, 1963. Mayavathi: Mayavathi Memorial Edition.
- Parameswaran, E.G. and Beena, C. (2002). An Invitation to Psychology. Hyderabad: Neelkamal Publishers.
- Collected Works of Sri Aurobindo. Aurobindo Ashram, Pandicherry.

❖ ❖ ❖

Teacher Education
A Pleasurable Experience
Principles of Integral Education

– *Prof. Y.F.W.Prasada Rao,*
Dr. Padma

Human life as we can all experience, is a combination of being able to do; i.e., see, hear, smell, taste and at the same time enjoy in doing so. We are told in our childhood, "edaina manasupetti cheyali" [do any thing by putting your mind into it] and then one will enjoy it. It would mean, do anything, read, eat, play or sing, put your mind and heart into it. Then you will enjoy or derive joy from it. This was a strategy suggested by 'The Mother' and in the expressions of Sri Aurobindo. However, there is a rider and that is, we shall not be seeking pleasure only or do things for the sake of pleasure. We feel on the basis of our, though humble but considerable, years of experience as teachers and teacher educators, that any and everything done and being done in the name of teacher education, is felt as burdensome by those who do it and also those who get it done as it were. It seems to be like something 'one *has* to do' like a routine approach. Though all those activities, concepts and what not are well thought out, discussed, deliberated and formulated, something, somewhere there seems to be a gap, a missing of the *real spirit*. It was always felt that in a college/department of education even one does everything, there would seem to be much more to be done and at the same time, someone who does not do any thing there is nothing to be done. It was and is a paradox. With this background as a basis this paper is attempted.

✍ **Prof. Y.F.W.Prasada Rao,** *Former Dean, Faculty of Education, Andhra University, Visakhapatnam.*

✍ ***[Dr.] Padma,*** *M.A., M.Ed., Teacher, Z.P. School, Srikakulum.*

The thought/s that came was/were, whether one of the core ideas of integral education could be applied to the area or arena of teacher education. Whether being conscious of this natural inclination to '*enjoy*', be able to do the magic as it were to the teacher education, especially in the context of growing numbers of institutions. Whether the humanistic psychological principles enshrined in the integral education, thoughts of Sri Aurobindo and The Mother be able to give us a new light.

As Sri Aurobindo wrote

"The traditions of the past are very great in their own place, in the past, but I do not see why we should merely repeat them and not go farther. In the spiritual development of consciousness on earth a great past ought to be followed by an ever greater future." (Sri Aurobindo 1971, p88)

A study into the past is warranted. At the same time it must be remembered what is it that made the past meaningful to them. What were the conditions and the forces at operation in those days needed to be researched into? There seems to be a need, also to look into what went wrong with those things that went wrong along with things that were good enough to be emulated now too.

With this theoretical thought behind us shall we indulge in putting forward the idea that in the process of preparing syllabi for teacher education, instead of somebody, though may be experienced, or expert as we may call her/him, let the clientele, the user; the learner engage in reflective reasoning as in the words of Sri Aurobindo "help the children to develop their intellectual, emotional, moral, spiritual being?" And this shall be the process through which they are provided opportunity to deliberate and decide upon what needs to be experienced by them through the course. Being their own impressions, would they not be enjoying experiencing them? This is in comparison with what we have now, i.e., some high and mighty decide what needs to be in the syllabi, both theory and practicum. Neither the taught nor those in the process of teaching really are involved in its full sense. Syllabi are made hastily, and given out for implementation. This is really devoid of much to think and much to deliberate based on empirical research. Hence, in spite of the best intention of those powers that be, the entire exercise ends up as a mere Xerox or cut, edit, and or paste of the old.

But then there needs to be readjustment in our thinking. What is the needed correction? It is the thinking on the part of the elders/ curriculum framers/the experts that even those young ones, the teachers to be, can contribute with their experiences as learners and can give out wholesome ideas. If we think and feel that the learning experience needs to be enjoyable, then they, i.e., those who are to experience need to have their own conceptual framework: need to be familiar; need opportunities to express their feelings; need to reconstruct: need a variety of kinds of opportunities for experience. It would be an educational experience that is liberating and empowering. It would be more than conceptual learning, because they are really involved in the entire process. This is termed as Deep Intelligence.

What is this idea of 'deep intelligence'? *Deep Intelligence is that ability to prosper through conscious and intentional coordination of the inner and outer faculties of our being with the inner and outer qualities of the world through which we live. Seaton A., [2007]* It is a holistic function of intelligence. It gives importance to feelings and impressions.

It is time that we realize and make use of those thoughts that were ancient as it were; integral educational thoughts and the modern as they are presented for the education more so teacher education of today. A combination of integral education and deep intelligence can develop broader set of abilities in the teacher to be. It would also be more effective and at the same time more satisfying to the persons involved by giving their better arenas of thinking, feeling, knowing, relating, living and being in the world of today, not just in a competitive scale but on a cooperative panel.

References

- Mohanty, S.B., [2007] Theory & Practice of Integral Education, Manu Publications, 4 Dr.Annie Besant Street, Pondicherry
- Seaton, Andrew [2007] Plenary Address, at Internation Conference of All India Association for Education Research, HP, India
- www.askjeeves.com

Let the Child's Mind Develop

– *P.S.A.S.K. Sudha*

The child is the father of the man. – **William Wordsworth**

Every child has innate powers. These have to be trained to develop fully in a child. The training is the education. Sri Aurobindo writes, "The chief aim of education should be to help the growing soul to draw out that in itself which is best and make it perfect for a noble use". Hence education must be based on the psychology of child's nature. He should be enabled to educate himself and grow independently as an organic being.

In enabling the child's mind to grow, Sri Aurobindo proposes steps in this process. They are:

i) The training of the senses,

ii) Sense improvement by practice,

iii) The training of the mental faculties and

iv) The training of the logical faculties.

Training of the Senses

Sri Aurobindo writes, "Every child is an enquirer, an investigator, an analyzer and an intellectual scientist". For a child's mind to grow and accumulate these skills, the senses have to be developed. As part of the total education, he lays stress on the training of the senses to begin with. "There are six senses which minister to knowledge –sight, hearing, smell, touch, taste and mind". The teacher should take great care in the perfection of the senses as ministers to thought. Sri Aurobindo writes, " The two things that are needed of the senses are accuracy and sensitiveness". The unobstructed activity of the nerves is necessary for making the senses

✍ **P.S.A.S.K. Sudha,** *Lecturer, St. Joseph's College of Education for Women, Guntur.*

accurate and sensitive. The organs do their work perfectly in themselves. For example, the eye forms a correct image on the retina. The fault comes in the nerve currents.

The nerves are nothing but channels. They cannot alter the information but a channel can be obstructed and accuracy is lost. Sri Aurobindo says, " The case of a physical defect in the organ can be removed by physician". He also advocates, "The obstructions can be removed and sensitiveness remedied by the purification of the nerve system –the regulation of the breathing through Yoga i.e. Nadi – suddhi."

If the nerve channels are quiet and clear, the only possible disturbance of the information is from or through the mind. "The manas is both a sense organ and a channel". It is automatically perfect as a sense organ but can be obstructed as a channel. According to Sri Aurobindo the development of the sensitiveness of the mind can be done through yogic discipline Suksmadrsti or subtle reception of images.

Sri Aurobindo deplores that the development of the sixth sense –manas (mind) has never been part of the education of man. He says, " Mind should be trained to give a correct report to the intellect with the full impressions absolutely correct".

Sri Aurobindo observes the second obstacle as emotions. "Emotions wrap the impression as it comes". He gives the remedy that the discipline of the emotions, and the purifying of the moral habits can remove this. The interference of previous associations formed in the citta or passive memory also distorts the impressions. Sri Aurobindo advises the process of Yoga –Citta suddhi to get rid of this obstacle. "The purification of the citta is essential for the liberation, purification and perfect action of the intellect".

Sense Improvement by Practice

Sri Aurobindo says, "Another cause of the inefficiency of the senses as the gatherers of knowledge, is insufficient use". The child has to be trained with sufficient attention. "Attention is the first condition of right memory and of accuracy. This attention to a single thing is called concentration". Sri Aurobindo advocates that the child can be trained in this discipline if the object of attention is made interesting.

By attention, it does not mean only centering the mind on one thing at a time. Sri Aurobindo writes, ".... it is quite possible to develop the power of double concentration, triple concentration, multiple concentration". He insists that through steady natural practice or Abhyasa the child can be trained to observe and remember perfectly several simultaneous happenings –a sight, a sound, a touch or several of these occurring at the same moment or same short pace of time.

Sri Aurobindo advocates, " The imitation by the hand ensures accuracy of observation". The practice of imitation by the hand through the drawing helps the mind to notice the objects of sense and register accurately as seen.

Training of the Mental Faculties

Sri Aurobindo reinstates that the first qualities of the mind that have to be developed can be grouped under observation. The first thing the teacher has to do as he says is to accustom the pupil to concentrate attention. Full concentration of the faculty of observation gives all the knowledge that the five senses can tell. For example the flower -the form, colour, beauty, scent and texture.

Memory and judgment are the next qualities to be encouraged in the same unconscious way. The student should not be made to repeat the same lesson over again to remember it. He should be encouraged to note the similarities and differences. It becomes a habit and it lays foundation to scientific attitude. For example –the observation of flowers, plants, animals, stars etc.

Judgment comes from making distinctions –the right idea of colour, sound, scent etc. At first they make errors. The best way to accustom the child to compare his judgments is with those of others. The wrongs being corrected first by the elder or teacher and later these are to be corrected by him. This develops analogy.

The last of the mental faculties is imagination. It has three functions. They are forming of the mental images, the power of creating thoughts, images, imitations, or new combinations and the appreciation of the soul in things. Sri Aurobindo emphasizes that the mental faculties should first be exercised on things, later on words and then on ideas. The learning should create interest and curiosity and avoid set teaching and memorizing of rules.

Training of the Logical Faculty

Sri Aurobindo realizes the necessity of training the logical faculty. For this he recognizes three steps –to make the child interested in drawing inferences from the facts, tracing cause and effect, to mark its successes and failures and to notice the cause of the success and the failure.

The training of the logical reasoning should proceed from example to the rule and accumulating harmony of rules to the science.

Role of the Teacher

According to Sri Aurobindo, "The teacher is not an instructor or the taskmaster; he is a helper and a guide. His business is to suggest and not to impose. He does not actually train the pupil's mind, he only shows him how to perfect his instruments of knowledge and helps him and encourages him in the process. He does not impart knowledge to him, he shows him to acquire the knowledge within; he only shows him where it lies and how it can be habituated to rise to the surface".

Conclusion

Sri Aurobindo says, "The past is our foundation, the present our material, the future our aim and summit. It's God's arrangement that they should be children with the past, possessors of the present and creators of the future". Hence, let the children grow and develop to be worthy citizens of the world.

References

- SRI AUROBINDO AND THE MOTHER ON EDUCATION, published by Sri Aurobindo Ashram, Pondicherry, 1978. Pg. 36 to 54 and 21-22.
- Chaube, S.P., SOME GREAT INDIAN EDUCATORS, Sri Aurobindo, Published by Bharat Publications, Agra, 1957. Pg. 96 to 120.

❖ ❖ ❖

Part-IV

Psychology from Krishnamurti's Teaching

– G. Venkata Mohan

J.Krishnamurti speaks of 'Nirvana' or 'Moksha' in English. There is nothing wrong in instincts and their expression according to him. Sex in itself is not wrong. Without procreation there is no continuity to the life of humanity. He spoke about not having attachment to the mate, possessiveness and jealousy as they cause aggression. Sex and aggression are related. He spoke about not having emotional worries. Worries of the monk, the rich and the poor are not different to him. Monk pursues his own ambition of salvation; the rich pursue their greed for wealth and the poor struggle to satisfy their day-to-day needs. The basic nature of the human beings is the same. What makes a difference is realization of that - 'you are the world'.

Many proposed meditation in which one is to control one's thoughts and concentrate the mind on something. But to Krishnamurti, meditation is not concentration on an object, on an idea, on a symbol but paying attention to what goes on in the mind, even when the mind goes inattentive. He wants us to see who is observing apart from observation. While one is conscious of one's observation that very observation ceases to happen. Nisargadatha and Ramana Maharshi of the twentieth century are the nearest seers to Krishnamurti in this respect. It is not holding onto whatever passes through the mind. It is like not holding the air that is passing through. When one tries to control thought it may be put off for a while, but it becomes stronger due to its suppression. For instance, people promise to give up smoking. But they promise so many a time! Krishnamurti proposes to pay total attention to be aware of it choicelessly, so that there is possibility, in that intensity, to be aware of it.

✍ **G. Venkata Mohan,** *Author and Faculty, UIAS, Delhi.*

To Krishnamurti the problem is the self, its longings and cravings. When one understands the reality of the self as has formed on birth, strengthened on growth and would be ended along with the body on death, then there is the possibility of 'self' not becoming a problem. Biologists appreciate the surviral value of the 'self', the instinct of self-preservation. Krishnamurti is not antagonistic to the preservation of body rather he says that the instrument of body has to be cared enough. He talks about the psychological self, rather emotional self that stands and holds everything to evaluate and judge. He talks about the dissolution of 'self', 'I'. When 'I' is dissolved there is the possibility of enlightenment.

A strikingly unique aspect of Krishnamurti's teaching is his opposition to self-control. Many Indian philosophers insisted on controlling one's thoughts to purify one's mind. Gandhi, for example, advised fasting to control sexual thoughts. Krishnamurti is against such control over thoughts.

Krishnamurti's opposition to self-control extends to his views on meditation. Many view meditation as trying to control thoughts with the goal of having a mind that is under one's control with no unnecessary thoughts. Many propose focusing on some word or breathing to keep away unnecessary thoughts. We can call that meditation, by the method of concentration.

That kind of meditation is what Krishnamurti was opposed to. In his view, meditation should be resistant-free awareness of everything going through the mind. And that awareness is supposed to cleanse the mind of the distractions, that may bring the quietness, and with that the ability to focus.

More radically, the end of the road to such resistance-free awareness is not simply a kind of superior understanding of oneself. Krishnamurti really didn't bother much about the so-called 'self-knowledge'. Rather he wanted an end to all knowledge about one's self.

Knowledge of self is really not very difficult –all reasonably serious introspection only leads us to see in us, craving for sex, success and love and that history of self is history of pleasure and pain recorded. This understanding no doubt makes an individual a better one; but it doesn't give freedom from these processes. This gives no fundamental transformation, in which Krishnamurti is interested.

In this way, Krishnamurti didn't value much self-knowledge, much the way people like Socrates did. Instead, the ending of all knowledge or emptying the mind is what Krishnamurti valued. Obviously, Krishnamurti's proposals are unusual and truly radical. To that extent, it is really difficult to work out their educational implications.

Implications of Krishnamurti's Philosophy to Education

These enlightened people always wanted to educate others about what they found and also encouraged to start schools to educate children differently. Krishnamurti mainly highlighted the relationship between the teacher and students, which is devoid of the quality of authority, so that there is transparency about our concreteness, reactions and feelings. In conversational style so much of openness can be facilitated in relationships. The key here is relationships. When there is space for children and teachers there is freedom of the mind to be aware of any thing.

Then the spirit of inquiry could be such that of 'Prahlada'. When his father wished Prahlada to worship him as God, the mightiest, 'Prahlada' found that his father was not the ultimate. Such must be the inquiry of learners. Schools should produce children like Prahlada. But as of today, there is an ambition-oriented school life. School is a part of the bigger society. School is answerable to the society. Today's spirit is conversion of everything into measurable form. What current is flowing in the society has to be cared by the school and do accordingly. School should know the constraints. School should function within the constraints in the society where it is situated. The teacher has to tell the students what constraints the school has.

However we can be more certain that schools should promote that culture in which feelings and sentiments are freely expressed and understood. Maintaining secrecy and condemnation of 'wrong' is not the way.

If two students fight, the teacher shouldn't lecture on discipline or ideal of cooperative living. That conflict should be brought into open to help both and the others to see the nature of conflict. No sermonizing. Those two students can be encouraged to write a good essay on their conflict. Others can join and give their views.

There should be no effort to end the conflict at the earliest with the idea they should focus on studies. Rather that conflict is the topic for their study; we should let it prolong till the participants are tired of it or they become more curious and excited about something else, say how poor performance affects one's image among the friends and teachers.

Love, hate, conflict, sorrow... are usually regarded as distractions to study. But in a school inspired by Krishnamurti, they are the chapters, along with electricity, magnetism, and cell division. Life is the centre of their learning. It is the highest book for a student. It is not that teachers should appear evolved and students should learn from them. Instead all should be involved and encouraged to understand human problem.

How about the teachers who don't believe in all this? They should be helped to learn in their own way. All this may not lead to any fundamental transformation that Krishnamurti talked about. But it creates appropriate conditions for that, since no transformation is possible without inquiry into the way we live.

J. Krishnamurti's Perception of Intellect, Authority and Intelligence

– G. Yashoda

The idea that teaching every human being to read and write will solve human problems is proved to be false. The so-called educated are not peace loving, integrated people; they too are responsible for the confusion and misery of the world.

The right kind of education is the means to foster an integrated life. Such an education is for the awakening of intelligence, which alone can create a new culture and a peaceful world. To bring about this education we must make a fresh start.

When we hear truth and do not act upon it, it becomes a poison within our selves, and that poison spreads, bringing psychological disturbances and ill health. Only when intelligence is awakened in the individual there is a possibility of a peaceful and happy life. Many of our problems exist in the present, and it is only in the present that they can be solved.

To understand the problem the nearest step is oneself feeling the problem. One is to understand oneself and verify whether his conditioned way of the living is resisting the change, which is inevitable. Human problems are not simple; they are very complex. To understand them requires patience and insight, and it is of the highest importance that we as individuals understand and resolve them for ourselves. Our many problems can be understood and resolved only when we are aware of ourselves as a total process, that is, when we understand our whole psychological makeup, nobody can give us the key to that understanding.

✍ *G. Yashoda,* Asst. Professor, Dept. of EducationA. N. U

For a True Revolution in Human Relationship

If we are to bring about a true revolution in human relationship, which is the basis of all society, there must be a fundamental change in our own values and outlook, but we avoid the necessary and fundamental transformation of ourselves, and try to bring about political revolutions in the world, which always lead to bloodshed and disaster. Whereas, if we apply our minds and hearts to the task of knowing ourselves, we shall undoubtedly solve many of our conflicts and sorrows.

Modern education is making us thoughtless entities; it does very little towards helping us to find our individual vocation. We pass certain examinations and get a job, which means endless routine for the rest of our life. We may dislike our job but we are forced to continue it for the rest of our life. Commitments and responsibilities hold us down, and we are hedged in by our own anxieties and fears.

Whenever ambitions are thwarted we give undue importance to that which should be normal and we develop a psychological twist. Until we have a comprehensive understanding of our life we shall have ever increasing problems in our relationships, leading us to misery and destruction.

Opinion and tradition mold our thoughts and feelings from the tenderest age. The immediate influences and impressions produce an effect which is powerful and lasting and which shapes the whole course of our conscious and unconscious life. Conformity begins in childhood through education and the impact of society. It is what we think that matters, not how we are thinking. When we conform to tradition, we soon become mere copies of what we should be.

Freedom from Authority

Our lives are not just on the surface; their greater part is concealed from casual observation. If we would have our obscure fears come into the open and dissolve, the conscious mind must be somewhat still, and not occupied forever. One of the results of fear is the acceptance of authority in human affairs. Authority is created by our desire to be right, to be secure, to be comfortable, to have no conscious conflicts and disturbances. The wise wield no authority, and those in authority are not wise.

The following of authority is the denial of intelligence. To accept authority is to submit to domination. To subjugate oneself to an individual, to a group or an ideology is the denial not only of intelligence but also of individual freedom. The acceptance of authority may help us temporarily to cover up our difficulties and problems, but to avoid a problem is only to intensify it and in the process self-knowledge and freedom are abandoned.

We worship authority in various forms -knowledge, success, power and so on. We exert authority on the young, and at the same time we are afraid of superior authority. Man himself has no inward vision; outward powers, and position assume vast importance, and then the individual is more and more subject to authority and compulsion; he becomes the instrument of others.

If we can understand the compulsion behind our desire to dominate or to be dominated, then perhaps we can be free from the crippling effects of authority. We crave to be certain, to be right, to be successful, to know, and this desire for certainty, for permanence, builds up within ourselves the authority of personal experience, while outwardly it creates the authority of society, of the family, of religion and so on. The self, the 'me' and the 'mine' is very strong in most of us; sleeping or waking, it is ever alert, always strengthening itself.

Education is to Awaken Intelligence not Intellect

Modern education, in developing the intellect, offers more and more theories and facts, without bringing about the understanding of the total process of human existence. We are highly intellectual; we have developed cunning minds, and caught up in explanations. For understanding of the total process of existence, there must be an integration of the mind and heart in action. Our education cultivates the intellect to be sharp, cunning, and acquisitive and so it plays the most important role in our life. Intelligence is greater than intellect, for it is the integration of reason and love; but there can be intelligence only when there is self-knowledge, the deep understanding of the total process of oneself.

Our attitude towards life, towards our fellow beings can come about only through the right kind of education, which develops right thinking. Self-knowledge is the beginning of freedom, and it is only when we know ourselves that we can bring about order and peace. We can bring about a change in the world of our every day relationships, a fundamental change which will have it's own effect. Individual transformation does affect large groups of people , but only if one is not eager for results. If one thinks in terms of gain and effect, right transformation of oneself is not possible.

References

- Krishnamurti, J. *Education and the Significance of Life*, Chennai: Krishanamurti foundation India. (2000)
- Krishnamurti, J. (1976) Freedom from the Known. Chennai: Krishanamurti foundation India.
- Krishnamurti, J,.(2006) *"the whole moment of life is learning"* England: Krishanamurti foundation trust Ltd.

A Religious Mind is Like Clear Water

– Mubasharah Tahseen

When we look into the history of mankind we find that many battles were fought in the name of religion or religious sect along with the other causes. While every religion is for the good of man and for the liberation of man, why did man attach himself to his religious sect? Is it due to his ignorance or sheer fanaticism? In this context it is puzzling to hear what Krishnamurti of the 20th century says – "development of religious mind is the only solution for the human problem of degeneration".

What is a religious life? The present religions throughout the world seem to be just words, a great deal of belief and faith, years of propaganda, idol worship, symbolic worship and repetitive rituals day after day -that's not surely religion. So, what could we consider a religious life? Who is a religious man? Which type of life is considered a religious life? What is a religious mind?

Talking about something and doing it are quite different things. First of all, one must enquire into what the religious mind is, not what religion is, and also the quality of the mind and the heart that is religious. One can give great many meanings to that word religion, depending on one's conditioning –either accepting emotionally or devotionally or totally denying the whole question of a religious attitude, a religious way of life, as a great many people do. A religious mind is difficult to describe – 'the description can never be the thing described' according to Krishnamurti.

✍ ***Mubasharah Tahseen,*** *M.sc., B.Ed. (M.Ed), St.Joseph's College of Education for Women, Guntur.*

Fearless Mind

Krishnamurti says: "Only the fearless mind is capable of looking at things directly and understanding things immediately". (Krishnamurti. J, 1970-Talk).

A religious mind is not burdened with fear, or seeking out any form of security and pleasure. For a mind that is not burdened with experience it is absolutely necessary to find out what meditation is. Any mind is fearful of going wrong when it is dependent on authority, incapable of standing alone, incapable of understanding and incapable of looking directly. It cannot be sure of doing the right thing. Only the fearless mind is capable of looking at things directly and understanding things immediately. Krishnamurti proposes: "A religious mind is a light to itself". (1995, p.125). Such is the religious mind, because it is light to itself. It's light is not lit by another –the candle that is lit by another can be put out very quickly.

Harmony Leads to Silence

Krishnamurti points out: "Quietness is not a thing to be cultivated, it can happen, it does happen if you are attentive". Krishnamurti 1995,p131

Religious mind has great harmony among the mind, the heart and the body. Obviously there must be complete harmony, because if there is any contradiction, any division, then there is conflict. 'Conflict is the very essence of waste of energy'. Therefore, harmony is necessary so that the mind, the brain, the organism and the depth of the heart are whole, not broken up. Complete harmony means that the mind as well as the organism must be extraordinarily sensitive. The mind, the brain and the body in complete harmony must be silent. Silence of the mind comes naturally, easily, without any effort if we know how to observe, how to look. One looks at a tree, at a cloud, at the light on the water, without judgement. Similarly, we can look at our self without the image, the conclusion, the opinion, etc. In such alert but passive observation, the mind, and the brain become extraordinarily quiet. 'This quietness is not a thing to be cultivated; it can happen, it does happen if you are attentive'. So, silence comes about when there is profound attention, not only at the conscious level but also at the deeper levels of consciousness. And it is not a thing to be practiced –according to Krishnamurti. 'It comes when you have understood the whole structure and the beginning and the living of life'.

The sensitive man cares to live properly. He looks into the routine –to question diet, exercise, how he talks, answers, cares or uncares. Thus he can make himself orderly by looking at the disorder if at all there is. He doesn't create conflict by having the ideal of good behavior, good communication, but looks at his actual behavior, understands it, so that he can overcome if there is any pretension or hypocrisy. Thus he can have cooperating body and mind to go inward.

Religious Mind is Unprejudiced

A religious mind is a mind, which looks at things without prejudice. Krishnamurti further says, 'A mind that is holistic means – A mind which is able to see its own state in relation to the outside'. That is, it sees what is happening outside, and feels not only a sense of responsibility for the condition that exists outside but also the impact of it on its own self. To him, it is "A serious mind which is a mind that is willing to go to the very root of things and discover what is true and what is false". It means 'the complete destruction of what has been, so that the mind is capable of seeing what is true without distortion, with out illusion'.

Religious Mind cannot be in Religious Dogma

Krishnamurti feels "Revolution is synonymous with religion". (Krishnamurti, 1991, p111)

A mind that has broken down, destroyed all the barriers, all the lies, dogma, religion, belief which society has imposed upon it, and gone beyond to discover what is true, is the true religious mind. The religious mind is not the mind that belongs to some church, some belief, and some dogma. These only condition the mind. Going to temple, church, mosque every morning and worshipping this or that does not make us a religious person and respectable though society may accept us as such.

Religion doesn't mean simply believing and worshipping an idol or a symbol or performing rituals. Religion is re-legion which means uniting with the source. If such a state is to be attained, the mind, which is ordinary and performing all the religious activities is not enough. It needs to have total transformation in itself, which is nothing but a total psychological revolution. "The religious mind is capable of thinking precisely, not in terms of the negative and positive, therefore, that mind can hold within it the scientific mind because it is based on time, knowledge, it is rooted in success and achievement". (Krishnamurti. 1961, Bombay talk).

The religious mind is the real revolutionary mind; it is not a reaction to what has been, but it is only when there is seeing of the totality. The innumerable problems of life like the economic and social injustice, the conflicts between man and man, woman and man, the conflict between groups and social divisions, and the division of religions have little meaning. The inward revolution of the mind is necessary to answer all such problems. The religious mind is the only mind to Krishnamurti that can respond totally to the present challenge and to all challenges, at all times. He feels that religious mind is inclusive of a scientific mind.

Living and Dying Every Minute

Krishnamurti describes, "A mind that is alone is completely living and in that living there is dying every minute". (Krishnamurti, 1991, p114).

The mind must be uninfluenced, such a mind is a pure mind, and a pure mind can proceed. Then the brain can function with reason, with sanity, with clarity, inwardly because inwardly it is completely quiet. Biologists say that it has taken millions of years for the brain to develop to its present state and that it will take millions of years to develop further.

Krishnamurti finds "The religious mind does not depend on time for its development". (Krishnamurti, 1991, p115). So, for the religious mind, there is no time. The religious mind has destroyed the authority of the past, the traditions, and the values imposed upon it. Religious mind is the pure mind which is totally alive and attentive to the present because it is capable of dying to the past whether it is minutes past or millions of years of past.

Love and Beauty go together in a Religious Mind

Krishnamurti discovers a different sense of beauty. "A religious mind has that beauty, which is not the mere appreciation of nature, the lovely mountains and the roaring stream –but quite a different sense of beauty, and with it goes love". (Krishnamurti, 1991, p116)

Love doesn't mean jealousy, hate and possessive instincts. If any mind has hatred or jealousy or possessiveness it limits its expression, otherwise love has no limitations. As the fragrance of a flower is smelt by anyone so is love, which is boundless and is experienced by whoever comes into relationship. To Krishnamurti the sense of beauty and love are indivisible. Beauty can only be when there is a passion, which is austere. The religious mind being in this state has a peculiar quality of strength.

Krishnamurti enforces "the religious mind exists if only one has gone so deeply in discovering of oneself". (Krishnamurti, 1991, p117)

To find out what beauty is, and therefore what love is, there must be the understanding of self, the knowing of oneself, the learning about oneself, not according to any pattern, not according to any system, but just learning about oneself as one actually is. So, if one has gone so deeply in discovering his self, then the religious mind does exist and it does not belong to any individual.

The highest form of sensitivity when the brain completely still is the quality of love. We know love is the most extraordinary thing if we have it in our heart. Love is the quality of the mind that is free, sensitive, and intelligent when brain is not responding in terms of the past and is therefore still. Then the heart comes upon this perfume called love. That is the foundation of meditation according to Krishnamurti.

Without Meditation there is no Perfume in Life

According to Krishnamurti "Meditation is emptying of the mind; not only the conscious mind but also all the hidden layers of the mind, which are called unconscious. He also finds that 'the unconscious is as trivial and absurd as the conscious. The wakefulness of the mind sees something, which the conscious mind can never see. So silence is not a thing to be practiced –it comes when you have understood the whole structure and the beginning and the living of life". (Krishnamurti, 1995,p132)

Meditation is a part of life, just as we are going to our office, as we are eating our meals, or we are speaking, or our acting is a part of life. And meditation, being a part of life, is not to be neglected any more than we neglect to clean our teeth, to bathe, to go to our office etc. So, if we pursue self-knowing, we begin to inquire into what we are, our daily activities, the way we talk to our servant, the way of treating a wife or a husband, the way we play up to important people, the everlasting desire to be 'somebody'. Without knowing the whole field of the conscious and the unconscious of our being, do what we will, we will never know what meditation is. "The beginning of meditation is the knowing of our self". (Krishnamurti.J, 2001, p.69)

Generosity is the Beginning of Meditation

"The flowering of meditation is goodness, and the generosity of the heart is the beginning of meditation. The flowering of generosity cannot take place in the arid soil of the mind. The mind can never be generous, but only the heart and the hand. The mind can imagine what the qualities of generosity are and try to cultivate generosity, but the cultivation of generosity is not to be generous". (Krishnamurti J, 2001, p66).

There can be no meditation with out generosity and goodness-, which is to be free from pride, from longing for success and to be famous. It is to die for whatever has been achieved, every minute of the day. It is only in such fertile ground that goodness can grow and flower.

Meditation is the way of life, i.e.; meditating all day, looking, observing, moving, and learning. Through this we can attain a religious mind.

Educational Implications

According to Krishnamurti: A human being is a true human being when the scientific spirit and the true religious spirit go together. The teacher as well as the student must care to develop the religious mind. It means being fearless, free from religious dogma, and fanaticism, being unprejudiced, and being totally attentive to the present. In such a mind are goodness, generosity, love, beauty etc. Discovering oneself or knowing of self is the most important factor, which is nothing but meditation, and it is lagging behind. The spirit of knowing oneself is to be free of all the fixations of mind. It is rather cleansing of the mind. The function of education according to Krishnamurti is the development of two states of mind –the true religious mind and the true scientific mind.

References

- Krishnamurti.J. (2001) *The Nature of New Mind* California: Krishnamurti Foundation of America
- Krishnamurti.J. (1991) *Meeting Life* Hampshire: Krishnamurti Foundation Trust Ltd.
- Krishnamurti.J. (1995) *Beyond Violence* London: Krishnamurti Foundation Trust Ltd.

Depth and Breadth of Human Conditioning from the Teaching of Krishnamurti

– G. Showrilu

Introduction

Human beings are influenced by the society, its culture in which they are born and raised. They are habituated or conditioned to live in certain patterns set up by the society; economic and political pressures also shape them. Society is the outcome of mans relationship with man, which is fairly obvious.

Human Conditioning: External Consequences

Individuals have created the structure of the society throughout the world. The outward social structure is the result of the inward psychological structure of our human relationships, for the individual is the result of the total experience, knowledge and conduct of man. Each one of us is the storehouse of all the past. The individual is the human who is all mankind.

"For centuries we have been conditioned by nationality, caste, class, tradition, religion, language, education, literature, art, custom, convention, propaganda of all kinds, economic pressure, the food we eat, the climate we live in, our family, our friends, our experiences, every influence you can think of and therefore our responses to every problem are conditioned". *Krishnamurti. 1999 p. 25*

When we struggle against any kind of disturbance to defend ourselves against any outer or inner threat, we know that we are conditioned, we are disturbed about life, politics, the economic situation, the horror, the brutality, the sorrow in the world as well as

---

✍ **G. Showrilu,** *Lecturer, St. Paul's College of Education, Giddaluru*

in ourselves, and from that we realize how terribly narrowly conditioned we are. There is a tendency in all of us to put up with things, to get used to them, to blame them on circumstances. "'Ah, if things were right I would be different' we say, or, 'Give me the opportunity and I will fulfill myself,' or, 'I am crushed by the injustice of it all'; always blaming our disturbances on other or on our environment or on the economic situation". Krishnamurti, 1999. p 28:

To understand a fact we must look at it but not run away from it. Most of us are afraid of living as well as of dying. We are afraid of our family, afraid of public opinion, of losing our job, our security and hundreds of other things.

How is one to be Aware of one's Conditioning?

It is possible only by understanding another process, the process of attachment. If we can understand why we are attached, then perhaps we can be aware of our conditioning.

" Just try to be aware of your conditioning; you can only know it indirectly, in relation to something else. You cannot be aware of your conditioning as an abstraction, for then it is merely verbal, without much significance". Krishnamurti,1995, p17.

We are only aware of conflict. Conflict exists when there is no integration between challenge and response. This conflict is the result of our conditioning. Conditioning is attachment; attachment to work, to tradition, to property, to people, to ideas, and so on. We are attached to our country through identification with it we become somebody. We identify ourselves with work, and work becomes important. Like that we are attached to family, property and so on. The object of attachment offers the means of escape from our own emptiness. Attachment is escape, and it is escape that strengthens conditioning. Attachment to our work is our escape. There are escapes at all the levels of our being. One escapes through work, another through drink, another through religious ceremonies, another through knowledge, another through God, and still another is addicted to amusement. All escapes are the same; there is no superior or inferior escape. God and drink are on the same level as long as they are escapes from what we are. When we are aware of our escapes, only then can we know of our conditioning.

Krishnamurti questions us relentlessly

First of all, do you know that you are conditioned? How do you know?

Is it only because somebody has told you that you are conditioned that you know?

Do you see the difference? That is, somebody tells you that you are hungry, that is one thing and to know for yourself that you are altogether different. These two statements are different, aren't they? In the same way, do you know for yourself without somebody telling you that you are conditioned, as a Hindu, a Muslim? Do you know it for yourself? Are you aware that you are conditioned without being told? Do you know what it means to be aware?

When there is a pain in the thumb, you are aware there is pain; nobody tells you there is pain. You know it. Now, in the same way do you know that you are conditioned, conditioned into thinking that you are a Hindu, that you believe in this, that you do not believe in that, that you must go to temple, that you must not go to a temple? Are you aware of it?

Now I am conditioned as a Muslim and you are conditioned as a Hindu, right? We may live in the same street, but because of my conditioning, my belief, my dogma, and you with your belief with your dogma, though we may meet in the same street, we are separate, aren't we?

So where there is separation there must be conflict. Where there are political, economic, social, nationalistic divisions, there must be conflict. So conditioning is the factor of division. Therefore in order to live peacefully in this world, let us be free of conditioning, cease to be Muslim or Hindu. This is the factor of intelligence, becoming aware that one is conditioned, then seeing the effect of that conditioning in the world, the divisions, nationalistic, linguistic and so on, and seeing that where there is division, there is conflict. 'When you see this, when you are aware that you are conditioned, that is the operation of intelligence'.

Creation of Psychological Time

Krishnamurti finds how the individual is caught in his creation of psychological time. Man lives by time. Inventing the future has been a favourite game of escape. Time is deceiver, as it does not do a thing to help us bring about a change in ourselves. Time is a movement, which man has divided into past, present and future, and as long as he divides he is always in conflict. Time being not only chronological time by the watch, as yesterday, today and tomorrow, but also psychological time, the remembrance of yesterday, the pleasures of yesterday, and the pains, the grief and the anxieties of yesterday. The root of fear is time, time to fulfill, time to become, time to achieve, time to realize God, or whatever we like to call it. Psychologically what is time?

"Tomorrow I shall be happy; tomorrow I will achieve something, tomorrow I will become the executive of some business; tomorrow I will become the enlightened one; tomorrow the guru promises something and I'll achieve it". . Krishnamurthi,1995 p 78.

To us tomorrow is tremendously important. And is there a tomorrow psychologically? We have accepted: it is our whole traditional education, that there is a tomorrow. So thought as time, thought as becoming, is the root of fear. Time is necessary to learn any technique. In order to learn about oneself, what one is, what one has to achieve.

One says, "I may be able to get rid of conscious fears, but it is almost impossible to be free of the unconscious fears with their roots in the unconscious". Krishnamurthi 1992 p 79).

We say that it is much more difficult to be free of unconscious fears, that it is the racial fears, the family fears, the tribal fears, the fears that are deeply rooted and instinctive.

Internal Conditioning: Consequences

The problem of FEAR:

"If you can be totally free of fear, then heaven is with you". Krishnamurti 1992 p 72. The human mind has lived for so long, so many, centuries upon centuries, putting up with fear, escaping from it, trying to rationalize it, trying to be together, or completely identifying with something that is not fear. One asks if it is at all possible to be free totally, completely of fear, psychologically. Fear is one of the greatest problems in life. A mind that is caught in fear lives in confusion, in conflict, and therefore must be violent, distorted and aggressive. It dare not move away from its own patterns of thinking, and this breeds hypocrisy. Until we are free from fear, though we climb the highest mountain, invent every kind of God, we will always remain in darkness.

Desire Conditions Us

Krishnamurti leads us to have insight into the problem of desire. Desire is the want of something. That is one fragment of desire. Then there is the longing for something, whether it be social longing or psychological longing or so called spiritual longing. And how does this desire arise?

"Desire is the want of something, the lack of something, missing something; then the longing for it, whether imaginative, or actual want, like hunger; and there is the problem of how desire arises in one". Krishnamurti, 1995 p 73). In coming face to face with fear, we have to understand desire not the denial of desire, but to have insight into desire.

'Desire may be the root of fear'. The religious monk's throughout the world have denied desire, they have resisted desire, they have identified that desire with their gods, with their saviours, with their Jesus, and so on. But it is still desire. And without the full penetration into that desire, without having insight into it, one's mind cannot possibly be free from fear, which is the movement of desire, which is also the movement of thought in time, as time and measure.. Therefore desire arises from this urge to fill that emptiness. 'When you are seeking enlightenment, or self-realization as the Hindus call it, it is a form of desire. This sense of ignorance will be wiped away, or put aside, or dissipated by acquiring tremendous knowledge, enlightment. It is never the process of investigating "what is", but rather of acquiring; not actually looking at "what is", but inviting something which might be, or hopeful of a greater experience, greater knowledge. So we are always avoiding "what is", and the "what is" is created by thought. One's loneliness, emptiness, sorrow, pain, suffering, anxiety, fear, that is actually" what is", And thought is incapable of facing it and tries to move away from it. So in the understanding of desire, that is perception, seeking, contact, sensation, and the want of that, which he has not, and so desire, the longing for it –that involves the whole process of time. 'I have not, but I will have'. So desire is the movement of thought in time as measure.

How can one be Free from Conditioning?

Krishnamurti leads us to go into the whole process of conditioning. Only by understanding, being aware of our escapes, our attachment to a person, to work, to an ideology, is the conditioning factor; this is the thing we have to understand, and not seek a better or more intelligent escape. All escapes are unintelligent, as they inevitably bring about conflict. To cultivate detachment is another from of escape, of isolation; it is attachment to an abstraction, to an ideal called detachment. The ideal is fictitious, ego-made, and becoming the ideal is an escape from 'what is'. There is the understanding of 'what is', an adequate action towards 'what is', only when the mind is no longer seeking any escape. The very thinking about "what is" is an escape from the problem; for thinking is the problem, and the only problem.

The mind, unwilling to be what it is, fearful of what it is, seeks these various escapes; and the way of escape is thought. As long as there is thinking, there must be escapes, attachments, which only strengthen conditioning. Freedom from conditioning comes with the freedom from thinking. When the mind is utterly still, only then is there freedom for the real to be. If we can actually free ourselves from fear, not theoretically, not ideally, not merely outwardly but actually, inwardly, deeply, then we can be different human beings. Then we can become the coming generation. The older people are ridden with fear –fear of death, fear of losing jobs, fear of public opinion. They are completely held in the grip of fear. So their gods, their scriptures, their puja, are all within the field of fear and therefore the mind is curiously wrapped, perverted. Such a mind cannot think straight, cannot reason logically, sanely, healthily, because it is rooted in fear.

'Watch the older generation and you will see how fearful it is of everything –of death, of disease, of going against the current of tradition, of being different, of being new.

Life at Reality Level

Everything that thought has put together is reality. This tent in which we meet has been put together by thought; it is a reality. The tree has not been put together by thought; but it is a reality. Illusions are reality –the illusions that one has, imagination, all that is reality. And the action from those illusions is neurotic, which is also reality. So when one asks this question. 'What is right livelihood', one must understand what reality is. 'Reality is not Truth'.

Now what is correct action in this reality? And how will we discover what is right in this reality? We are to discover for ourselves, not be told. So we have to find out what accurate, correct, right action, or right livelihood is in the world of reality, and reality includes illusion. 'Don't escape, don't move away' Belief is an illusion, and the activities of belief are neurotic; nationalism and all the rest of it are another form of reality, but an illusion. So taking all that as reality, what is the right action there? We all want to achieve truth, whatever that is. And all these paths lead to that. That means truth is fixed. It must be, otherwise there would be no path to it. It must be stationary, it must have no movement, it must be dead. Then there can be paths to it.

References

- Krishnamuri, J. (1999). Freedom from the Known. Chennai: KFI.
- Krishnamuri, J. (1998). On Education. Chennai: KFI.
- Krishnamuri, J. (2006). On Truth. Chennai: KFI.
- Krishnamuri, J. (1995). Truth and Actuality. Chennai: KFI.
- Krishnamuri, J. (2000). Commentaries on Living Second Series. Chennai: KFI.

❖ ❖ ❖

Nature: Human Nature

– G. Sasikala

"Mind is the pivotal point to the orderly functioning of Nature".

A Mantra from EsoUpanishad.Ranganadhananda (1992), p-132.

Nature is so fascinating. The lushy green forests, hills, the beautiful birds, the bewildering varieties of animals, insects, pests, tiny and invisible microorganisms, the magnificent mountains, the great rivers, the oceans and seas with all biota, the blue lagoons and lakes, marvelous reservoir of underground wealth, water and minerals, sky and many more constitute Nature. Nature has embedded in itself the beautiful, varied living functions. As can the knowledge goes till date, among the nine planets of the solar system, mother Earth is the only known Cosmos that sustains life with all the components of nature. We, the humanbeings, live on the mother earth in nature, which is aesthetically enjoyable and functionally helpful in all aspects of life.

Design with Nature

Man's living in following the concept of design with nature is not new in the Indian context. Nature, the embodiment of the spirit of the creator is admired, adored and worshipped by poets, aesthetists, sages and seers since ages. It is true that it all started from time immemorial. All our scriptures glorified each and every component of nature as gods and godesses that created a feeling of reverence towards nature. Most of the rituals say that would help in the conservation of nature and natural resources.

The following extracts from Vedas in translation prove it:

✍ **G. Sasikala,** *Lecturer, St. Joseph's College of Education for Women, Guntur.*

Earth's Inhabitants

The earth is not the races of men alone but for other creatures also.

Born of these, on thee move-mortal creatures,
Thou bearest them-the biped and the quadruped;
Thine, O Earth, are the five races of men, to
Whom mortals, Surya (Sun) as he rises spreads
With his rays the light that is immortal. (A.XII,1,15)

Earth's Variety

The earth does not belong to a single race, but to the different races, speaking different languages.

May the Earth that bears people speaking varied languages, with various religious rites according to the place of abode.

Enrich me wealth in a thousand streams,
Like a milch-cow that never fails. (A.XII.1,45)

In Hindu Dharma, Aadibhootha, the five primary elements of nature are given a place. During the earliest formative period of the society, human beings perceived the nature as the manifestation of an almighty creator called Brahman. So, to please the creator, they felt that one should live in harmony with his creation including earth, rivers, forests, mountains, sun, air etc. This belief spawned many rituals that are still followed in Hinduism in India.

The Jainism preaches that even the smallest of the small living beings (Jeevas) should be given protection and should not be hurt. Mahaveer preaches "Live and Let Live". It means that along with the human beings the other living beings are also having the equal right to live. Therefore every human being should protect every other living being.

Buddhists find that consumerism and the other ways of living are the fundamental causes of destruction of nature. Buddha points out that for all the limitations, our ancestors were aware of the need for harmony between human beings and nature; they loved their environment and revered it as a source of life and well-being.

Maharatnakuta Sutra points out "Dwelling in the forest is a spiritual path related to the nature". In Buddhism, right views, right action, right livselihood, right mindfulness, right effort etc; bring out ecological vision that has compelling relevance for our own time. The concept of 'ahimsa' (non-violence) in Buddhism and Jainism ensures due respect to all forms of life.

According to the Holy Sikh book, the Guru Granth Sahib, humans are formed from five elements of nature that teach us and give us power during the time of the personality development.

The Earth teaches us Patience and Love

The Air teaches us Mobility and Liberty

Fire teaches us Warmth and Courage

Sky teaches us Liveliness and Broadmindedness

Water teaches us Cleanliness and Purity.

Environmental Consciousness is not a new concept for Indians, which is evident from the account of rulers, historians, visitors, rock and pillar edicts etc. In Kautilya's Arthasastra it was stated 'the stability of an empire is dependant upon the stability of its environment'. Dr.A.V.V.S.Swamy (1998) p-14.

Rabindranath Tagore established his schools Shantiniketan (abode of peace), amidst nature (trees, plants, flowers, birds, animals, small muddy huts) all over the world for educating about the components of nature.

Human beings' Dominating Nature

Ancient man identified himself as part of our nature, lived as one among the various components. But because of his superior mental faculties, he started dominating all other living species and used several of them for his comforts. In this pursuit, man slowly alienated himself from nature.

Since the dawn of evolution of man on earth, he has been trying to evolve newer ways of survival. His basic philosophy had been one of the harmony with nature is in sharp contrast to the present concept of conquest of nature. If man's intellectual mind is responsible for all the so-called progress, his arrogant mind and lack of wisdom to live in harmony with nature are responsible for all the harmful effects of the nature, which we call 'pollution' in all possible means. He deserves praise for converting wild forests into parks, gardens, orchards and cities, in his attempts to make life more and more comfortable. But his thoughtless destruction of forests accelerated soil erosion, decline in soil fertility, increased global warming that leads to drought conditions, melting of icecaps, flooding that results in famine etc. Out of man's greed, desperation, short sightedness, ignorance and selfishness he had been using all the natural resources without conserving in the name of industrialisation, urbanisation, globalisation etc. and causing the ecological crises. Now it has become a serious global problem with all kinds of pollution that affects health too.

Moreover in the background of growing violence, terrorism, rebellious fights in the society and corruption, human relationships are turning unhygienic. Religious, linguistic, caste, political and communal conflicts are increasing along with the polluted air, water, atmosphere and polluted human minds. Thought pollution is predominating endlessly. In this context, we can recall Gandhiji for what he has told about nature, i.e; "Nature has given us enough to meet every man's need, but not for his greed."

If the mind is getting polluted, who can take care of the mind?

Why is the mind failing to keep the relationships with nature?

Man's inward disorder brings about the outward structure of disorder. Modern man tends to pursue pleasure constantly, the pleasure of possession, of domination, the pleasure of money that gives power and so on. He is ambitious, proud of his belongings, his fame and achievements. He acts egoistically narrowing the whole of this vast life into little 'me' and causing every sort of disorder. If that 'me' feels the responsibility towards the co-existing beings in the form of tree or animals, there remain no complaints but caring of each and every thing that he comes in touch with. Is it possible!

With this disorder of egoistic 'me', man is becoming very very poor at maintaining relations with the other and is becoming more mechanical in his living. In familial, social, occupational and political spheres, human relationships are very much disturbed. Jiddu Krishnamurti, the world-renowned philosopher, says, "Life is a movement in relationship". Dr.G.Aruna (1998), p-194. Man cannot live by himself. Humanity exists in relationships. But man is failing in his relations with the fellow beings and nature. When we realise this reality and when we live with concern for all, then only we can develop relationships in life; otherwise the mental pollution reflects on the environment outside. Our culture is addicted to nature-disconnected 'progress' and 'economics' that is sensitively exploiting our fellow beings and the nature.

How can we be sensitive by seeing and feeling the nature, that hightens the sensitivity, that silences the mind to deepen the feeling for others according to Krishnamurti?

Retreat in the Lap of Nature

Nature is a source of happiness to man and his happiness will be hightened if he learns to love and appreciate nature, its various phenomena and its systematic functioning. Nature is always in order. It becomes disordered only when the human beings interfere with it. The whole inner nature is disturbed and reflects the same outside. The question of what can be done to prevent or reverse the escalation of the dominating patterns, is therefore of enormous urgency.

According to Krishnamurti, Nature is the solitary tree in the field, the meadows and the grove, it is that squirrel shyly hiding behind a bough. Nature is the ant and the bee and all the living things of the earth. Nature is the river, not a particular river, Whether the Ganga, The Thames or Mississippi. Nature is all those mountains, snow-clad, with the dark blue valleys and range of hills meeting the sea. The Universe is part of this world. One must have a feeling for all this, not destroy it, not kill for one's pleasure. So one must intelligently discern.

Nature is part of our life. He turns our hearts to have a feeling for the tree, to look at it, see the beauty of it, listen to the sound it makes, be sensitive to the little plant, to the little weed, to that creeper that is growing up the wall, to the light on the leaves and the many shadows. One must be aware of this and have that sense of communion with nature around us. We may live in a town but we do have trees here and there. A flower in the next garden may be ill-kept, crowded with weeds, but look at it, feel that we are part of all that, part of all living things. 'If we hurt nature, we are hurting ourself'. One knows all this has been said before in different ways but we don't seem to pay much attention. Is it that we are so caught up in our network of problems, our own desires, our own urges of pleasure and pain that we never look around, never watch the moon? If we watch it, with all our eyes and ears, our sense of smell; if we look as though we are looking for the first time; if we can do that, that tree, that bush , that blade of grass as though we are seeing for the first time, then we can see our teacher, our mother and father, our brother and sister, for the first time. There is an extraordinary feeling about that, the wonder, the strangeness, the miracle of a fresh morning that has never been before, never will be. Be really in the communion with nature, not verbally caught in the description of it, but be a part of it, be aware and feel that we belong to all that, be able to have love for all that, to admire a deer, the lizard on the wall, that broken branch lying on the ground. It is to look at the evening star or the new moon, without the word, without merely saying how beautiful it is and turning our back on it, attracted by something else, but watch the single star and new delicate moon as though for the first time. If there is such a communion between us and nature, then we can commune with man, with the boy sitting next with our educator, or with our parents. We have lost all sense of relationship in which there is not only a verbal statement of affection and concern, but also this sense of communion, which is not verbal. It is a sense that we are all together that we are all human beings, not divided, not broken up, not belonging to any particular group or race, or to some idealistic concepts, but belong to the extraordinary beautiful earth.

The Greatest Possible Rest to the Mind is Silence

Man's inward observation, his understanding of responsibility to the present day calamities and urgency to come out of them, his observation of his mind, the contradictory desires and the conflicts exhausting his energy, the ideals and ambitions making him greedy, the images about others and about him, are turning him competitive, aggressive, uncertain and selfish; his blindness to his fragmenting approaches, his longing for pleasure, his false pursuits of security and so on are to become part and parcel of his knowing. The answer to all these catastrophies is to do something with the mind.

The mind indulges in various activities, which are sometimes excessive and often incoherent. This creates a great stress, which leads to fatigue and diminution of all the intellectual faculties. The fact is that like all other parts of the body, the mind too needs rest and it will not have this rest unless we know how to provide it. The art of resting one's mind is something to be acquired. Changing one's mental activity is certainly the way of resting, but the greatest possible rest is silence. And as far as the mental faculties are concerned a few minutes passed in the calm of silence are a more effective rest than hours of sleep. Mind must be very clear. It happens through observation of the sunlight reflecting on the dew drops, the sound of the breeze, the soft green leaf moving gently, the bird singing hidden in a mango groove, all are so enchanting and enthralling.

There must be the observation of the outer silently which take a course of looking into the self or inner that sharpens the brain and helps in flowering of knowing oneself with clarity. That clarity is stability, that clarity can then examine any problem. Without this clarity, the mind is confused, contradictory, broken up, it is unstable, neurotic, seeking, striving, and struggling. Therefore mind with clarity is extraordinarily stable and yet pliable. When the mind is silent, even the most violent external storm cannot disturb us. It is based on a process of separating our consciousness from the spell of the mind through the discipline of observation.

The Bhagavadgita says that the true yogin, whatever may be his outerlife, has an innerlife, is really what constitutes the true life of a man. Sri Aurobindo said that evolution requires that the light from the soul should illumine our inner being and through it our outer being.

It is clear with Tagore, that the joyous realisation of the self is possible through the profound interaction of man and nature.

For Krishnamurti, Nature's appeal is in the silence that resonates between him and the nature. "When there is silence of the mind, action springs from it and this action does not cause confusion and misery". (The Only Revolution p31). Silence is a metaphor for egolessness or desirelessness -the state of annihilated mind. Hence time and again it is mentioned in the scriptures, Silence is very essential through which one can link with his true nature, the pure self. According to Sri Ramana Maharshi "The more you get fixed in the self, the more other thoughts will dropoff of themselves. The mind is nothing but a bundle of thoughts, and the 'I' thought is the root of all of them. When you see who this 'I' is and find out where it comes from, all thoughts get merged in the self".

That stillness is very active, very alert, very watchful, intensive and passive to enquire and such a mind asks a question, it has validity, vitality, significance and depth in knowing oneself and also about how the nature functions in cooperation.

When the mind is quiet, it can see and hear much more, see things as they are. It is not to invent or imagine but to perceive directly as in our relationship with other beings, things or events and ideas, which fall into an order that brings humility. This self-knowldge is the beginning of transformation or regeneration. This seed of transformation in one-self, our own self is the maker of our own destiny.

Educational Implications

We can understand from Brihadaranyaka Upanishad that says: "We are what our deep driving desire is. As our deep driving desire is, so is our will. As our will, so is our deed. As our deed is, so is our destiny". Dr. Aruna (2006), p-133.

As educators can we realize the existence and co-existence, dependence and interdependence, relationship and interrelationship with all the components of nature?

Can we convey the same to our students? We and our students are to be sensitive and feel for the co-beings whether with living systems like air, water, light, temperature etc; or living beings like tree, bird, lion, and the like. Can we see the depth of Krishnamurti's proposition "If you establish a relationship with nature, then you have relationship with mankind." Krishnamurti (1983), p-9.

This is not a sentiment or romantic imagination but a reality of a relationship with everything that lives and moves on the earth. "If you could establish a deep, abiding relationship with nature, we could find ways to heal our bodies. Healing of the mind also gradually takes place, if we are with nature." Krishnamurti (1983), p.10. Nature is the supreme beauty; Man is joyous in the context of nature. One must feel that the world, the world of nature, the world of man are inter-related. Man cannot escape from that. When he destroys nature, he is destroying himself. To live in such harmony with nature, with the world, naturally brings about a different world and makes living blissful.

Can we impress upon our students, the significant role of the world of nature, which is intricately interwoven with the world of man?

Can we care to see that the destruction of nature is nothing but the destruction of ourselves?

Once white people said that they have difficulty in understanding the Indian way of looking at the world. The Indian replied: "It is easy. You only have to remember two things. One is, everything in the Universe is alive. The other is, we are all relatives. The bear, the deer, the eagle, these are our brothers. The rocky crests, the juices in the meadow, the body heat of the pony, and the man, all belong to the same family. We teach our children that the earth is our mother. What befalls the earth befalls all the sons of the earth."

On understanding such an inevitable relation between the Nature and Human nature, can we live in harmony with the Nature around and with the world of human beings?

References

- Sasikala(2006). Being to Well-being-An ethical consideration towards Environment. Vijaya Bharathi and Vanaja (eds.), Value-oriented education, p.160, Hyderabad, Neelkamal publications.
- NCTE(1999), Sri Aurobindo On Education.

- Lalith Kumar Jain (2006). Jainism and Value-oriented Education In Vijaya Bharathi and Vanaja (eds.), Value-oriented education, p. 40, Hyderabad, Neelkamal publications.
- Aruna Mohan. G. (2006). The Value of Mind as the way of Truth, The Absolute value. In Vijaya Bharathi and Vanaja (eds.), Value-oriented education, p. 133, Hyderabad, Neelkamal publications.
- Sarma, V.B.B. (1998). Environmental Education Curricular changes. In Ramesh Ghanta and D. Bhaskara Rao (Ed.), Environment and it's Problems, p.123-124, New Delhi, Discovery Publishing House, .
- Aruna.G (1998). The Man inside is the environment out side. In Ramesh Ghanta and D.Bhaskara Rao (Ed.), Environment and it's problems, p.190-191 &193-196, New Delhi, Discovery Publishing House.
- Krishnamurti (1998), Krishnamurti to Himself His Last journal, Chennai, Krishnamurti Foundation India .
- Swami Ranganadhananda (1992). Upanishathula Sandesam, Hyderabad, Ramakrishna Mission.
- Krishnamurti, Meeting Life, Chennai, Krishnamurti Foundation India.
- Krishnamurti, Letters to schools – 1st Nov,1983, pg.no.70-73, Chennai,Krishnamurti Foundation India.
- Krishnamurti, Letters to Schools – 25th Feb, 1983, Chennai, Krishnamurti Foundation India.
- Maitra S.K.(1965), An Introduction to the Philosophy of Aurobindo, Pondicherry, Sri Aurobindo Ashram.
- Krishnamurti (1998). Only Revolution, Page-31 is taken from World Future-1998 Vol.251, pg-239-267, Green Earth Foundation, Ralph Metzner, EI Verano, CA-95433.
- Dr. Michael J.Cohen, Director, Organic Advanced Ecopsychology in Action, Natural systems in Action- Thinking Process, Institute of Global Education. http:/ www.eco.psycho.com.
- Krishnamurti (2001). The Nature of the new mind. Chennai, KFI.

❖ ❖ ❖

Development of Integrated Individual from the Perspective of J. Krishnamurti

– A. Srinivasa Murthy

Education is for preparing children for life, a life that is pain, joy, beauty, ugliness and love. When we understand child as a whole, at every level, that understanding creates its own technique while educating children.

Present day education appears to be a failure because it has overemphasized this technique. In overemphasizing a technique we destroy man. To cultivate capacity and efficiency without understanding life, without having a comprehensive perception of the ways of thought and desire, will only make us increasingly ruthless, which results in wars and jeopardizes our physical security. The exclusive cultivation of technique has produced scientists, mathematicians, bridge builders, and space conquerors but do they understand the total process of life?

The greatest need and most pressing problem for every individual is to have an integrated comprehension of life, which will enable him to meet its everincreasing complexities.

Education is for Understanding Oneself

Education has become only a matter of accumulating information, and knowledge from books, which anyone who can read can do. Such education offers a subtle form of escape from ourselves and, like all escapes it inevitably increases misery.

For Krishnamurti the ignorant man is not the unlearned, but he who does not know himself, and the learned man is stupid when

✍ ***A. Srinivasa Murthy,*** *Lecturer, Nova College of Education, Ibrahimpatnam, Vijayawada.*

he relies on books, on knowledge and on authority to give him understanding.

"It seems to me that without understanding the way our minds work, one cannot understand and resolve the very complex problems of living." Understanding comes only through self-knowledge, which is awareness of one's total psychological process. This education, in the true sense, is the understanding of oneself for it is within each one of us that the whole of existence is gathered. Without understanding ourselves, mere occupation leads to frustration with its inevitable escapes through all kinds of mischievous activities.

Buddha also said that our life is shaped by our mind; we become what we think. Suffering follows an evil thought. Joy follows a pure thought like a shade that never leaves. The mind is the only instrument we have, the instrument with which we think, we act, in which we have our being. If we do not understand that mind in operation as it is functioning in each one of us, any problem that we are confronted with will become more complex and more destructive. So it seems to understand one's mind is the first essential function of all education. According to Krishnamurti, it is essential that education should, above all, help the individual to understand his own psychological process.

Teacher in Educating the Child

The right kind of education consists in understanding the child as he is without imposing upon him an ideal of what we think he should be. If the teacher is of the right kind, he will not depend on a method, but will study each individual. In his relationship with children and young people, he is not dealing with mechanical devices that can be quickly repaired, but with living beings that are impressionable, volatile, sensitive and affectionate; and to deal with them, he has to have great understanding, the strength of patience and love. When he lacks these, he looks for quick and easy remedies and hopes for marvelous and automatic results. Even teachers feel confident with teaching techniques ignoring the lively learners. Krishnamurti says that the caring teacher gives proper place for any technique without giving all the place.

The highest function of education to him is to bring about an integrated individual who is capable of dealing with life as a whole. Life cannot be made to conform to a system; it cannot be forced into a framework, however nobly conceived and a mind that has merely been trained in factual knowledge is incapable of meeting with its variety, its subtlety, its depths and great heights. When we train our children according to a system of thought or a particular discipline, when we teach them to think within departmental divisions, we prevent them from growing into integrated men and women, and therefore they are incapable of thinking intelligently, which is to meet life as a whole.

Education, at present, in no way encourages the understanding of the inherited tendencies and environmental influences which condition the mind and heart and sustain fear, and therefore it does not help the learners to break through the conditioning and bring about an integrated human being. Any form of education that concerns itself with a part and not with the whole of man inevitably leads to increasing conflict and suffering.

If the teacher demands respect from his pupils and has very little from them, it will obviously cause indifference and disrespect on their part. Without respect for human life, knowledge only leads to destruction and misery. The cultivation of respect for others is an essential part of right education, but if the educator himself lacks this quality, he cannot help his students in an integrated life.

Rightkind of Freedom

The right kind of educator, seeing the inward nature of freedom, helps each individual student to observe and understand his own self-projected values and impositions; he helps him to become aware of how his conditioning and his own desires influence him. Both of them limit his mind and breed fear. Education helps the student to observe and understand himself in relation to all things.

Freedom can never come through discipline and through resistance. Discipline is an easy way to control a child, but it does not help him to understand the problems involved in living. Some form of compulsion, the discipline of punishment and reward, may be necessary to maintain order and quietness among a large number of students herded together in a classroom.

"Freedom is not a goal, an end to be achieved. Freedom is at the beginning, not at the end, it is not to be found in some distant ideal". *(Krishnamurti, 2000.P:31).*

Freedom does not mean the opportunity for self-gratification or the setting aside of consideration for others. The teacher who is sincere will project the children and help them in every possible way to grow towards the right kind of freedom; but it will be impossible for him to do this if he himself is addicted to an ideology, if he is in any way dogmatic or self-seeking.

There can be no compromises with freedom. Partial freedom for the individual is no freedom at all. Conditioning of any kind, whether cultural, political or religious, is not freedom.

Freedom from Fear

As long as success is our goal we cannot be rid of fear for the desire to succeed inevitably breeds the fear of failure. That is why the young should not be taught to worship success.

Krishnamurti shows the nature of life as follows: "Life is a well of deep waters. One can come to it with small buckets and draw only a little water, or one can come with large vessels, drawing plentiful waters that will nourish and sustain". While one is young it is the time to investigate, and experiment with everything. The school should help its young people to discover their vocations and responsibilities, and not merely cram their minds with facts and technical knowledge; it should be the soil in which they can grow without fear, happily and integrally.

Teaching should not become a specialist's profession. When it does, as is so often the case, love fades away; and love is essential to the process of integration.

To educate a child is to help him to understand freedom and integration. To have freedom there must be order, which virtue alone can give; and integration can take place only when there is great simplicity.

Fearlessness brings independence without ruthlessness, without contempt for another and this is the most essential factor in life. Without love we cannot work among conflicting problems, without love the acquisition of knowledge only increases confusion and leads to self- destruction.

Right Relationship

The purpose of education is to cultivate right relationship, not only between individuals, but also between the individual and society. The right kind of education will encourage thoughtfulness and consideration for others without enticements or threats of any kind.

If we are to have right relationship between human beings there should be no compulsion or even persuasion. How can there be affection and genuine cooperation between those who are in power and those who are subject to power? The real problem in education is the educator. Even a small group of students becomes the instrument of his personal importance if he uses authority as a means of his own release, and if teaching is for him a self-expansive fulfillment.

To understand a child, a teacher has to watch him at play, study him in his different moods; he cannot project upon him his own prejudices, hopes and fears or mould him to fit the pattern of his desires. If he is constantly judging the child according to his personal likes and dislikes, he is bound to create barriers and hindrances in his relationship with him and in his relationships with the world.

Where there is love there is consideration, not only for the children but also for every human being.

References

- Krishnamurti, J. (2000), Education and the significance of life, Chennai: Krishnamurti foundation.
- Krishnamurti, J. (2003), What are you doing with your life? Chennai: Krishnamurti Foundation.
- Krishnamurti, J. (1992), The collected works of Krishnamurti: Kendall – Hunt.
- Krishnamurti, J. (1989), Think on these things, Chennai: Krishnamurti foundation.
- Narada Thera, (1993), The Dhammapada, secunderabad: The corporate body of the Buddha Educational foundation.

❖ ❖ ❖

Promotive and Destructive Factors of Integrated Human Being

– ***Sr.Santha***

We, the human beings are the result of evolution through millions of years. The human being has inherited animal instincts like aggression, violence and hatred. He also has love, concern, compassion and unity.

What is LIFE all about? *The human being is greatly affected by the conflicts of life, the physical disasters, the fear of death, the mental twists, miseries and inward struggles. The reason for all this may be*, the society in which we live, and the culture in which we are brought up, which influences the entire nation and conditions everybody. Life has become a threat to man's own existence. At this stage an attempt is made through education to wipe away the ugly thinking of man, with the help of self-knowledge, which is the beginning of wisdom.

Jiddu Krishanamurti's view on education is broad in its perspective "The highest function of education is to bring about an integrated individual who is capable of dealing with life as a whole". K (2000) P.25.This is only possible when man is holistic in his approaches and understands the deep-rooted conditioned mind. This can be possible only when he cares to know about the inner world apart from the outer world. Self-knowing only makes him understand and be free of his conditioning to relate rightly with anything and everything.

'Self-knowledge is self-discovery.' Through self-knowledge alone the learner discovers truth. This cannot be learnt through a

✍ **Sr. Santha,** *Lecturer in Psychology, St. Joseph's College of Education for Women, Guntur.*

book or through another. It is to be aware of the conscious and unconscious process of learner's thoughts, feelings and activities. To transform oneself, self-knowledge is essential because without knowing what an individual is, there is no basis for right thought. Without knowing oneself there cannot be transformation. So it is very essential to *be aware of one's mental and emotional activities that are going on.*

Krishnamurti rightly expresses "Self-knowledge is the understanding of the process of oneself, the process of the mind; it is to be aware of all the intricacies of the passions and their pursuits, and as one knows oneself more and more deeply and widely, extensively and profoundly, there comes a freedom, liberation from the entanglements of fear." K (2006) P 44.

But it seems that the learner is having many obstacles in his journey into himself. Krishnamurti observes and exposes the following obstacles, which actually prevent the integrated development of the human being. Some of them are: Conflict, sorrow, violence, cruelty, fear, comparison, competition, authority, conditioned mind, anger, jealousy etc.

Destructive Factors of Integrated Human Being

Fear

JK finds *"fear is the heavy burden which man has always carried."*

Both the older and younger generations live with fear. There are many varieties of fear, the immediate fear and the fears of many tomorrows. Franklin Roosevelt warned, "The *only thing we have to fear is fear itself.*" It is part of human tradition to accept fear. From the highest person to the lowest is frightened and held in the grip of fear. The function of education to Krishnamurti is to eliminate fear. Because fear in any form *cripples the mind, destroys sensitivity and kills the inner abilities and shrinks the senses.* From this fear arise various forms of superstitions. It destroys the nature of relationships between human beings. It dominates progress and freedom.

Fear is found to be one of the barriers even to intelligent actions and prevents the flowering of mind and goodness. The fearful man is insensitive to himself, to his own sorrows, to the movement of the birds, to the smiles and miseries of others and to whatever is going on around him. What does fear do? It makes the learner's mind dull, curbs his initiative and destroys his flame of good qualities like generosity, affection and love. It destroys intelligence and prevents the learner from examining, questioning, and inquiring, preventing him from finding out what is true.

Krishnamurti expresses, "the understanding of fear comes through self-knowledge not through resistance to fear" K (2006) p 49. So it is the responsibility of every teacher to understand the cause of fear and help the child to overcome it.

According to Krishnamurti, the highest function of education is to help the learner, from childhood to be completely free of fear so that when he goes into the world he will be an intelligent human being full of real initiative. A learner can learn a new thing only when there is no fear. He has to free himself from fear, not theoretically, and merely outwardly but actually inwardly and deeply; then he can become a different human being and flower into an integrated human being.

Learner learns mostly when he is not frightened, not threatened by authority and not competing with his neighbour. So the right kind of education should help the individual to know what fear is and how fear comes into being and how it destroys the integration of the human being. When the learner knows and understands fear it goes away.

Responsibility of educators is to help the child understand the sources of fear through self-knowledge. Creativeness comes only when there is no fear and when the mind is not occupied with its own problems. This is possible only in an atmosphere of freedom, *freedom means not doing whatever one likes, but free to question, to investigate, to find out and to reason*. To be free requires a great deal of intelligence and this intelligence cannot be there when the learner is frightened. All this requires a great deal of thinking and that is real education.

Comparison

Another form of conditioning pointed out by Krishnamurti is comparison.

Having the past knowledge one compares oneself with what one thinks, noble or heroic with what one would like to be as opposed to what one is. The entire schooling system depends on comparison. Assessments that teachers make of children are comparative. Most thoughtful people would surely accept that comparison is destructive and certainly should not have a place in education.

Krishnamurti explains, 'The better is the outcome of comparison'. He says that *comparison is dangerous and competition is disastrous*. This is really a fact, a great truth that every teacher and parent must realize. No two children should ever be compared; each child is an individual with his unique personality and characteristic beauty. Surely one cannot compare lilies and daffodils. Some say that competition is healthy. But competition in its nature has disintegrity. Krishnamurti says when there is no comparison, there is integrity; when there is measurement, there is a fragmentation.

What does Comparison do?

It brings dissatisfaction in the life of an individual and destroys his initiative. He feels himself inferior and the feeling of indifference and isolation steps in. When A is compared with B he feels angry and irritated at once. He develops jealously over B and develops enmity or A can have only B as his goal and intends to overdo B without understanding whereever he is not up to the mark. Thus he fails to understand the reality in him. He is emotionally led by the ideal of surpassing B, which may or may not be possible. If he probes into the fact of him he can really surpass his limitations. Comparison hinders the spontaneity of the learner and he may become rebellious towards the teacher. Comparative mind is the most stupid mind and stops thinking and no longer has it investigated to find out what is true.

The responsibility of every teacher is to identify the uniqueness of a person and help him to flower in his total development. Teach him to act as he is, without wearing a mask.

Competition

Krishnamurti says competition exists only when there is comparison. Where as the field of education is full of competition and teachers and parents indulge in comparison. Competition is essentially selfish and promotes excessive self-regard to the exclusion of the legitimate rights of others. It promotes secrecy, greed, trick and hatred. It is the most widely prevalent spirit of the day and we can see this in every individual from the school to the business magnet. Wiggin's comments "Competition destroys the communal aspect of interpersonal interaction and destroys the most important of the distinctly human qualities."

Our education system implicitly and often crudely assumes that fear and anxiety are part of the price our children need to pay to be educated. Several common pracitices in schools seem to provoke anxiety in the students. Among them are the insidious role of examinations, comparative methods of assessment, very little true learning due to the comparative grading and competition. Furthermore the teacher in the classroom is still an object of fear and authority in many schools.

What does Competition do?

It destroys the relationship and mutual understanding among students and real learning will not take place when the learner has this attitude. . He develops the attitude of rivalry and will never be quiet in his mind as it distracts. He may not be able to do any creative and productive work and fails to live a happy and peaceful life. It brings a lot of harm to the individual when expected result doesn't come. It creates jealousy and the individual undergoes a lot of mental stress. The individual never likes to have failure in life but always likes to win. In a competitive society the individual cannot have the feeling of brotherhood and no reformation can be brought about.

Promotive Factors of an Integrated Human Being

Besides Krishnamurti explored the nature of mind in its pristine quality and proposed to care for it. He expressed many promotive aspects for the development of an integrated human being.

Some of them are: love, goodness, sensitivity, freedom, intelligence, self-knowledge etc.

The responsibility of every teacher is to identify the natural capacities of the learner and try to motivate him to develop in the natural settings with the attitude of awareness.

Love

'LIFE IS LOVE'. Krishnamurti says, "Love exists only when there is no self"

Krishnamurti expects that one must have the feeling of being wholly concerned and committed to the environment around, nature and totally responsible for one's actions. This absolute care is Love. Then love is not conditioned for a particular group, community or for a particular deity but for all mankind. Love has no cause. When love is taken as pleasure, then man has cut himself off from beauty and the sacredness of life. It is not an achievement. Humility is the essence of love and intelligence.

Love is the total responsibility. The Bible speaks, 'If I speak in the tongues of men and of angels but have not love I am only a resounding gong or a clanging symbol'. Love is a natural instinct of every human being. Jerrold said 'It is a beautiful necessity of our nature to love something.' The Bible says, 'Knowledge puffs up but love builds up'.

Love is like an opening to beauty. When love exists all other qualities will follow. Krishnamurti also says, "Love is the natural fragrance of nature. It gives itself abundantly as a flower gives its perfume' (2000) 10.

Gandhi felt that the only true religion of man is the religion of love. He believed to see the universal and all prevailing spirit of truth face to face one must be able to love the nearest of creation as oneself. Thus his love attains the form of universal love. If a person has this loving nature, that person gets peace of mind.

Krishnamurti says,' Without this love there can be no change in the society.' So the responsibility of every teacher and the parent is to show love to the students and thus teachers can develop the feeling of integrity in the students. The quality of love brings humility, gentleness, consideration, patience, and courtesy. Possessing all these qualities the learner can blossom and spread that fragrance of love to everyone.

Goodness

Krishnamurti says *Goodness has no opposite.* Many people consider goodness has opposite like bad or evil. Throughout history in any culture goodness has been so considered. Man has struggled against evil in order to be good. But goodness can never come into existence if there is any form of violence or struggle. Many people think that goodness will come out of struggle and violence. But it is not, instead it harms and gives pain to other human beings and disturbs the relationships. Elder Hubbard expressed "Do not be disturbed about saving your soul it will be saved if you make it worth saving. Do your work. Think always good, and evil can be swallowed by good. Think no evil and if you think only good, you will think no evil". If one can think there is no evil, he will freely move with his neighbor without any fear and he can develop a good relationship.

Goodness shows itself in behavior and this behavior is based on sensitivity. This goodness can be expressed in action. The flowering of goodness does not lie in knowing mathematics and biology or in passing exams and having a successful career. One must bear in mind constantly that 'freedom is essential for the beauty of goodness.' We must become aware of our actions, thoughts and feelings in everyday life so that goodness may flower and blossom and release one's total energy. Goodness cannot flower in the field of fear. It can flower only in freedom. If freedom is lacking he never experiences the feeling of goodness. He may only do some good habitually, which is taught by his elders.

The right kind of education helps the educators and the students to flower in goodness. Krishnamurti says, "Goodness shows itself in ones behavior in relationship." More important is, not making the child technologically proficient, but creation of the right climate in the school for the child to develop fully as a complete human being. This means giving him the opportunity to flower in goodness so that he is rightly related to people, things and ideas and to the whole of his life. It is very much necessary to encourage the development of a good mind in the children –a mind that is capable of dealing with many issues of life as a whole.

Sensitivity

According to Krishnamurti, '*Sensitivity is not the thing to capture but to grasp*'.

Krishnamurti explains that in the very perception one can be sensitive. There is no resistance in sensitivity. It is immediate and limitless. He expects everyone to be sensitive to nature, to hills, to rivers and the trees around one, and 'to be sensitive to the man who is sitting next to you.' This sensitivity has in it no choice, no complaint and it is not critical. If the educator is concerned with this, he is helping the student to become sensitive to other people's sorrows, struggles, anxieties and worries. 'Beauty is supreme sensitivity not to the sense of one's own pains and anxieties, but in encompassing the whole existence of man.' Beauty brings pleasant thoughts to the mind. Inspiration comes when we are open to beauty. Beauty and action are inseparable from man's life. Awareness implies sensitivity. The very nature of intelligence is sensitivity and this sensitivity is love to Krishnamurti.

When the learner becomes the only importance, sensitivity fades away and then the teacher shall really lose contact with the learner. To teach mathematics or how to run a computer is not the only responsibility of the teacher. Far more important is to have communion with other human beings who suffer, struggle with great pain and the sorrow of poverty.

Krishnamurti says,' *Diligence has the quality of sensitivity*'. The word diligence implies care, watchfulness, observation and sense of freedom. Sensitivity creates desire to know others sufferings. Diligence is not self-centered watchfulness, but to be sensitive to all relationships. Diligence is to be aware of reactions to the world outside and to the inner whispering responses.

Educational Implications

Holistic education is more concerned with the cultivation of latent capacities rather than stuffing the young minds with lots of information. It is education that prepares young people to live purposefully, creatively and morally in a complex world. It brings a sense of great responsibility for things connected with human beings, how one behaves, relates with others and things. Krishnamurti says, 'you're the world and your relationship with another is society' so that the students develop as the citizens of the world rather than as nationalists.

Holistic education is possible when the teacher and learner are ready to inquire, to discover and to think about their acquired knowledge of the outer world and also aware of themselves. Such an education prepares the child in totality to live in peace with themselves and with the people around and the world at large, so that they exercise the natural capacities, observe and overcome various fears, jealousy, envy, anger, aggression, anxiety etc. that prevent the flowering of mind. The right kind of education can therefore help the individual to face his problems and lead a happy and peaceful life.

Psychologically, the individual human being is inseparable from the whole of mankind. His goodness, responsibility, relationship and love are associated with life of humanity as a whole.

Teachers are to allow the child to examine what happens in his life, perhaps every problem, every incident, every thought and every emotion, which helps him to be aware of his doings. As a teacher we can examine all these problems not superficially or casually but more and more deeply so that the mind is free to be creative, free to think and free to love. As a teacher we can help our learner to do what he loves to do and not get stuck in something unnatural and irrelevant, which makes his life miserable for the rest of his life.

We are to provide an atmosphere of freedom to the child to flower and blossom into an integrated human being. We are also to create an atmosphere to be aware of his inner self and attune to the workings of the mind. It is impossible to realize the worth of what Krishnamurti says, about the function of education, 'to bring a mind that will not only act in the immediate but go beyond, a mind that is extraordinarily alive not with knowledge, not with experience but alive'. So the function of educators is surely freeing the mind to function in freedom without any twist, without any corruption.

References

- Krishnamurti, J (1992) Education and the Significance of Life. Chennai: KFI.
- Krishnamurti, J (2001) Talks with Students: Varanasi 1954. Chennai: KFI.
- Aruna Mohan, G (2003) Consciousness. New Delhi: Neelkaml Publications.
- Krishnamurti, J (2000) Life Ahead, Chennai: KFI
- Krishnamurti, J (2008) Self Knowledge, Chennai: KFI
- Krishnamurti, J (1997) Letters to Schools. Vol. I Chennai: KFI
- Krishnamurti, J (1996) Letters to Schools. Vol. II chennai: KFI

Psychological Health in J. Krishnamurti's Perspective

– J. Padmavathi

In the world there is an astounding advance in science and technology on one side and war, poverty, violence, mental pollution on the other side. It is obvious that one has undergone a lot of struggle to develop outwardly, totally neglecting the inward nature. Many eminent sages explore their own ways of knowledge through examples and experiences. But the teachings of the world teacher, J.Krishnamurthi are remarkable for their depth, clarity and vastness. His perception is simple and direct. He explored deeper and wider the application of natural faculties of one's mind.

Most of our lives are routine from childhood. Throughout our lives we never try to look inward. We never question how the anxieties, fear and agony are disturbing our psychological health. The contents of our consciousness are desires, senses, feelings, past experiences, memories, ambitions, greed, anxiety, shame, fears, thoughts and emotions. J.Krishnamurti says " The uniqueness of the individual does not lie in the superficial but in the total freedom from the content of consciousness 2001". When we do not understand these contents properly we become psychologically ill. To live happily, a harmonious development of mind and heart in oneself is essential. J. Krishnamurti wants us not only to understand the cause for ill health but also its removal. He says "Disease has a cause and until the cause is removed there cannot be good health .The dissolution of the cause is not a matter of health but of immediate perception. (1998, p. 17)

✍ ***J. Padmavathi,*** *PGT English, APR School (Urdu Minority Girls), Vijayawada.*

Envy Leads to Violence

When we watch all our actions sometimes we are found craving for more and more. In this craving we compare with others. The moment we compare, envy comes into being, envious of somebody, another's capacity, and prestige or physical personality. This envy begins in a small way and then grows into a stream of action in which jealousy, greed, anxiety and fear come into being. All these actions lead to violence.

Attachment to Desire Causes Conflict

To satisfy our daily needs desire must be there. A desire to go to space needs enormous technical knowledge but that is limited Psychologically when man is haunted by desire then the problem of conflict begins. If we do not understand the place of desire, it brings about degeneration of the mind.

Krishnamutrti warns us saying that there are both psychological and physical sensory activities, the body seeks warmth, food, sex; these sensations are natural but when they enter into psychological field the problem begins.

"I must have and I must have not". This contradiction itself leads to confusion. One is to do if there is necessity and not to change it, respecting what one wanted. If the learner is learning ambitiously, the very nature of ambition itself intervenes in his studies. The role of the teacher is to make him understand the nature of the ambition destroying the joy of learning.

Psychological Hurts become Wounds

In daily life psychological hurts are common. When a man is hurt he thinks 'I am hurt. I don't want to be hurt in future and is thus caught up in these opposites. Consequently it becomes a psychological wound. It is comparatively easy to deal with the physical pain but to understand the hidden psychological wounds is difficult. With the lack of inward looking the wound itself builds a wall around to escape pain and when unwatched it consequently leads to ill health.

Imaginary Fears Cause Psychological Ill Health

When we see a snake or placed in any dangerous situation we are afraid. In fact it is natural and factual. But most of us have specific psychological fears. We have many imaginary fears, like fear of teacher, parents, water, death or devil, of being left alone, losing property, having no prestige, position, fear of wanting something, fear of particular situation. Sometimes it comes into being while we are travelling in a train or walking that some disaster may happen.

Sometimes we are afraid from the stories we listen and the imaginations that we gather, by watching incidents that those images begin to work which hinder perception. If any of these fears are experienced again and again they become a habit unconsciously, such a fear is called phobia. We come across such neurotic behaviors.

Conflict in Relationship Creates Psychological Pain

We have relationship with members of the family, neighbors, friends and with nature. But many a time these relationships are not harmonious whether with the family members or strangers. But these relationships are between the images. Mostly we have misunderstandings due to the images.

These build a wall of continuous resistance and create distortions of the mind. This leads to false relations and attachment due to psychological dependence, dominance and possessiveness. This is because of inward psychological insufficiency which gives rise to fear of loss of close relationships. Being fearful we long to be secure emotionally, and mentally. Then for security we maintain dependence. Sometimes we adjust in relationships but it merely intensifies struggle.

When we are attached, there is a pride of position or fear of losing; therefore jealousy, and anxiety come up. For most of us love means a terrible conflict between human beings. So relationship becomes a perpetual anxiety. To be free of attachment doesn't mean its opposite -detachment. When we are attached we know the pain of detachment and anxiety of it. Then we say 'I must detach myself', so the battle of detachment begins.

When there are right relationships among students and teacher there is mutual cooperation, friendliness and understanding and learning is meaningful.

The Suppressed Anger Leaves a Mark

Sometimes one may think that he is more intelligent than all others; then the image has already been formed about himself psychologically. If anybody calls him a fool, anger comes into being which hurts his image.

Then he begins to think that he has to take revenge against the one who has hurt. The whole energy is being directed towards that person, to take action. There is suppression of emotions and reactions.

But whenever we meet that person the image of anger comes again. When we remain in that state of anger partially, it leaves a mark which itself is memory. When we conclude that we should not be angry it creates further conflict.

When we observe the state of anger completely with full attention the whole process of image itself reveals everything and we can be free from it. If teachers and students are learning in peaceful physical and psychological environment, students become confident and good human beings. The teacher is to help himself and the students to understand the consequences of separation.

Suffering Develops Resistance

We suffer as we have with in us the contradiction of desires, one desire trying to dominate another. The majority of us try to escape from suffering through illusions, rituals or god, interests entrusted in social activity. We may escape temporarily but there is suffering which has been lingering in the mind and hinders the understanding of itself.

When we make an effort to come out of it, to get rid of it, a wall of resistance is there. Suffering is inherent in the very nature of that effort. Suffering is still there as long as one does not totally comprehend the process of desire. J.Krishnamurthi warns us " The mind that wants to change or improve itself will always remain mediocre however great its effort". (1999, p. 105.)

Man is Suffering from Ambition

When we want to achieve something or become some thing we are caught up in constant struggle. When the state of mind is always seeking result the important thing is achieving result but not the thing we do in itself. Ambition always tortures the mind. The momement we are thwarted and prevented from carrying out our ambition we fall ill. When our mind is occupied with success of becoming something it never understands the present state of mind. J.Krishnamurti warns us, "You love yourself and not what you are doing". (p.73)

To come out of all these J.Krishnamurti teaches us:

- To watch oneself that brings about understanding of the nature of jealousy or fear and also freedom from them.
- To watch the mind constantly with care and concern directly.
- When a man is hurt, it is not to carry it day by day, but finish it then and there only by understanding in complete attention which tells its story.
- By watching and by knowing the things associated with fear, they are wiped out.
- To understand this problem of relationship requires patience and pliability of mind and heart. When we observe deeply without the burden of yesterday or judgment or acceptance or rejection then out of the total observation a different kind of movement comes in to being.
- If we observe deeply and directly every movement of the mind with out denial, accepting or rejecting slowly the mind becomes silent. In that state of silence things connected with suffering are understood and the mind is free.
- J.Krishnamurti spoke of the need to understand oneself as one is, to look into oneself in relation to others. Then there is the possibility to understand and face the world as it is. 'If you really faced the world as it is and tackled it you would find in it something infinitely greater than any philosophy, greater than any book in the world, greater than any teaching, greater than any teacher'.

- If students and teachers are learning in peaceful physical and psychological environment, free from psychological habits, comparison and competition, various fears and conflicts, then there is right relationship, mutual cooperation, friendliness and understanding, and meaningful learning. Then, there comes a different kind of creative human beings.

References

- Krishnamurti, J. (1974). On Education. London: KF Trust limited.
- Krishnamurti, J. (2001). Talks with Students. Varanasi: Krishnamurthi KFI.
- Krishnamurti, J. (2000) On the Teachings. California: KF Trust Ltd.,
- Krishnamurti, J. (1999). The Revolution from With in. Chennai: KFI.
- Krishnamurti, J. (1983). A Flame of Attention. London : KFI Ltd.
- Krishnamurti, J. Bulletin June 1991. Chennai: KFI Ltd.
- Krishnamurti, J. (1998). On Transformation of Man. Sahyadri: KFI Education Centre.

Care for the Caring Nature of the Child

– J. R.Priyadarsini

"Life is like a river, never still, always moving, always alive and rich, we all have to prepare for it" -Krishnamurti

Fortunately when we are young most of us are not yet on the battlefield of life. But as we grow older, the problems, the miseries, the doubts, the economic and internal struggles all begin to crowd in on us and then we want to find out the significance of life; we want to know what life is all about.

When the children are young, they are sensitive, active, alive, and full of curiosity and imagination. When an atmosphere, where they are given every opportunity to grow uninfluenced, unconditioned, untaught, is provided when they grow older they can meet life intelligently without fear and solve the problems of their life. Such an atmosphere is lacking today.

Parents pack off their kids who are just three to kindergarten and then for the next fourteen years it is the same routine. At school, they learn to read and write, learn different subjects, learn discipline and perhaps may discover their interests and talents. "Is it the only thing to care?" Krishnamurti questioned.

According to Krishnamurti the pursuit of knowledge does not liberate man from his ignorance. We should look at, observe, feel and care for everything around us. When children are young they can really observe, feel and care for every thing. Krisnamurti says "When you do not feel everything now itself when you are young, alive, then when you grow you notice nothing."

✍ ***J. R. Priyadarsini,*** *Lecturer in Mathematics, St.Joseph's College of Education for Women, Guntur.*

What it is to feel, to look, to watch, to observe and to care?

To watch the river, to look at the moon for a long time, to feel the movement of the tree, to hear the breeze in the morning among the leaves, to see a bird –how it flies, how delicate its wings are and yet how extraordinarily strong they must be to support it through a storm etc. demand a great deal of feeling.

To hear, not the technique, not the repetition over and over again of a particular note, but a song sung really well by someone with a full heart and who does not care whether anyone is listening or not, to listen to the call of a bird in the morning and to listen to the fisherman across the river calling, makes one very very sensitive –it makes one truly alive.

It is also very important for everyone to have feeling about our lives i.e. the way we dress, the way we sit, the way we play games, how we talk to our servant, how people treat us, etc. It is possible only when the children are young. But when they grow up all the emotions would have been destroyed and they have no strong feeling about anything.

Krishnamurti cared deeply for children. He gave many talks and also had personal interaction with the young by visiting schools and answering their questions. His intention was to help the young understand and deal with the world within themselves i.e. the world of hurts, fears, pleasures, ambitions, success, failures and so on. Krishnamurti felt that one should observe and feel about everything around us and should have care and concern towards them. But most of us have very little feeling about any thing. We can feel and care about small things because caring leads to real affection and love. Caring is really a part of love, a profound feeling.

Love is Absolute Care

"Love is absolute care which brings change in the society" says Krishnamurti.

We should care everything around us i.e. the birds, the plants and trees, the poor people, the dirty roads and cows that have no shelter, the dogs that are hungry, diseased etc. We care when we look after a pet animal, when we keep our clothes in order, taking care of the plants we plant. Krishnamurti says that caring begins with the caring of little things. It should begin right from the early childhood of the child because when he grows up he has to live a life with speed, strain, stress and anxiety and all the feelings of sensitivity may probably disappear.

To have real affection for people, one must not only look and listen but also care. Caring means looking after others, being kind to them and not treating cruelly.

To see everything as it is, is quite an art. It is difficult to see things as they are, as it is. When we go out for a walk we really do not see the squalor and misery of the poor, the filth on the road and the diseased dogs. If we began to see all this we would do something about it and that is beauty of seeing. Seeing is action. If we see, if we observe, if we listen we cannot but act. But most of us are blind, so we do not act.

Responsibility of Teachers and Parents in Developing Caring Nature in the Child

Though by profession we are teachers, we should not forget that we are human beings. As a human being with a special profession of education, the teacher's life is not only the classroom but is involved with the whole outer world as well as inner struggles, ambitions and relationships.

The communication of knowledge is not the only function of the teacher. But surely a teacher has far greater responsibility than this. He must be concerned with behaviour, with the human complexity of action, with a way of life, which is the flowering of goodness. When the relationship between the teacher and the student has this element of companionship of mutual understanding then humility, sensitivity and affection are natural. A teacher might say all this is impossible.

Nature is part of our life. We grew out of the seed, the earth, and we are part of all that but we are rapidly losing that sense. Far more important is to have communion with other human beings who suffer, struggle and have great pain and the sorrow of poverty and with those people who go by in a rich car.

If the teacher is concerned with this he is helping the student to become sensitive to other people's sorrows, other people's struggles, anxieties and worries. It is the responsibility of the teacher to educate the children to have such communion with the world. This brings about natural consideration, affection for others, courtesy and behaviour that is not rough, cruel, and vulgar.

"Train up a child in the way he should go, And when he is old he will not depart from it." *—Holy Bible-Proverbs:22:6*

The teachers and parents must deeply understand, feel that the total responsibility is to develop love for all mankind and without this love there can be no change in the society. Without love, life is like a shallow pool. In a deep river there is richness and many fish can live, but the shallow pool is soon dried up by the strong sun, and nothing remains except mud and dirt. For most of us, love is an extraordinarily difficult thing to understand because our lives are very shallow.

If there is love there would be no wars, no starvation, no class differences, no fears, no rich and no poor. If we try to reform a society without love in our hearts, we cannot bring about a social structure free of conflict and misery. According to Krishnamurthi any feeling which is accomplished by a sense of gratitude, emotional dependence, sense of owning, sense of possessing someone, sense of comparison etc is not real love i.e anything with selfish motive is not love. But giving without expecting, helping wholeheartedly, having real feeling, concern and caring is real love.

'The fullest development of every individual creates a society of equals'. Equality is not in terms of economic level or social status or some spiritual level .With right education, there is no need to seek equality through social and other reforms, because envy with its comparison ceases. Therefore only through right education and total development of the human being a radical transformation of the mind is possible. This is easy when the child is young and it is the function of not a single person but it is the joint responsibility of the parents, teachers and society to develop this absolute care in the minds of the small ones so that their sensitivity allows them to perceive essential, which is intelligence.

Educational Implications

Right education, thus, is development of caring nature in the children; feeling of responsibility; self-awareness that brings orderliness; concern for everything in the surrounding; concern for everyone; feeling of sensitivity; real affection and love and taking the things as they are. Development of free mind gives scope for the communion with the entire world. The fullest development of every individual is to be cared by the teachers.

References

- Krishnamurti. J. (1987) Letters to the schools-Volume one, Chennai, Krishnamurti Foundation, India.
- Krishnamurti. J. (1996) Letters to the schools-Volume Two, Chennai, Krishnamurti Foundation, India.
- Krishnamurti. J. (2004) Life Ahead, Chennai, Krishnamurti Foundation India.
- Krishnamurti. J. (2004) 'What is it to care?' California, Krishnamurti Foundation America.
- Krishnamurti. J. (2002) 'Why are you being educated' - England.: Krishnamurti Foundation Trust.

Learner cannot Flower in the Field of Fear

– Kezia. A

Fear is a feeling inside us. It is very important to understand fear. Students experience innumerable fears -fear of the parent, of the teacher, of an older student, examinations and failure, the fear of being alone or the fear of natural phenomena and so on. Krishnamurti proposes, "The mind must know why it is afraid, is fear something apart from the mind? Does not the mind itself create fear, either because it remembers the past or it projects itself into the future". (Krishnamurti, 2004 p.17).

One has to understand how the mind creates fear. There is no such thing as fear except what the mind itself creates. The mind wants shelter and wants security. The mind has various forms of self-protective ambitions. But as long as the mind wants to be not fearful it is having fear. It is very important to understand ambition, to understand authority; both are indications of this fear, which is so destructive.

Krishnamurti says, "The central issue is understanding the nature and structure of fear by facing it. To face it is not through the screen of words but to observe the very happening of fear without being away from it, a moment away from it confounds the fact of fear. Our tradition and our education encourage control, acceptance or denial or very clever rationalization". (Krishnamurti, 2006 p.16). Fear is something, which exists in relation to something else. It doesn't exist by itself. If exists in relation to a snake, to what parents or teachers might say, to death, it is in connection with something. Fear is not a thing by itself. It exists in contact, in relation, in touch

✍ **Kezia. A,** *M.Ed. Student St. Joseph's College of Education for Women, Guntur.*

with something else. In the field of fear there are many varieties, the immediate fears and the fears of many tomorrows.

Fear is not a concept, but the explanations of fear are conceptual and vary from one pundit to another or from one intellectual to another. The explanation is not important; what is important is facing the fact of fear. Fear is the heavy burden which man has always carried.

We have to see our own fear; simply we have to observe the fear not only with intellect but also with the actual eye. Krishnamurti says, "Fear is a very complex business, as ancient as the hills, ancient as human kind. If we allow fear to tell it's ancient story, listen to it attentively without interference, for it is telling you the history of your own fear. When we listen we can discover that the fear is not separate from us". He further says, " Facing the fact of fear without any movement of thought is the ending of fear. We must know the art of listening; there is a great beauty in that listening, there is only listening and the story does not exist" (Krishnamurti, 2006, p.17).

To be free we must first know that we get frightened and secondly we must not run away from it. We must not escape from fear, but look at it; we have to face it. It is like examining a bird –the shape of its wings, its legs, its beak. We must go very close to it. Similarly if we are afraid, we must look very closely at our fear. When we run away from it we only increase our fear.

Causes of Fear

Why are we afraid of public opinion? We want to look alike, dress alike, we do not want to be even slightly different. We want to conform and accept the pattern; when we begin to question the pattern there is fear. Krishnamurti speaks on how comparison is one of the causes of fears. When one teacher or parent compares us with a clever boy or with somebody else fear begins in us. Our whole society is based on comparison. We think comparison is necessary for growth. So we compare ourself with another and say 'well I must beat him, I must be better than him.'

"When teacher compares us with another who is perhaps a little cleverer it raises in us envy and jealousy. Jealousy is the beginning of fear. We start struggling to become like somebody else. In that struggle is born envy and fear………" (Krishnamurti. 2004, pp11 to 12).

According to Krishnamurti there are some causes. We, human beings are cruel people. Among the animals the stronger destroys the weaker and that is what we also do in human society. The strong man pushes out his chest and beats everybody and the weaker one gets angry with the still weaker. For this very simple reason we want to do it. If we are beaten by a big man, we want to take it out on the little man. The desire to hurt is very strong in us. We want to hurt people. There is pleasure in hurting people, in saying cruel things and ugly things and in belittling them. We rarely speak of people with kindness, and speak of their goodness but always talk with a sneer. That is what has to be understood. Fear is not separate from pleasure.

Outcomes of Fear

Fear restricts the capacity of thought. From this fear arise various forms of superstition -religious, scientific and imaginary. One lives in a make-believe world and the essence of the conceptual world is born of fear. . "Obedience is born of fear - Fear of going wrong. Fear breeds authority, resistance and aggression" (Krishnamurti. 2006, p.211).

If one has fear, there can be no initiative in doing something original, to do spontaneously, naturally without being guided, forced and controlled. We have to be free from fear. If there is fear then one cannot take initiative anywhere, he becomes insensitive and does not observe what is going around to respond spontaneously.

Fear conditions the mind; we are unconsciously conditioned by the past. "This conditioning is the result of many centuries of fear, anxiety, conflict and the search for security both inwardly and outwardly, both biologically and psychologically" (Krishnamurti. 2006, p.151). Most of our images have been built by thousands of years of thought of fear. The self-centredness increased throughout the world because of fears, pleasures and anxieties. 'Goodness cannot exist where there is fear'. It cannot flower in the field of fear. Tyrannical governments and tyrannical parents have tried to establish order through fear and punishment. Mind cannot flower in the field of fear. It only flowers in freedom and order.

"Order cann't possibly exist when there is fear. Fear and disorder go together. The social structure, in which we live, by its very nature, produces this disorder. It is this disorder that we are frightened of and we cultivate morality to overcome this fear. So, our so-called morality is no more than adjustment to disorder" (krishnamurti. 2006, p 219).

Role of Educator in Dealing with Fear

Education is the real cultivation of human mind, for the flowering or the total unfoldment and cultivation of our minds, our hearts and physical being. When the mind, the heart and body are in complete harmony, the flowering comes naturally. The educator has the responsibility to see that the children are free of fear because fear in any form cripples the mind, destroys sensitivity and shrinks the senses.

Teacher has to point out these acts of cruelty and animosity in the pupils; he has to initiate everyone to watch all the things that are taking place about us and around us, how chickens fight with each other, how the strong bulldog dominates everything else. Then he has to make us find that the same spirit of domination, anger, hatred, and animosity is in each one of us. Krishnamurti points out that to dispel this we have only to be aware of it, and not consider it as wrong or right. It is not at all difficult; rather it is easier than academic subjects. So the students are to give time to see how their mind works, how it operates and responds and it is very important to begin to understand their own mind while they are young. Otherwise they grow up with fear, without taking any initiative and so turn imitative.

Krishnamurti advises teachers by saying, "If there is any kind of fear in the relationship of teacher and student, then the educator cannot possibly help the student to be free of it. The student comes from a background of fear of authority of all kinds of fanciful and actual impressions and pressures. The educator too has his own pressures and fears. He will not be able to bring about understanding of the nature of fear if he has not uncovered the root of his own fears.

He must be free of his own fears in order to help the student to be free. The teacher can point out that he himself is afraid, if he is as the student; in conversation, they can together explore the whole nature and structure of fear. It is not a confessional aspect or a fact of emotional or personal emphasis. It can be in the spirit of a conversation between good friends. It requires a certain honesty and humility" (Krishnamurti 2006, pp 11,12).

References

- Krishnamurti. J., (2006) *"The whole moment of life is learning"* England: Krishnamurti Foundation Trust Ltd.,.
- Krishnamurti. J, (2004) "*What does fear do to you*" England: Krishnamurti Foundation Trust Ltd.,

Need for Self-Knowledge Apart from Knowledge from the Perspective of J. Krishnamurti

– *Sr. Kochuthresia*

What is Knowledge?

Knowledge is the process of converting data into meaningful information and actually acting on such information. Every person is just gathering pebbles on the seashore of knowledge. In this sense knowing what to know is just as important as knowing. Man's mind can be compared to a garden, which if not cultivated properly gets destroyed by waves of impure and useless thoughts. Like any other living creature, we all need to eat in order to survive. With appropriate knowledge tastes and skills, knowing can be a joyous experience. Through conscious involvement, many of our mundane and routine activities can be converted into expressions of art.

What we call education is a matter of accumulating information and knowledge from books, which anyone who can read can do. Such education offers a subtle form of escape from our selves and it inevitably creates increasing misery. Children come to school, learn some technique by which they can eventually earn a livelihood and secure economic position.

Another factor in the cultivation of technique is that it gives us a sense of security, not only economic, but psychological as well. It is reassuring to know that we are capable and efficient. When we establish for ourselves psychological zones of safety in the form of systems, techniques and beliefs, we are seeking inward security. Then the total process of life cannot be understood. It is necessary to know how to read and write, and to learn engineering or some other

✍ **Sr. Kochuthresia,** *K. K. Research Scholar, ANU.*

profession. But will technique give us the capacity to understand life? The question here is, does the cultivation of a technique enable us to understand ourselves?

Krishnamurti says that life is pain, joy, beauty, ugliness, love, and when we understand it as a whole, at every level, that understanding creates its own technique. To him the ignorant man is not the unlearned, but he who does not know himself, and the learned man is stupid when he relies on books, on knowledge and on authority to give him understanding. Understanding comes only through self-knowledge, which is awareness of one's total psychological process. Thus education, in the true sense, is the understanding of oneself, for it is within each one of us that the whole of existence is gathered.

Hence he says right education comes with the transformation of ourselves. We must learn to be compassionate, to be content with little and to seek the Supreme for only then can there be the true salvation of mankind. The right form of education, while encouraging the learning of a technique, should help man to experience the integrated process of life. Education in the true sense is helping the individual to be mature and free, to flower greatly in love and goodness. This can come true only through self-knowledge.

What is Self-knowledge?

Light is the best protection against thieves; sunlight is considered the best disinfectant. Similarly knowledge and self-knowledge are our best defenses against the confusions of life. Self-knowledge is the beginning of freedom, and it is only when we know ourselves that we can bring about order and peace in us.

Krishnamurti says, "Without knowing yourself, do what you will, there cannot possibly be the state of meditation. I mean by "self-knowing", knowing every thought, every mood, every word, every feeling... And merely to try to meditate without first establishing deeply, irrevocably, that virtue which comes about through self-knowing is utterly deceptive and absolutely useless."

What is the Significance of Self knowledge?

At the dawn of the third millennium the Education Commission led by UNESCO affirmed that "education has a fundamental role to play in personal and social development' as one of the principal means available to foster a deeper and more harmonious form of human development and thereby to reduce poverty, exclusion, ignorance, oppression and war". Jacques Delors, P13

When we look at the present scenario the outward progress seems to open any number of opportunities but complicating the very living. Man is amidst all the marvels of the progressing science and technology, but is not at ease with his neighbour. His excellent abilities to measure and calculate are weighing whether there is any benefit in any of their relationships or not; his rich abilities to think, reason and imagine are invested in his activities to beat out the other; his memory abilities to store up the ill feelings, fears, hurts, failures that keep up aggression, prejudice and revenge. The well-developed cognitive capacities are invested to generate negative emotions, negative thoughts and negative actions. It is high time to critically examine the very saying, 'knowledge is wisdom'. Is this, the knowledge of academic subjects? Or any other sort of knowledge?

The Education Commission of UNESCO points out that education is to enable "each person to grasp the individuality of other people and to understand the world's erratic progression towards a certain unity, but its process must begin with self-understanding through an inner voyage whose milestones are knowledge, meditation and the practice of self-criticism". Jacques Delors, P19.

Need for Self-knowledge

We understand how the life is becoming superficial due to the kind of living interims of the immediate. Living such an empty life and shallow life we are always trying to fill with cars, books, sex, drink, more clothes or trying to escape into more beliefs, more gods, more dogmas, more authoritarian attitudes, and more cricket. Education, hence, is to take the totality of life. Lack of place to self-knowledge, perhaps is the reason behind the lack of long vision about the totality of life. Krishnamurti points out: “Ignorance is this unawareness of the whole structure and nature of the mind, the brain, and of all its movement, that is the very essence of ignorance. You learn from books and from your professors, pass examinations, get a few degrees and get a job - that is nothing, that is necessary in this mad world, but to be totally aware of the extraordinary movement, the beauty, the ability, the quickness of all that inward movement; to be unconscious, to be unaware of it is not only ignorance, it brings its own destruction”. Krishnamurti, 12. P39

Acquisition of knowledge of various things -literary, scientific, technological, sociological and economic knowledge are obviously necessary to acquire a job, to keep up the job by performing well. Man is doing extraordinary things, fantastic technological advancement; is able to meet the world, nature and its storms; going to the moon and beyond with such knowledge. But we have not inquired into the whole field of man's ignorance. Ignorance is utter disregard and utter neglect of the complicated and extraordinarily subtle, psychological world. Krishnamurti finds that the outward crisis in any form in any field mostly is due to crisis in the human consciousness. It needs a fundamental revolution, inward revolution that affects the outer.

So we should not disregard the inner, because the inner demands, the inner urges, appetites, drives, and compulsions change the outer -the outer form, the outward expression and outward morality. As of today education is considering the outer and neglecting the inner. We are not to neglect the outer in considering the inner. It means though we change the outer with new laws, new structures of society, new economic and social conditions; without understanding the inner nature of our own selves we do not solve our problems. The little order brought by outer changes will be destroyed by our inner demands, greed and fear, which may even bring out total perversion of the human mind. Hence it is very important to inquire into understanding the inner i.e., learning the inner.

How to Gain Self-knowledge?

Meditation is Silence that Comes in Self-knowing

"You will find that all the barriers drop away where you yourself are beginning to listen, to observe, to find out. There is no reason for removing the barriers; and the moment you bring in a reason, you are not removing them. The miracle, the greatest blessing is to give your own inward perception an opportunity to remove the barriers".Krishnamurti, 7, P133

When we want to remove the barriers and practice it that is the work of the mind. The mind, which created the barriers, cannot remove. No attempt on its part can remove them. Then the mind becomes silent, quiet, very still, and in that stillness the barriers drop away without leaving a residue. This self-awareness is meditation. Meditation begins in self-knowing. When one knows oneself as one is, without the accumulating centre, out of that self-knowing comes intelligence, which can meet life, and that intelligence is creative. So, what is important is to understand our psychological dependence in relationship. It is in uncovering the hidden things of the heart and mind, in understanding our own loneliness, and emptiness, there is freedom, not from relationship, but from psychological dependence, which causes conflict, misery, pain and fear.

"Thought is the response of memory accumulated through various experiences, real or imagined, which are stored as knowledge in the brain".

Krishnamurti Says "In a world of vast organizations, vast mobilizations of people, mass movements, we are afraid to act on a small scale; we are afraid to be little people clearing up our own patch… and the small scale is the "me" and the "you". When I understand myself, I understand you, and out of that understanding comes love."

Krishnamurti further says, "Awareness of this whole process, both the conscious and the hidden, is meditation; and through this meditation the self, with its desires and conflicts, is transcended. Self-knowledge is necessary if one is to be free of the influences and values that give shelter to the self; and in this freedom alone is there creation, Truth, God, or what you will".

What's the outcome of self-knowledge?

- With self-knowledge comes immeasurable joy.
- Resolution of negative emotions; Elimination of bad habits;
- Improved relationships; Knowing and loving what one really is
- Seeing the magnitude of our potential; Realizing that we can achieve that potential; Establishing a plan of action to move us to where we want to go;
- Developing the skills to take us where we want to go;
- Removing any fear that is preventing us from taking the action that we know, we need to take; True freedom.
- Self-knowledge helps us to unlearn prejudices and discard redundancies. Any gardener will tell us that in order to have a beautiful garden it is not enough to love flowers, one must also hate weeds.

Discontent may bring what appears to be disorder; but if it leads to self-knowledge, then it will create a new social order and enduring peace. Freedom comes into being only through self-knowledge in one's daily occupations, that is, in one's relationship with people, with things, with ideas and with nature.

How does Self-knowledge Help Us?

Self-knowledge as we see it, is knowing our selves well. It makes us aware of our strengths, our weakness, our capabilities, and our value system, which together reflect in our actions. E.g.: Methanol yellow is a pigment widely used in India in cooking particularly in sweets. It is used in the kitchens of educated families even though the packaging clearly mentions not for human consumption and for industrial use only. The producer and seller are not violating any law. The buyer is not illiterate. Absence of law is not the problem. Lack of education is also not the problem. What is it then? It is lack of awareness and attention.

What can we expect if we have self- knowledge?

We can expect to have our world of possibility opened up and appear within reach. Our confidence, happiness, gratitude and love for life will grow which will all result in bringing us a greater sense of freedom.

- We have a deep desire to grow;
- We know that there is more for us in life than we currently are experiencing;
- We are successful high-achievers and want to move to higher levels of success and fulfillment in relationships, business, health, athletics, creativity, spirituality, wealth or freedom.
- Our time and energy are precious, and we are not going to waste either of them.
- A belief in the existence of some power beyond us (e.g. Spirit, Divine Energy, God, etc. - the name is not important).

The Mind of a Whole or True Human Being is Religious and Scientific

Jiddu Krishnamurti of the 20th Century points out that the function of education is to cultivate both the religious mind and scientific mind. The word religion comes from the root 'to bind', to bind ourselves to something greater. 'The scientific mind is very factual; discovery is its mission, its perception'. Such a mind moves from fact to fact. Religious mind is a creative and compassionate mind. Such a mind only can experience what is called God, which is immeasurable. In Krishnamurti's view there are two attitudes in the world. These are the only two states of mind that are of value, the true religious spirit and the true scientific mind. Every other activity is destructive, leading to a great deal of misery, confusion and sorrow.

The scientific mind is very factual. Discovery is its mission, its perception. It sees things through a microscope, through a telescope; everything has to be seen as it is; from that perception, science draws conclusion, builds up theories. Such a mind moves from fact to fact. The spirit of science has nothing to do with individual conditions, with nationalism, with race, with prejudice. Scientists are there to explore matter, to investigate the structure of the earth and of stars and the planets, to find out how to cure man's diseases, how to prolong man's life, to explain time, both the past and the future. But the scientific mind and its discoveries are used and exploited by the nationalistic mind, by the mind that is in India, by the mind that is in Russia, by the mind that is in America. Scientific discovery is utilized and exploited by sovereign states and continents.

Then there is the religious mind, the true religious mind that does not belong to any cult, to any group, to any religion, to any organized church. The religious mind is not the Hindu mind, the Christian mind, the Buddhist mind, or the Muslim mind. The religious mind is not the mind that goes to churches, temples, or mosques. Nor is it a religious mind that holds to certain forms of beliefs, dogmas. The religious mind is completely alone. It is a mind that has seen through the falsity of churches, dogmas, beliefs, and traditions. Not being nationalistic, not being conditioned by its environment, such a mind has no horizons, no limits. It is explosive, new, young, fresh, and innocent. The innocent mind, the young mind, the mind that is extraordinarily pliable, subtle, has no anchor. 'It is only such a mind that can experience that which you call God, that which is not measurable'.

A human being is a true human being when the scientific spirit and the true religious spirit go together. I think the purpose of education is to create this new mind, which is explosive, and does not conform to a pattern which society has set. A religious mind is a creative mind.

We cannot have a religious mind without knowing ourselves, without knowing all about our body, our mind, and our emotions, how the mind works, how thought functions. And to go on beyond all that, to uncover all that, we must approach it with a scientific mind, which is precise, clear, unprejudiced, which does not condemn, which observes, which sees. When we have such a mind we are really cultured human beings, who know compassion. Such a human being knows what it is to be alive. Religion is not a form of conditioning. It is a state of tranquility in which there is a reality, God; but that creative state can come into being only when there is self-knowledge and freedom. When there is self-knowledge, the power of creating illusions ceases, and only then is it possible for reality or God to be.

How does one bring this about?

There is no existence without relationship; and without self-knowledge, all relationship, with the one and with many, brings conflict and sorrow. 'Educate' in the real sense of that word is not transmission from the teachers to the students some information about mathematics or history or geography, but is the very instruction of these subjects to bring about a change in the minds. The education we receive fills our brains with a clutter of thoughts. It succeeds in creating a crowd in our mind but miserably fails to explode our potential. Our education may prepare us for a career, but it fails to prepare us for life. For it is imperative to help the student to be scientific, to think very clearly, precisely, to be sharp, as well as to help him uncover the depths of his mind, to go beyond words, his various labels as the Hindu, Muslim, and Christian.

Conclusion

The essence of Krishnamurti's teachings is that only through a complete change of heart in the individual can there come about a change in society and peace in the world. His teachings help us to see ourselves as we really are. Education, according to Krishnamurti, is holistic if it is to know the outer world and inner world. Knowledge about the outer world is given its right place only when there is self-knowledge, which is the knowledge about the whole humanity. The highest function of education is to bring about an integrated individual who is capable of dealing with life as a whole.

"Wisdom comes with Self-knowledge"

References

- Delors, Jaquis(1996) Learning the treasure within UNESCO
- Krishnamurthy (2006) Education and Significance of life. Chennai; KFI
- Krishnamurthy (2006) On Education Chennai KFI
- Krishnamurthy (2006) On Self Knowledge Chennai KFI
- www.antiqbook.com/boox/uhr/034962.shtml - 5k
- plato.stanford.edu/entries/self -knowledge/
- en.wikipedia.org/wiki/Self-knowledge - 20k –
- www.poornamadam.blogspot.com/ - 132k
- www.creative-personal-growth.com/ - 24k
- thinkexist.com/quotations/self -knowledge/ - 35k
- www.academyofselfknowledge.com/ - 4k
- www.satramana.org/html/self_knowledge .htm - 11k

❖ ❖ ❖

Holistic Learning
The Rhythm of Life

– Dr. T. Swarupa Rani

"The whole movement of life is learning" – J. Krishnamurti

The highest function of education is to mould an integrated individual who is capable of dealing with life as a whole. Education is a continuous process throughout the life. Essence of education is learning. The word learning has a great significance in psychology and in education. Psychologists theorized learning in various ways. Stimulus response theorists defined learning as habit formation. This learning can be seen in acquiring smooth running skills and stereotyped responses. Thorndike explained learning as bonds or connections between S-R. Hull proposed drive reduction theory and related learning to the needs of organization. Skinner introduced the concept of operant behavior of positive and negative conditioning Cognitive theorists emphasized learning as a cognitive process rather than a specific product. Lewins learning theory explained learning as the behavior of cognitive structure. Tolman proposed a system of purposive behaviorism and explained about the development of cognitive maps.

J. Krishnamurti (1895–1986), the well known philosopher, psychologist and spiritual sage of the 20th century, observed and proposed different dimensions of learning, which are challenges to the teachers and learners in particular and to the system of education in general. J.Krishnamurti was born in a traditional south Indian family, trained to become a great seer to guide humanity. His enquiry peeps through the hidden corners of mind. His propositions on learning are applicable in physical, psychological and spiritual fields.

✍ **Dr. T. Swarupa Rani,** *Lecturer, St. Joseph's College of Education for Women, Guntur.*

J.Krishnamurti starts at the level of human behavior and reaches the heights of transpersonal psychology or spiritual psychology. His approach breaks through the frontiers of present learning in education, and establishes a holistic learning.

The concept of holistic learning drawn from the letters and writings of J.Krishnamurti is presented as follows.

Meaning & Nature of Learning according to Krishnamurti

Learning about the outer world in the form of academic subjects and learning about one's inner world is of value to him. The present paper reflects more on the latter aspect.

a) The whole movement of life is learning

The whole of life from the moment one is born till the moment one dies is a process of learning. There is never a time when there is no learning. Every action is a movement of learning and every relationship is learning. Relationship is the process of understanding of oneself from moment to moment in daily life. Hearing is nothing but understanding the relationship of the individual with himself, with society, with the environment, with his friends and relatives. Learning continuously, knowing himself from each and every moment is self-knowledge. Self-knowledge is bringing the wisdom to seek the absolute. Learning is continuous and goes on endlessly without measure. So learning is nothing but knowing the life.

b) Learning is living with clarity

To enquire and to learn is the function of the mind. Learning is the capacity to think clearly and sanely without illusion. Learning requires full attention. Attention is the awareness of the dominance of intellect, without an instinctive urge to control it, or allowing emotion to take its place. This awareness brings about subtlety and clarity of mind. Discovering the true and clear self in relationship to nature, society, relatives, friends, and with everything requires alertness of mind and a keenness of perception and awareness. Awareness implies sensitivity and intelligence.

c) Learning is always in the active present

It has no past. It always exists in the present. It is nothing but learning and enjoying the moment that comes to us. In the present moment this learning is active and fresh. The moment we say that 'we have learned 'it has already become knowledge. Mere acquisition of information or knowledge is not learning. Learning implies the love of understanding and the love of doing a thing for itself. It is only the mind that can understand this whole entity that we call the 'me', the self.

d) Learning is pure observation

Learning is a continuous process but not a process of adding. Learning is observation from moment to moment. J.Krishnamurti has always stressed about pure observation, which leads the student in the right path. Pure observation means – observation, which is not concerned with the observer and about the background of the observed thing. Observation of things outside and inward without the observer. Krishnamurti points out "Learning is not limited to learn the things outside. It is only part of learning. But to observe which is happening inwardly is actual learning". It is a sort of self-observation in which one perceives one's own feelings, thoughts and tendencies to act. This observation facilitates deep learning.

A free and pure observation is the beginning to learn anything. Observation frees the mind from this mechanical world. It is the first step to learn things by one's actual perception.

e) Learning is never accumulative

Self-learning is not a process of addition, which gathers information as an idea, as an experience or as knowledge or as a tradition. It is not gathering information as memory. It is a constant movement of learning and ending to participate afresh in the next moment of learning. Learning is not a thought, organization of hypothesis and conclusion. It is not a moment of retrogression

f) Learning is not experience as tradition

Learning is not knowledge as tradition. It is not knowledge as an experience. It is a constant moment. Learning is not habit formation. Learning is not gathering information as memory, not protective, constantly through knowledge. It is not accumulative, not crowded, not filled with facts about oneself in relationships.

j) Learning takes place when the mind is very quite

Mind can be quiet only when it is simple. A simple mind is always fresh. In a fresh mind there is no storing up, condemning and judging. A simple mind understands the real; it is not the mind that is full of words, knowledge, information, analysis and calculation. A simple mind understands the relationships of life. Simple mind is always active but quiet -quietness through observation, investigation and constant alertness. Quiet mind is a silent mind. This silent mind is a sensitive mind and it is an intelligent mind.

k) Learning implies the love of understanding, and love of doing things

Love is total responsibility. Love is not conditioned for a particular group, community, but for all mankind. Humility is the essence of love and intelligence. It is possible only when there is no coercion of any kind. It is understanding of the relationships Learning is to know the structure, nature and significance of whole entity that we call the me, the self.

Nature of Learning

J.Krishnamurti (1985) clarifies further the nature of learning "Learning implies not only observing visually, optically, but also observing without distortion, hearing things exactly what the other fellow is saying without any distortion. So when we are seeing the disorder in ourselves, then order comes about very naturally, easily, and unexpectedly".

Learning implies listening and observing not only with ears and eyes but also listening and observing without distortion exactly as they are and as they say, "learning implies a great sensitivity ". If one is sensitive to oneself, environment, and relationship and to how the past shapes one's mind, heart and senses, there is freedom, which has its own order and discipline.

Kinds of Learning

J. Krishnamurti proposed two kinds of learning; one is to deal with the outer world and the second is for self-development. The first type of learning is as a skill, a language, a technique to earn livelihood.

The second type of learning is learning about the happenings of the mind, which give a wide scope for psychological and educational implications.

When is Learning Possible?

Learning is possible only with pure observation. Observation from moment to moment. In the observation, which is not reduced to knowledge, is learning.

J.Krishnamurti (1974) further explains when learning is possible.

"Learning can exist only in that state of communication between the teacher and the student. Communion means to communicate, to be in touch, to transmit a certain feeling, to share it, not only at the verbal level but also at an intellectual level and also to feel much more deeply, subtly". (P.74)

The essential ingredients required for learning, according to J.Krishnamurti (1972) are "If you want to learn, three things are absolutely necessary, curiosity, eagerness and you must have energy, that energy gives you the passion to learn".(P.150)

Learning born out of curiosity is not simply based on pleasure or some excitement. But it is far deeper and more extensive. In conflict there is wastage of energy while in learning in freedom there is total energy to perceive 'what is?'.

J.Krishnamurti's learning takes place when the mind is very quiet. Learning is always in the active present. It has no past. Mind is quiet only when it is simple, but not easy while demanding, judging and weighing. Simple minds understand the real. It is possible only in the fresh mind, which does not burden itself with innumerable memories. This mind carries no shadow of suffering, though it may pass through the valley of sorrow it remains unscratched.

Holistic learning is possible in the simple mind, which is quiet and understands the reality of oneself. It is an intelligent mind, which is creative and sensitive in which is flowering of goodness. Learning about oneself is found to develop sensitivity, gentle spirit, and great inward strength. His self-knowing from moment to moment also involves ending it. Each moment liberates from sorrow and misery. Such living and dying each moment may bring out a new personality enabling one to utilize one's full potentiality in any field of life. Observations, listening and learning everything from moment to moment develop relationship and right action.

J.Krishnamurti's holistic approach to learning is similar to Gestaltian, in its meaning but different in its nature, process and purpose. It is extending the 'Whole' for igniting the flame of self-learning i.e. Self-awareness or learning of total self in a state of silence.

Holistic learning is possible for a fresh mind or a new mind; a fresh mind is quiet and simple, which is incorruptible, not contaminated by tradition, fear, authority, conflict and ambition. It is not the mind full of words -knowledge, information, calculation and analysis. It uses all of them whenever necessary in the quiet, simple and silent mind. In the total psychological freedom, love, creativity, sensitivity, and pure observation are possible.

Outcomes of Holistic Learning

Krishnamurti observed that the attainment of the following qualities is possible with Holistic Learning.

Intelligence: J.Krishnamurti (1981) shows when intelligence is awakened: "Intelligence comes naturally and easily when the whole nature and structure of relationship is seen. An intelligent mind is an inquiring mind, a mind that is watching, learning.......". So, intelligence comes into being with the understanding of our self.

Krishnamurti finds "When intelligence and love exist all other qualities will follow. It is like opening the gate to beauty. Totality of intelligence is compassion". The very understanding of the nature of freedom is the awakening of intelligence. Intelligence has no authority. Intelligence is not knowledge, though acquisition of knowledge depends to a great extent on intelligence.

J.Krishnamurti says, "Tradition is knowledge and the ending of knowledge is the birth of intelligence". Such a quality of intelligence develops relationship between human beings and among nations.

Sensitivity: J.Krishnamurti (1974) shows how sensitivity takes its place in one's awareness. "A human being who is aware of his environment, as well as of every movement of thought and feeling, which is a harmonious whole, is sensitive". P.28. According to Krishnamurthi, "Sensitivity is not the thing to capture but to grasp". He explains that in the every perception one can be sensitive. There is no resistance in sensitivity. Beauty is supreme sensitivity not in the sense of one's own pains and anxieties, but in encompassing the whole existence of man. Awareness implies sensitivity. The very nature of intelligence is sensitivity and this sensitivity is love.

Freedom: Freedom is found to be the beauty of nature. Flying birds, running streams, everything in the nature indicates their freedom. The very understanding of the nature of freedom is the awakening of intelligence. J.Krishnamurti proposes: "First human beings must be free from their concepts, prejudices and so on". This is real freedom. Clarity of perception comes from the freedom from self. Freedom facilitates psychological discipline in the child. 'Learning is the nature of discipline'.

J.Krishnamurti (1974) describes the nature of total psychological freedom. The flowering of the mind can take place only when there is clear, objective, and non-personal perception unburdened by any kind of imposition. Understanding the whole habit forming mechanism, and elimination of the comparative evaluation, both academically and ethically, are possible only in freedom. Freedom brings silence of the mind. In freedom creation comes into being as one has extraordinary energy in the silence of the mind, due to operation of all the senses and the wholeness of brain.

Love: Love is total responsibility not to a particular group, community, but for all mankind. Humility is the essence of love and intelligence. If the educators love children, they can understand how children are nervous, frightened, and defensive, how they are conditioned by them, their parents and the society and how they themselves are imposing their opinions, conclusions and judgments. If children are so loved both by parents and teachers, learning and living become extremely interesting to them.

Creativity: J.Krishnamurti (1974) maintains that the creative mind can be had only after knowing the self in freedom. "When the mind, which is scientific and religious in spirit, is fully aware of the movement of time and thought, one is highly sensitive, open, and free to be in the present moments, then there is something fresh like a new flower coming out". It is possible only 'when the mind is still, extraordinarily clear without a shadow of conflict which does not expect expression or fulfillment'. When the mind is still one finds creative joy.

Creativity begins with initiative, discovery, and compassion, when all the senses are active, when the mind is empty of the contents of consciousness and when the heart is full of love and initiative. Creativity is deep insight.

Beauty: J.Krishnamurti (1973) maintains: "Beauty is in abandoning the self. Beauty is part of this understanding, but beauty is not merely a matter of proportion, form, taste and behavior. Beauty is that state in which the mind has abandoned the centre of self in the passion of simplicity".p.21.

Goodness: J.Krishnamurti (1976) shows how goodness is order. "Goodness is total order. Not only outwardly, but especially inwardly.......... That order can be absolute... And it is disorder that leads to chaos, to destruction, to the anarchy, to the so called evil".p.109. The selfless can be good, considerate, orderly and responsible for good action appropriate to the situation and for the common good.

Concern, love, and good behavior reflect the inward beauty, which brings joy to everybody. Happiness thus results in the abnegation of self when thought and time end.

Truth: When there is harmony between body, mind and heart i.e., in the absence of comparison, conflict, envy, effort and when one lives with self-critical awareness from moment to moment and lives in right relationship with everything around, there is an integrated being. He can see "What is" without any illusions.

The Role of Teacher-Learner in Holistic Learning

As a great teacher J.Krishnamurti feels, "teaching another is the highest in the world'. It is not just passing on some information but creating generations of human beings. Teaching is not a technique but a way of life.

Krishnamurti (1974) proposes a state of relationship between teachers and students. Understanding and communication between the teacher and the student are possible in freedom and in deep affection for each other but not in dependence, attachment, suppression and imitation. Learning is facilitated in an atmosphere of happy affection and thoughtful care.

He proposes a unique approach to teachers while dealing with students to preserve their originality without killing their sensitivity. He advises teachers not to convince or influence the student, not to talk to him in terms of condemnation, agreement and persuasion but to show him the fact. Learning specific facts is important to the extent that it helps to promote the formation of ideas about the external life.

Krishnamurti proposes that the key role of teachers is to help the student to find out his relationship to the world, the world not of imagination or romantic sentimentality, but to the actual world in which all things are taking place. So, the teacher must be concerned with behavior, with the human complexity of action, with a way of life, which is the flowering of goodness. The educator and the student should find out what actually is learning. So both are learning in the deeper sense of the world.

Krishnamurti gives importance to relationship. According to him learning is relationship. Krishnamurti observes that when the teacher and the taught are involved in really understanding the extraordinary importance of relationship then they are establishing in the school a right relationship among themselves. The relationship between the teacher and the student has the element of companionship, of mutual understanding; then humility, sensitivity and affection are natural.

Krishnamurti proposes: "To learn the art of living one must have leisure". Through proper use of leisure time one can get physical and psychological energy to achieve things. Learner's learning is possible in leisure.

There can be no discipline without love. So, loving teachers, with their kindness and love, can surely develop inner-discipline in learners. If the educators love children, they can understand how children are nervous, frightened and defensive, how they are conditioned by them, their parents and the society and how they themselves are imposing their opinions, conclusions and judgements. If children are so loved both by parents and teachers, learning and living become extremely interesting to them. It is important that the teacher should feel secure both economically and psychologically in the schools. Then, the teacher being happy, secure in feeling that he/she is at home, can create in the student this quality of security, this feeling that the school is his/her home. If the educator is concerned with this he/she is helping the student to become sensitive to other peoples sorrows, struggles, anxieties and worries.

Educational Implications

Krishnamurti's holistic learning is inclusive of learning academic subjects and learning about oneself.

Competition breeds problems

Competition is the established pattern of existence in modern civilization. It is breeding innumerable problems.

J.Krishnamurti (1974) exposes how competition is a barrier in learning.

"Real learning comes about when the competitive spirit has ceased. The competitive spirit is merely an additive process which is not learning at all".p.76.

If learning depends on competition or past experiences in life, it is accumulation of conditioning which develops fear.

Discard comparison

Another barrier pointed out by J.Krishnamurti (1956) is comparison. "Memory compares, modifies, condemns, justifies or identifies; but it cannot bring understanding". p.132.

J.Krishnamurti (1969) shows how this comparison leads to confusion. Trying to become somebody else or like your ideal is one of the main causes of contradiction, confusion and conflict. A mind that is confused, whatever it does, at any level, will remain confused, any action born of confusion leads to further confusion". p.66.

J.Krishnamurti points out the barriers in learning. 'Comparison prevents learning and breeds fear'. It also breeds jealousy, anxiety, rivalry, conflict, aggression, guilt, and other such negative feelings. In the absence of comparison children are open, sensitive and flower to their fullest capacities, provided, both the teachers and students have a desire to teach and learn.

Avoid Conflict

Krishnamurti (1956) brings out how conflicts are created in life. "Naming is the recording of memory. The past meets the new, challenge is met by memory, the past. The response of the past can't understand the living, the new, the challenge; the responses of the past are inadequate, and from this arises conflict, which is self-consciousness". p.174

The mind can't be silent with its experiences stored in the brain. It responds to any, present or new experience from its memory as a note of recognition from the past experience. Thus there is conflict between the past memory and the present demand.

Break Conditioning

Krishnamurti accepts the inevitability of conditioned learning in doing the mechanical jobs, in language learning and so on. He also finds the human devaluation to the mechanical level as human beings are having only conditioned living without questioning its place and worth.

Human being is just nothing but his dead past i.e. 'he is dead'. Either he is living the life of his ancestors or the life of his previous day. There is nothing 'present' for him because every fresh present moment is based on the past, either one day or one million years. The known, the experience fashions his life. This associated memory of the past is pulling man to conform to that groove by promising him security. That is why man is unable to be dynamic to perceive the new and fresh moments of the present. J.Krishnamurti makes parents and teachers, alert by emphasizing how psychological conditioning is killing the original nature of man and how it is mechanizing his relationship.

Teach the art of observation

Observe what one thinks, feels, and does from moment to moment, to face the fact and act immediately.

The teacher is to teach the art of living in four seasons in a day, to live each experience as fully and deeply as possible, to think it out, and feel it out extensively and profoundly.

Live anonymously

There is richness and great beauty in living anonymously. So teach the life's purpose, and make them observe the purpose of life.

Make a living in the present

Accumulation of knowledge and experience leave the ashes of memory that make the mind old. The mind that dies everyday to the memories of yesterday and to all the joys and sorrows of the past is fresh.

Develop deep sensitivity

Teach the art of watchfulness. Care deeply for the feelings of children, allow them to feel every moment, every sound, and establish relationship, develop kind concern towards fellow beings, make them understand the nature of pleasure and teach the feeling of responsibility.

Awaken intelligence

Teachers concern would enable the children to have a clear perception and a free mind resulting in the awakening of intelligence. It should be a passionate concern of every teacher to light the flame of holistic learning, which would culminate in bringing radical transformation in them.

Conclusions

As teachers let us feel passionately to the very need of transforming children as Holistic beings, whose minds are always enjoying in a state of psychological freedom, and silence, which allow their sensitivity, pure observation and creativity. It should be our passionate concern to light the flame of Holistic learning which will lead them towards their total transformation.

References

- Aruna Mohan (2003) Consciousness- Krishnamurti's Observations on Life and Relationship, Neelkamal Publication, Hyderabad.
- J.Krishnamurti.J (2006) The whole movement of life is learning KFI Foundation Trust Limited, Brockwoodpark, England.
- J.Krishnamurti.J.(2005) A flame of learning KFI Foundation Trust Limited, Brockwoodpark, England
- J.Krishnamurti.J.(1974) On education, KFI Trust Limited England, Sudarsan Graphics, 14 Neelkantha Mehata Street, Tamilnadu.
- Santha Kumari (2002) J. J. Krishnamurti's perspectives on significance of education in life – M.Ed. Dissertation.
- J. Krishnamurti, (1998). On Self-knowledge. Chennai: KFI.

Explosion of Psychological Fact in the Fasting Mind, Not in the Feasting Mind

– Dr. G. Aruna Mohan

Man of these days is seen talking about himself all the time, evaluating his position in life. He is also seen battling with others in the name of nationality, religion or some organisation, ideology; in the name of left and right parties, republican and democratic fronts to bring a new world order. As a result the present world is full of conflicts, competition, violence, turmoil, ruthlessness, brutal acts, immorality, and the agony of man.

Old Instruments did not Solve the Problem

> ***"Our crisis is not in the world but in the consciousness itself"***
>
> *- Krishnamurti, 1968, p.14*

Krishnamurti insists that regeneration in society can come about only through a radical revolution in consciousness of the individual because he finds that the crisis is not economic or social but is in human consciousness. The way out of such a crisis is not to stop war, to reform univerersities, to give more work or less work and pay more. Such an intellectualism could so far invent theories, explain the human problem, and fragment people into classes, races, religions and so on. Krishnamurti identifies, "The intellect, the emotion, the tradition, the accumulated knowledge, those are the old instruments". *Krishnamurti (1968) p. 14.*

Intellect itself being a fragment of the human being cannot solve the whole problem of man's existence. Likewise the

✍ **Dr. G. Aruna Mohan,** *Reader, St. Joseph's College of Education for Women, Guntur.*

emotionalism and sentimentality cannot do anything, as they are also the fragmentary responses. That is why they have failed to bring about a different world. Though the intellect and emotion have value at certain levels of existence i.e., in learning and earning livelihood, in the development of communication and technical production of varied things, we are not to use them endlessly. If we do not respond to the crisis in consciousness we will be adding consciously or unconsciously to the confusion and misery.

Krishnamurti further says that the crisis is due to overimportance being given to the material life than to mental life. "The confusion has arisen because we are dominated by sensate values. We have to rediscover eternal values. The discovery of eternal values must be made by each one, the reformation must begin with each one". *(Krishnamurti (1968) p. 10)*

The Fact of Consciousness

Another yogi of the twentieth century, Sri Aurobindo also asserts the importance of consciousness. "Consciousness is a fundamental thing, the fundamental thing in existence, it is the energy, the motion, the movement of consciousness that creates the universe and all that is in it......consciousness that works in the energy and determines the form and the evolution of form. When it wants to liberate itself slowly, evolutionarily, out of matter, but still in the form, it emerges as life, as animal, as man and it can go on evolving itself still further out of its involution and become something more than mere man". *(Aurobindo, pp. 236-7.)*

Nisargadatta also says, "Consciousness is the only actor enacting all the multifarious roles. It is not various human beings, each possessing consciousness, it is consciousness which possesses the millions of forms through which the nouminon can objectify itself" and he further asserts, "The fact is that all manifestation, all phenomena, are appearances in consciousness, perceived by consciousness and cognized by consciousness through the interpretation by the mind". (*Nisargadatta, 1999, p. 222*)

In the words of Buddha "....The world is led by mind (thought); by mind the world is drawn along; all have gone under the sway of the mind, the one Dharma" (*B. Abhidamma, ii p. 177*)

All our psychological experiences are not attributed to any external agency. They are the result of our own thoughts and their resultant actions. The mind or consciousness is the core of existence.

Consciousness arises through the interaction of the sense organs and objects. Consciousness is not created by sense organs. Thus consciousness is the only 'capital' of every human being. Moreover Krishnamurti says that it is an evolutionary product - "Our consciousness is not actually yours or mine; it is the consciousness of man evolved, grown, accumulated through many, many centuries. The whole activity of man is the activity of thought. *(J. Krishnamurti, 1987, p. 32.)*

Buddha also asserted in his teachings that the collective consciousness, the strata of mind, is shared by every individual creature. The seeds of our evolutionary heritage are stored in the race -old instincts, desires, urges, and experiences of a primordial past.

Krishnamurti finds its content "In consciousness, there is the good and the bad; the bad is increasing; it is increasing because the good has become static, the good is not flowering. One has accepted certain patterns of what is thought to be good and one lives according to these patterns. So, the good, instead of flowering is withering and thereby giving strength to the bad". *(J. Krishnamurti, 1978, p.157-8)*

Aurobindo's urge is to clarify to us, that surface manipulation through reason is not enough but the humanity has to turn inward to bring in essential change of consciousness. The sages of Upanishads, Buddha, Jesus, J. Krishnamurti, Ramana Maharshi, Ramakrishna Paramahamsa, Nisargadatta also had their inward explorations and expositions to teach the truths of life to the humanity. They have vitality, a sublime self-confidence, an emphasis on direct experience in meditation without reference to outside authority and a passionate trust in truth.

Life in the Process of Discovering Ourselves

Many an intellectual man, a successful and productive man is critical of this phase of inwardness or meditation or self-awareness, suspects it as escapism, waste of time and solely to be kept as the last phase of life, whenever he hears the statements like, 'the harmony inside is the first thing, but not the harmony outside'. 'The outward harmony is the result of the harmony in the mind. To find out the harmony in oneself we have to enquire tremendously into ourselves.'

Ishopanishad puts forward: 'Life in the world and life in the spirit are not incompatiable. Work or action, is not contrary to knowledge of God' but indeed, if performed without attachment, is a means to it. On the other hand, renunciation is renunciation of the ego, of selfishness, not of life. The end, both of work and of renunciation, is to know the self within and 'Brahman' without, and to realise their identity. The self is Brahman, and Brahman is all". *(Isha Upanishad, 1957 – p. 26)*

They contain no trace of world denial, no shadow of fear, and no sense of diffidence about our place in an alien universe. Besides they taught that self-realisation means health, vitality, long life, and harmonious balance of inward and outward activity. They insist on direct experience of truth, the one reality underlying life in multiplicities. To know the truth one must make it real, must live it out, in thought, word and action. Human destiny lies ultimately in human hands for those who master the passions of the mind. One must be free of all hypocrisy, pretension, double standard of life saying one thing and doing another. Every form of self- deception must be ruled out and one must be honest.

In the words of Krishnamurti "The central issue is the complete, absolute, freedom of man -first, psychologically or inwardly, then outwardly. There is no division between the inner and outer; but for clarity sake one must first understand inward freedom. One must first find out whether it is at all possible to live in this world in psychological freedom, not neurotically retiring to some monastery, or secluding oneself in an isolated tower of one's imagination". *(Krishnamurti, 1968 p. 19)*

If there is no freedom, inwardly, then the chaos begins and there are the innumerable psychological conflicts, oppositions, indecisions, lack of clarity, lack of deep insight, which obviously express themselves outwardly. We have to follow the laws of our countries, but decision to obey, to comply, comes from inward freedom. The central issue is that our acceptance of the outer demand, outer law is from an inward freedom. But we are not inwardly free. We are heavily conditioned by the culture we live in, by the social environment, by religion, by the politics, by our ideological commitments. Being conditioned we are aggressive. Being conditioned, our lives are fragmentary, i.e., our everyday living -our everyday thoughts, aspirations all that is fragmentary. This conditioning makes each one of us a self-centered human being, fighting for 'self', his family, his nation, and his belief. And so ideological differences arise. In that very self-centerdness there is the process of isolation, of separation, of division. Each one of us is shaped or conditioned by every influence, by propaganda, by the books we read, the cinemas, the radios, the magazines and so on.

Why do we need Freedom, Psychological Freedom?

If we are not free we cannot see the actual facts but hang on to other people's ideas, opinions, judgements, worship public opinion, have heroes, breed fragmentation and division. If we are not free we do not have sense of beauty, we cannot love. If we see all these on our own we are completely free inwardly.

The way of life proposed by Buddha is also an intense process of cleansing the mind, one's speech, action and thought. It is self-development and self-purification resulting in self-realisation. In order to understand fully the importance of freedom of mind it is necessary to appreciate the role of mind. Of all the forces, the force of mind is the most potent. It predominates every other force. It is a power by itself and within itself. It does not deny the world of matter and the great effect that the physical world has on mental life. Mental actions are related to brain changes. It lies outside the realm of the physical world. 'Psyche' is not a fixed entity. Any individual's existence is a succession of change, something that comes into being and passes away not remaining the same for consecutive movements. It is the dynamic mind -flux that is termed as kammic energy. This mighty force, this will to live, keeps life going. Man is always changing either for good or for bad. This change is unavoidable and depends entirely upon his will and action. This is merely the universal natural law of conservation of energy. The root causes of all evil are: lust or craving; hatred or ill will and delusion or ignorance.

These motivate the people's actions. He has to be free from them. Buddha says, "Whatever there is of evil, connected with evil, belonging to evil, all issue from mind." Hence is the need for man to scrutinise his own mind with a view to understand how it works, how thoughts arise and pass away. There is no freedom if the mind is conditioned. The conditioned mind functions in a very limited specialised area.

The centuries of human living has conditioned man deeply and vastly. Apart from this, 'The conditioning of a mind that has been going on for many years or many centuries, that very conditioning is the system, the tradition, the habit and so on". *(Krishnamurti (1968) p. 34)*

Krishnamurti emphasises the need for freedom from conditioning by putting forward the question, can the mind put away all its conditioning so that it is - actually, not verbally or theoretically or ideologically, but actually - free, completely?

Inner Observation Without Reaction

Our consciousness is conditioned through education, through various inherited or acquired states, through various contradictions and the conflicts of the opposites. The conditioned state of mind can only be discovered, by each one of us, by looking at ourselves objectively. It is to examine every thought and every feeling but not with the eyes of experience and not with the eyes that have looked at so many things -such tragedies, such thoughts, such despairs and sorrows because those eyes never see anything clearly.

"Seeing is one thing and seeing something is another. . . . . seeing through knowledge, the object, the image, the symbol, and seeing -these are entirely different. *(Krishnamurti (1974) p. 144)*

He differentiated between seeing from one's background knowledge and seeing as it is and moving without any interpretation, evaluation and judgement. He contributed a way of looking at ourselves totally, without going through all the complications of introspective analysis, that will reveal the whole content of our conditioning. It is observation of 'what is' without the division between the observer and the observed. Because "When there is the division between the observer and the observed, the observer says, 'I must get rid of it', 'I must suppress it' or 'I must understand it', 'I must look at the cause of it' and so on....which is all a waste of energy because of the conflict involved in it". *Krishnamurti (1968) p. 45*

When there is anger in anybody he is nothing but anger. If he does not react to that but simply sees and sees that fact of anger it flowers and drops. There is no effort, struggle, battle with the 'what is'. Whether it is jealousy or whatever it is, if there is no contradicting thought of it, it comes to an end. Krishnamurti says that in such seeing in which there is no division of me and that 'a new state of energy comes into being. This new state of energy is going to dispel that fact altogether'.

Thus there is freedom from the fact in the mind's screen in seeing without the duality of the seer and the seen. When there is no association with the past -thought, memory, experience or recognition of the arising on the mind or in the mind, the mind is left empty. When the mind is silent, there is explosion of contents of consciousness accumulated through centuries. "You will see for yourself that all that psychological accumulation that you have gathered can be put aside with such ease; only then you know what living is. Living is to die, to die everyday to every thing that you have fought with and gathered, the self-importance, the self pity, the sorrow, the pleasure, and the agony of this thing called living." *(Krishnamurti 1968, p. 84)*

Buddhist way of living also proposes that one can dive into these waters of consciousness only when he takes off or leaves his individual personality. He has to see whatever comes to him with calmness, courage, compassion and kindness to clear his accounts. Thus the seed of separate personality is burned out. Thus consciousness is unified from surface to seabed. If we can get hold of the thinking process, we can actually re-do our personality and remake ourselves. Destructive ways of thinking can be rechanneled, and constructive channels can be deepened.

All these seers focussed their attention intensely on the contents of consciousness. They had predictable and replicable results from their experimental observations on the mind and by the mind.

Dhyama, 6
Disobedience, 49
Divine Life, 151
Divine Love, 151
Divine Nil, 151
Divine traits, 44-48
Divine Working, 151

E

Ego-oriented people, 2
Eightfold path, 109
Emotion, 290, 291
Energy balanace, 75-76, 77
Energy imbalance, 74-75
Evolution, 147

F

Faithful temperament, 98, 100-106
Fear, 240, 263-266
Fearlessness, 44
Five vows, 82
Flexibility, 46
Food, 18, 19, 31, 32
Four padas, 52
Freedom of mind, 235, 239-241, 283, 295
Functions of mind, 26

G

Glow, 47
Goodness, 218, 219, 284
Grades of consciousness, 161-170
Greed, 48
Greedy temperament, 98, 100-106

H

Hating Temperament, 98, 100-105
Higher Mind, 171-173
Holistic Development, 31, 131
Human body, 60

I

Ignorance, 48
Illumined Mind, 173
Imaginary fears, 254
Inconcient, 164-166, 195
Insights, 88
Integral Yoga Psychology, 194
Integrity, 47
Intellect, 20, 21, 211, 290
Intelligence, 209, 211, 282, 288
Intelligent Temperament, 98, 100-106
Intutive Mind, 173
Involution, 148
Inward journey, 52, 55

K

Kama, 51
Knowledge, 39, 40, 79, 80, 81, 276
Kundalini, 61

L

Learning, 277-286
Love, 217, 219, 241, 259, 261, 262, 282, 283

M

Mahavakyas, 4
Manipura Chakra, 63, 68, 69
Manomayakosa, 5
Manomulam, 13
Master mind, 15
Materialistic view, 48, 54
Meditation, 3, 22, 28, 29, 98, 99, 105, 111, 113, 206, 217-218
Mental attitude, 35
Mental Health, 9, 21
Mental plane, 35
Mercy, 47
Mind, 2, 9, 13, 14, 15, 16, 17, 20, 22, 23, 25, 26, 27, 88, 89, 206, 232-234, 238, 263
Modern psychology, 192
Moksha, 57, 205
Muladhara Chakra, 62, 63

N

Nation sould, 184-186
Nation-ego, 184-186
Nature, 227, 231
Nature's consciousness, 155, 156
Noble wealth, 132

O

Observation of what is, 295
Occult non-religious experiences, 28
Omnipresent consciousness, 17
Over mind, 174-175

P

Panchakosas, 5, 56
Patience, 47
Peace, 46
Perception, 88, 89
Personality, 4, 90, 192-194, 196
Physical mind, 171
Pingala, 62, 63
Positive thoughts, 13
Pranamayakosa, 5
Pranayama, 22
Pratyahara, 22
Pride, 48
Psychic being, 158-159
Psychoanalyst's method, 151, 152
Psychological environment, 257
Psychological health, 252
Psychological time, 223
Psychological wound, 253
Psychology, 195, 194
Purity of mind, 45
Purusha, 183-184
Purusharthas, 50

R

Raja yoga, 21
Rajsic food, 18
Ramakrishna teachings, 136-140
Realisation, 60
Reflections, 83
Relatigion, 28, 78
Religion of humanity, 188-189

Religion of man, 188-189
Religious mind, 213, 219
Religious virtues, 82
Renunciation, 39
Revolution in relationship, 210
Righteousness, 79
Rigveda, 1, 4, 78

S

Sachidananda, 152
Sacrifice, 46
Sahasrara chakra, 70
Samadhi, 22
Sattvic gifts, 35
Satwic food, 18
Scientific mind, 216, 219, 274, 274, 275
Self-awareness, 79
Self-complacent, 41
Self-culture, 88, 96
Self-knowledge, 206, 207, 238, 269-273, 298
Self-realization, 22
Sensitivity, 283, 288
Silence, 81
Simplicity, 47
Soul conscious people, 2
Speculative temperament, 98, 100-106
Spiritual crisis, 54
Spiritual Development, 199
Spiritual plane, 35
Spiritual way, 37
Subconconscient, 164-166
Subliminal consciousness, 166-169
Sufferings, 84, 255, 256
Super conscious, 17, 27, 169, 170
Super mind, 174-176
Suppressed anger, 255
Supreme consciousness, 149
Supreme qualities, 40
Swadhisthana chakra, 66, 67

T

Tamasic food, 18
Temperaments, 98-106
Therapy, 96
Thoughts, 13, 14, 15
Transcendentalist, 38
Truth consciousness, 171
Truth, 284, 46

U

Unbiased, 48
Uncomplaining, 46
Unconscious, 94, 95, 96
Upanishads, 1, 2, 3, 4, 8, 9, 10, 11, 12, 13, 18, 20, 21, 58, 60, 61, 78

V

Vedanta, 25, 26, 27, 28
Vijnanamaya kosa, 5
Vipasana Meditation, 97, 111-113
Vishudha chakra, 69

Visudhimagga, 98
Vital mind, 170-171

W

Watch method, 23
Way of work, 32
Way of yoga, 33
World stage, 187, 188
World union, 187, 188

Y

Yoga, 54-56, 29, 42
Yogasanas, 22, 55
Yogi's approach, 61

❖ ❖ ❖